Advance Pr:

"At a time when voluntary cultural amnesia about psychedelic research, psychotherapy, and spirituality is the norm, this fascinating book provides an essential antidote in the form of interviews with our cherished psychedelic elders. Skillfully selected and edited, these interviews testify to the remarkable healing, personal growth, and scientific potentials of these magical substances which they have evaluated throughout their lives."

—RICK DOBLIN, President, Multidisciplinary
Association for Psychedelic Studies

"In taking psychedelics out of the hands of professionals, the government may have taken away some of the most powerful tools that psychiatry has ever had. We still do not know the full range of what is possible with psychedelics, and we are still trying to grasp the profound implications of these substances for our understanding of mind, pathology, therapy, and human potential. Will we have another chance to use them properly? Listen to the wisdom of these elders."

—DAVID E. NICHOLS, Purdue University School
of Pharmacy and Pharmaceutical Sciences

"Brimming with the distilled experiences and perspectives of the first generation of Western psychedelic investigators, this is a terrifically rich resource for anyone interested in these unique, mind-altering substances."

—RICK STRASSMAN, MD, University of New Mexico School of
Medicine and author of *DMT: The Spirit Molecule:
A Doctor's Revolutionary Research into the Biology
of Near-Death and Mystical Experiences*

"This is a very welcome addition to the reexamination of the constructive potentials of psychedelics in society. The book presents a remarkably balanced survey of some of the key issues raised by experiences with these substances—issues like the nature of ultimate reality, how to handle expansions of consciousness, how to raise children, how to deal with social pathologies. None of the explorers suggest psychedelics are an answer to these problems; rather, they seem to agree, psychedelics stimulate us to ask questions in a new way, to explore with conscious intention, to see from a wider perspective."

—RALPH METZNER, author of *The Unfolding Self:
Varieties of Transformative Experience*

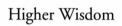
Higher Wisdom

SUNY series in Transpersonal and Humanistic Psychology
Richard D. Mann, editor

Higher Wisdom

Eminent Elders Explore the
Continuing Impact of Psychedelics

EDITED BY

Roger Walsh
and
Charles S. Grob

STATE UNIVERSITY OF NEW YORK PRESS

For information, address State University of New York Press,
194 Washington Avenue, Suite 305, Albany, NY 12201-2384

Production by Michael Haggett
Marketing by Fran Keneston

Library of Congress Cataloging in Publication Data

Higher wisdom : Eminent elders explore the continuing impact of psychedelics / edited
by Roger Walsh and Charles S. Grob.
    p. cm. — (SUNY series in transpersonal and humanistic psychology)
  Includes bibliographical references and index.
  ISBN 0-7914-6517-9 (hardcover : alk. paper) — ISBN 0-7914-6518-7 (pbk. : alk.
paper)
    1. Hallucinogenic drugs. 2. Transpersonal psychology. 3. Hallucinogenic drugs and
religious experience. I. Walsh, Roger N., 1946– II. Grob, Charles S., 1950– III. Series.

BF209.H34H54 2005
154.4—dc22

                                                                        2004021536

                              10 9 8 7 6 5 4 3 2 1

This book is dedicated to

WINSTON FRANKLIN
whose support of this and many other projects
contributed so much to so many.

and to

ALISE AGAR-WITTINE
whose work on this project culminated a life
of contribution and service

Contents

vii

Acknowledgments

The interviews published in this book took place during a year and a half period from late-1996 to mid-1998. This book project, and the meeting from which it stemmed, were funded and supported by the Institute of Noetic Sciences and the Fetzer Institute. Wink Franklin and Frances Vaughan supported the project in multiple ways. Betsy Gordon and Jeremy Tarcher supported the conference, and Betsy Gordon also supported photography of the interviewees, Bonnie L'Allier provided superb administrative and secretarial support, and John White served as our tireless agent.

In preparation for this book, some of these interviews have recently been updated. The task of the actual interviewing was shared with us by several good friends and colleagues, including Gary Bravo, Ralph Metzner, Rick Doblin, Robert Jesse, and the late Alise Agar-Wittine.

Throughout this and other projects we have received an unusual degree of collegial support and encouragement from our departmental chairmen William Bunney and Barry Chaitin at the University of California at Irvine, and Milton Miller and Ira Lesser at Harbor-UCLA Medical Center. Our SUNY editor, Jane Bunker, was a delight to work with, and Fran Keneston's enthusiasm was a gift. We are profoundly grateful for their contributions to this project, as well as for the expert editing provided by Jon Hanna.

Photos of elders were provided by Marc Franklin. For the full psychedelic pioneers' portraits' archives, see www.lordnose.com.

SUPPORT OF FURTHER RESEARCH ON PSYCHEDELICS

Those interested in supporting research on psychedelics can contact the Heffter Research Institute (www.heffter.org) or the Multidisciplinary Association for Psychedelic Studies (www.maps.org).

Psychedelics and the Western World

A Fateful Marriage

Roger Walsh and Charles S. Grob

For half a century psychedelics have rumbled through the Western world, seeding a subculture, titillating the media, fascinating youth, terrifying parents, enraging politicians, and intriguing researchers. Tens of millions of people have used them; millions still do—sometimes carefully and religiously, sometimes casually and dangerously. They have been a part—often a central and sacred part—of most societies throughout history. In fact, until recently the West was a curious anomaly in not recognizing psychedelics as medical and spiritual resources.[1] Consequently, the discovery of the powerful psychedelic drug LSD (lysergic acid diethylamide)—together with its chemical cousins such as mescaline and psilocybin—unleashed experiences of such intensity and impact that in the 1960s they shook the very foundations of our culture.[2]

Many of the world's societies are "polyphasic," meaning that they actively explore and derive their understanding of reality from multiple states of consciousness. Such states may include dreams, drugs, meditation, yoga, or trance—in addition to the normal waking state. By contrast, the West has been primarily "monophasic," valuing and deriving its view of reality solely from our usual waking state.

Yet with the explosion of psychedelics, suddenly millions of people were boggling and blowing their minds with states of consciousness and kinds of experiences that were, quite literally, beyond their wildest dreams. A Pandora's box of altered states, heavens and hells, highs and lows, trivia and transcendence cascaded into a society utterly unprepared for any of them.

Their effects reverberate to this day, and the Western world will probably never be the same. For better and for worse, psychedelics have
molded culture and counterculture, art and music, science and psychiatry,
and helped catalyze movements such as those for peace and civil rights.[3]
They continue to fuel spiritual practices, to inspire raves and rebellion, to
fertilize research on brain and behavior, and to suggest new understandings of consciousness, creativity, and cults.

At the same time, the War on Drugs continues unabated, making
thoughtful distinctions—such as the major differences between toxic
stimulants like cocaine, and problematic but potentially therapeutic substances like psychedelics—almost impossible. To a large extent, hype and
hypocrisy have overridden reason and research.

Yet from the beginning, serious researchers investigated psychedelics.
In fact, these curious chemicals have fascinated some of the greatest names
in psychology and psychiatry, sociology and anthropology, philosophy and
religion. Some of the foremost thinkers of the twentieth century zeroed in
on these substances as soon as they emerged, and in a period lasting
merely twenty years, an enormous amount of research was done. Some of
it did not meet today's more exacting research standards,[4] but the scientific, psychological, spiritual, and clinical implications of the findings were
nevertheless remarkable.

In the psychological arena, psychedelics revealed depths and dynamics
of mind rarely glimpsed by Western psychologists. They unveiled com-
plexes, archetypes, and early traumas that provided unexpected insights
into, and support for, depth psychologies such as those of Carl Jung and
Otto Rank.[5] They sometimes facilitated powerful transcendent experiences
previously available only to advanced contemplatives. In doing so, they provided new understandings of religion, spirituality, and mysticism, as well as
their associated practices such as meditation, yoga, and contemplation.[6]

From these insights emerged new and more expansive reviews of the
human mind and the human potential, the most sophisticated and best
known of these psychedelically informed theories being those of Stanislav
Grof.[7] Clinically, psychedelics showed therapeutic promise for a wide
array of difficult problems, such as chronic alcoholism, severe psychosomatic disorders, death anxiety in cancer patients, and post-traumatic stress
disorder. They even proved helpful in the most horrendous of all stress disorders: concentration camp syndrome.[8]

Of course, some of these clinical claims must be regarded as tentative
since, as described in more detail in the next chapter, many studies were

relatively unsophisticated. Given the enormous power of the psychedelic experience, strong expectation and placebo effects are likely. In addition, there is a saying in medicine which advises physicians to "use a new drug quickly while it still works," implying that the initial enthusiasm that often accompanies a novel treatment may be therapeutic in itself. Nevertheless, the net effect of over one thousand publications certainly suggests that psychedelics have significant therapeutic potential and deserve further study.[9]

In research studies, healthy subjects sometimes showed considerable psychological and spiritual benefits. For some of these people, including many of those interviewed in this book, the experience redirected their lives and initiated a lifelong spiritual quest.[10] For example, a significant percentage of Western students of Tibetan Buddhism report that psychedelics played a key role in initiating their practice.[11]

All this occurred with a remarkably low casualty rate. This was in stark contrast to the painful panic episodes (or worse) that sometimes resulted from unskillful use—such as among ill prepared, casual users or the unwitting victims of secret CIA experiments—that subsequently filled blaring newspaper headlines.[12] By contrast, clinical and research use of psychedelics resulted in very few complications and no deaths. The most comprehensive review of side effects concluded that "in well screened, prepared, supervised, and followed up psychiatric patients taking pure psychedelic drugs, the incidence of serious adverse reactions is less than 1 percent. It is even lower in 'normal' volunteers."[13] This makes psychedelics—contrary to the public's media-distorted perception—among the safest drugs in the medical pharmacopoeia, *when used carefully and clinically.*

Yet all this research crashed to a violent halt in the 1960s, banned by the United States government. Thus began "America's longest war," a war which most social scientists now agree is unwinnable and does more harm than good.[14] Although these drugs remain widely available on the street corners of many major cities, they are rarely available to researchers for study of their psychological and therapeutic effects. What many investigators regard as one of our most important research tools has largely been relegated to the museum of medical history.

Paradoxically, this makes the original psychedelic researchers a uniquely valuable and, because of their age, endangered resource. In their laboratories and clinics, they observed and recorded, puzzled over and analyzed, tens of thousands of psychedelic sessions. In doing so, they witnessed an unparalleled variety and intensity of human experience. In fact, probably no group in history has been privy to such a panoply of experience: painful and ecstatic, high and low, sublime and satanic, loving and hateful, mystical and mundane. The entire range of human experience, including some of the rarest and most profound, erupted in their subjects with an intensity seldom seen except in the most extreme existential conditions. Not surprisingly, many researchers reported that not only their subjects, but also they themselves, were transformed by their work.

In the late 1990s, several individuals and organizations realized that these researchers constitute an invaluable resource as an irreplaceable reservoir of knowledge and wisdom. A meeting of these researchers was therefore organized and funded by the Fetzer Institute and the Institute of Noetic Sciences. Given their advancing ages, this was probably the last time such a group would ever meet. The researchers were interviewed individually, and they convened in 1998 to recall and record their discoveries, and to reflect on what they had learned. For three days they talked, and their conversations were recorded. The result was a distillation of fascinating anecdotes, irreplaceable knowledge, and hard-won wisdom—the culmination of half a century of research and reflection on one of the most intriguing and challenging topics of our time. From these, *Higher Wisdom* was born.

NOTES

1. C. Grob, "Psychiatric research with hallucinogens: What have we learned?" *Heffter Review* 1 (1998): 8–20. C. Grob, ed., *Hallucinogens: A Reader* (New York: Tarcher/Putnam, 2002). M. Harner, ed., *Hallucinogens and Shamanism* (New York: Oxford University Press, 1973). R. Metzner, ed., *Teonanácatl: Sacred Mushroom of Visions* (El Verano, CA: Four Trees Press, 2004). R. Walsh, *The Spirit of Shamanism*, 2nd ed. (Minneapolis: Lewellyn, in press).

2. A. Hofmann, *LSD: My Problem Child* (New York: McGraw-Hill, 1980).

3. J. Stevens, *Storming Heaven: LSD and the American Dream* (New York: Harper & Row, 1998).

4. See note 1 (Grob 1998).

5. S. Grof, *LSD Psychotherapy* (Sarasota, FL: Multidisciplinary Association for Psychedelic Studies, 2001).

6. A. H. Badiner and A. Grey, eds., *Zig Zag Zen.* (San Francisco, CA: Chronicle Books, 2002). R. Forte, ed., *Entheogens and the Future of Religion* (San Francisco, CA:

Council on Spiritual Practices, 1997). T. Roberts, ed., *Psychoactive Sacramentals: Essays on Entheogens and Religion* (San Francisco, CA: Council on Spiritual Practices, 2001). T. Roberts and P. Hruby, "Towards an entheogen research agenda," *Journal of Humanistic Psychology* 42 (2002): 71–89. H. Smith, *Cleansing the Doors of Perception: The Religious Significance of Entheogenic Plants and Chemicals* (New York: Tarcher/Putnam, 2000). R. Walsh and F. Vaughan, eds., *Paths beyond Ego: The Transpersonal Vision.* (New York: Tarcher/Putnam, 1993).

7. S. Grof, *The Adventure of Self-discovery* (Albany: State University of New York Press, 1988). S. Grof, *The Cosmic Game* (Albany: State University of New York Press, 1998).

8. See note 5 (Grof 2001). R. L. Grinspoon and J. Bakalar, *Psychedelic Drugs Reconsidered.* 2nd edition. (New York: Lindesmith Center, 1997). Ka-Tzetnik 135633. *Shivitti: A Vision* (Nevada City, CA: Gateways, 1998).

9. See note 1 (Grob 1998, 2002); note 5 (Grof 2001); and note 8 (Grinspoon and Bakalar 1997).

10. See note 1 (Metzner 2004), and note 7 (Grof 1998). R. L. Grinspoon and J. Bakalar, eds., *Psychedelic Reflections* (New York: Human Sciences Press, 1983). F. Vaughan, "Perception and Knowledge: Reflections on Psychological and Spiritual Learning in the Psychedelic Experience," in *Psychedelic Reflections*, ed. L. Grinspoon and J. Bakalar, 108–14 (New York: Human Sciences Press, 1983).

11. C. Tart, "Influences of Previous Psychedelic Drug Experience on Students of Tibetan Buddhism," *Journal of Transpersonal Psychology* 23 (1991): 139–74.

12. See note 3 (Stevens 1988). M. Lee and B. Shlain, *Acid Dreams: The CIA, LSD, and the Sixties Rebellion* (New York: Grove Weidenfeld, 1985). T. Wolfe, *The Electric Kool-aid Acid Test* (New York: Bantam, 1968).

13. R. Strassman, "Biomedical Research with Psychedelics: Current Models, Future Prospects," in *Entheogens and the Future of Religion*, ed. R. Forte, 152–62 (San Francisco, CA: Council on Spiritual Practices, 1997).

14. E. Currie, *Reckoning: Drugs, the Cities, and the American Future* (New York: Hill and Wang, 1992). S. Duke and A. Gross, *America's Longest War: Rethinking Our Tragic Crusade against Drugs* (New York: Tarcher/Putnam, 1993). E. Nadelmann, "Common Sense Drug Policy," *Foreign Affairs* 77 (1998): 111–26. E. Schlosser, "Reefer Madness," *Atlantic Monthly*, August, 1994, 45–63. E. Schlosser, *Reefer Madness: Sex, Drugs and Cheap Labor in the American Black Market* (New York: Simon & Schuster, 2003).

The High Road

History and Hysteria

Charles S. Grob and Gary Bravo

> To make this trivial world sublime,
> Take a half a gramme of phanerothyme.

So wrote Aldous Huxley in 1956 to his new friend and colleague, British-born Canadian psychiatrist Humphry Osmond. Quick to reply, Osmond penned in return:

> To fathom Hell or soar angelic,
> Just take a pinch of psychedelic.

At the time, the names then in vogue for that peculiar class of compounds recently (re)discovered by Swiss research chemist Albert Hofmann were "psychotomimetic" and "hallucinogenic." Huxley and Osmond struggled to invent an alternative, less pathologizing name. As the full range of effects of this unusual class of psychoactive compounds became known, Osmond's term "psychedelic" became established parlance. Attracting widespread medical and public interest, psychedelics would soon emerge as one of the more controversial issues of the turbulent decade to come.

Psychiatrists were the first to study psychedelics, initially looking at their unique effects on the brain and capacity to successfully treat forms of mental illness often nonresponsive to conventional treatments. Unfortunately, as word of the highly unusual effects of psychedelics filtered out of laboratories and hospitals, naïve and inexperienced young people began to experiment.

The Pied Piper, for what was rapidly turning into an unprecedented mass social phenomenon of youth, was Timothy Leary. A distinguished Harvard psychologist who had established a solid reputation for his studies of personality and social theory, Leary had encountered psychedelic mushrooms while vacationing in Mexico in 1960. Returning to Harvard, Leary could not contain his enthusiasm and quickly redirected his research and teaching to focus on this new discovery. Attracting widespread media attention, Leary's irrepressible and provocative nature soon gathered clouds of disapproval and concern. As increasing numbers of young people followed the banner of Leary's crusade, serious and sanctioned studies were jeopardized and eventually, by 1972, terminated. In the eyes of many observers, psychedelics had become too hot to handle.

Meanwhile, other efforts to harness the power of the psychedelic experience were similarly undermining researchers and clinicians. Under the direction of U.S. military intelligence, secret programs were designed to test psychedelics as brainwashing and counter espionage weapons. Following Nazi scientists who had experimented with mescaline on prisoners at the Dachau concentration camp, an extensive program was developed in the United States in the 1950s and 1960s. These studies, under the code name MK-ULTRA, were designed to exploit the strong conditioning and suggestibility created by these drugs. Government-sponsored studies included surreptitiously spiking drinks of federal employees, resulting on some occasions in serious psychological trauma.

To the eventual regret of the psychiatric community, leading medical investigators received funding from the intelligence agencies to conduct unethical experiments on unsuspecting patients. These researchers included Canadian psychiatrist, Ewen Cameron, at one time President of the American Psychiatric Association as well as the first President of the World Psychiatric Association. In the late 1950s, Cameron developed a "treatment" which subjected his private patients first to "sleep therapy," where they were heavily sedated with barbiturates for several months. A "depatterning" phase of massive electroshock and frequent doses of LSD followed this, designed to obliterate past behavior patterns. Then the patients were further sedated, and finally they were subjected to a prolonged "psychic driving" reconditioning phase, where they received constant auditory bombardment from speakers under their pillows repeating tape-recorded messages, with some patients hearing the same message repeated a quarter of a million times. Cameron's questionable, and by today's standards unethical, treatment provoked severe mental injury in many unfortunate patients.

Ultimately, the combination of government misuse and a perceived public health crisis brought research to a crashing halt. Countless young people heedlessly ignored admonitions to be attentive to set and setting, and instead recklessly used psychedelics in dangerous and uncontrolled recreational contexts. Likewise, the ethically suspect activities of government intelligence operatives and grantees eventually surfaced, which also undermined legitimate and potentially valuable psychedelic research.

It is regrettable that promising medical investigations were abruptly forced to terminate. In spite of demonstrating encouraging preliminary results, inclusive of some very difficult patient populations, more comprehensive and methodologically controlled research studies with psychedelics were prevented from moving forward. Mainstream political agendas, along with heightened professional and public anxiety, overwhelmed the argument for further investigation designed to explore safety and effectiveness when these novel substances were administered under optimal conditions. This lost opportunity was particularly evident with treatment resistant conditions, where psychedelic therapies had raised hopes of effective interventions and alleviation of suffering.

A case in point was the treatment of chronic alcoholism. This is an illness notorious for its devastating physical, psychological, and spiritual damage to afflicted individuals, as well as to their families and communities. Within mainstream medicine, treatment advances over the last fifty years have been virtually nonexistent. Indeed, one would be hard-pressed to find any other clinical area in all of medicine where so little progress has been made. Yet, because of their increasingly negative reputation, promising and groundbreaking research using psychedelics to treat alcoholism never came to fruition.

An illustrative episode concerns Bill Wilson, founder of Alcoholics Anonymous. In the late 1950s and early 1960s Wilson volunteered to become a research subject for Sidney Cohen, a physician on the faculty of the UCLA School of Medicine, and one of the world's leading medical psychedelic researchers. After several profound and transformative LSD experiences facilitated by Cohen and his research psychologist, Betty Eisner, Wilson proposed to the Board of Directors of Alcoholics Anonymous that the psychedelic treatment model be incorporated into the AA approach. Wilson claimed that his LSD experiences were similar in content to the spiritual epiphany he had had while undergoing alcohol withdrawal-induced delirium tremens many years earlier, yet without the medical risks posed by DTs. Therefore, he asserted that psychedelics offered a safe and efficacious pathway to recovery from alcohol addiction. By the time of his proposal to the board of AA, however, disturbing reports had begun to filter out about Timothy Leary's activities at Harvard as well as of similar adventurers elsewhere, and it had become clear that this unusual class of drugs was developing a rather tarnished reputation. Consequently the AA board instructed Wilson to cease being a proponent of the psychedelic treatment model for alcoholics, or else face expulsion from the organization he had founded. Wilson, perceiving the futility of his efforts, abandoned his goal of bringing psychedelics into the Alcoholics Anonymous fold.

From our current vantage point of the early twenty-first century, the heady years of the 1950s and 1960s, when psychedelics were widely acclaimed as the cutting edge of psychiatric research and cultural transformation, should be something more than a period of obscure historical interest. The contribution of these novel chemical compounds as a catalyst for breakthroughs in neuroscience has often been poorly appreciated. As one example, LSD research facilitated the discovery of the serotonin neurotransmitter system, the vital brain chemical involved in regulation of mood, anxiety, sex, appetite, and sleep. And virtually forgotten was the development of depth psychotherapy with psychedelics, which demonstrated surprisingly consistent positive treatment responses in even the most seriously ill and difficult to treat patients. Regrettably, the lingering rancor and antipathy towards this provocative cultural symbol of the 1960s still impedes sober discussion on the potential psychedelics may hold for medicine and society.

History has moved on, and today's world is not the world of the 1960s. Cultural attitudes have evolved, as have the therapies designed to treat the mentally ill. In spite of impressive progress in understanding the underlying neuroscience of psychiatry, however, our commonly used treatments remain limited. Whereas major advances have occurred with conventional drug therapies in the 1990s, many devastating psychiatric illnesses often remain unresponsive to prevailing and acceptable treatments. Examples of such illnesses include drug addiction (including alcoholism), chronic post-traumatic stress disorder, obsessive-compulsive disorder, and the anxiety and depression often experienced by individuals with terminal illness.

In considering potential future uses of psychedelics, we must not forget or ignore that there was also a dark side to psychedelics. By the end of the 1960s, serious concerns had been aroused by high-profile disastrous responses to psychedelics in poorly prepared recreational users. In particular, cases of vulnerable young individuals who developed severe psychological problems aroused the understandable concerns of medical and legal authorities. The many warnings of competent investigators to scrupulously attend to the psychological "set" and environmental "setting" unfortunately were often ignored. The impressive safety record demonstrated under controlled research conditions did not necessarily extend to uncontrolled use. For years it was not possible to establish a fair and objective hearing on the relative risks and benefits of the psychedelic model, due to the fears based on the tragic outcomes of some cases of nonmedical use.

Yet it may be possible now, several decades from the chaos and dashed hopes of that prior generation, to reexamine the record and determine whether psychedelics have acceptable safety standards when used under carefully controlled and medically supervised conditions. From the late 1950s to the early 1970s, over a thousand clinical papers were published discussing the experiences of around forty thousand patients treated with psychedelics. When conditions were carefully and ethically controlled, the risk-to-benefit ratio was generally perceived as quite favorable and promising. Well beyond the glare of media and political attention, valuable research with psychedelics raised hopes that this novel treatment approach would make vital contributions to the development of the healing arts. While the cultural and political wars have continued to rage, however, critical questions concerning the untapped potentials of psychedelics remain unanswered.

A valuable resource, for whom limited time remains, are the veteran investigators and participants from that "Golden Age" of psychedelic research. Fewer in number now, as age and time have taken their inevitable toll, there still remain men and women from that period who were renowned for their leadership and important contributions. This book offers the experiences and insights of these elders. As we struggle to make sense of the potentials and pitfalls psychedelics hold for the twenty-first century, the words of these wise men and women, our predecessors on this path of exploration, may yield an unexpectedly hopeful message. Their collective vision of a world where the safe and efficacious use of these psychedelic medicines is tolerated still awaits us, our children, and our children's children.

AN ILLUSTRATIVE HISTORY OF PYSCHEDELIC RESEARCH

The modern era of psychedelic research began in an utterly unpredictable way. The eminent chemist Albert Hofmann, working in Basel, Switzerland in the midst of World War II, had a "peculiar presentiment" about a chemical he had created in 1938, while synthesizing a series of ergot alkaloid derivatives. The twenty-fifth compound he made, lysergic acid diethylamide (LSD-25), had proved uninteresting in animal tests and was quickly forgotten. Yet for some mysterious reason, Hofmann felt that the chemical "called to him." And so it was, that on April 16, 1943, Dr. Hofmann resynthesized it and subsequently experienced a very unusual state of mind.

Reasoning that he must have somehow absorbed some of this chemical, he eventually decided to cautiously replicate the experiment by taking what he believed was a very small measured amount three days later. Not realizing the remarkable potency of LSD, Dr. Hofmann inadvertently self-administered what was later recognized as a fairly large dose—250 micrograms—and thereby experienced the world's first intentional "acid trip." Of the thousands of substances he had synthesized in a long lifetime of chemical research, this was the only one, he claims to have resynthesized despite its failure in animal testing.

Dr. Hofmann immediately glimpsed the potential of this chemical for studying extreme altered states of consciousness, such as psychosis and mysticism. Over the next ten years, LSD was given to a wide variety of subjects, both normal and mentally ill, as the extraordinary potential of the drug was explored. This discovery captured the attention of the world's leading psychiatrists and neuroscientists. The profound implications that a drug administered in minuscule doses could cause such extreme alterations of mental functioning helped usher in the modern era of psychopharmacology. LSD and related chemicals became potent tools for psychology and neuroscience.

In addition, many proponents of the then dominant model in psychiatry, psychoanalytic theory, were excited by the potential of psychedelics to accelerate the process of uncovering the unconscious of neurotics. One young Czech physician, who took LSD as part of his psychiatric training, was Stanislav Grof. Grof, with his groundbreaking research programs in Prague, and later in Maryland, would go on to become one of the world's most eminent LSD therapists and cartographers of the various realms of human consciousness.

Far away in Southern California, during the late 1950s and early 1960s, two pioneering psychologists foresaw other potentials for these medicines. Betty Eisner used them for enhancing psychotherapy and creativity, in research programs at the University of California at Los Angeles. And Gary Fisher, a Canadian expatriate, was also on the faculty at UCLA. He used LSD to attempt to heal such devastating and intractable conditions as childhood schizophrenia and autism, as well as the existential anxiety often associated with end-stage cancer.

Psychedelics also sometimes elicited dramatic, even life changing, spiritual experiences. This was appreciated by none other than the great literary genius Aldous Huxley, who had just such an experience himself. He went on to call for a science of experimental mysticism in his landmark 1954 book, *The Doors of Perception*. At the close of his long and prolific career, Huxley gave much thought to how psychedelics might be utilized under optimal conditions, and what their impact might be on human development and society.

However, in his final novel, *Island*, Huxley despaired that the mainstream culture of his day could not tolerate the full implications of psychedelics. Predicting that the investigations he had endorsed would not be allowed to flower, Huxley anticipated the eventual repression of psychedelic research. But, true to his vision, when later diagnosed with cancer Huxley arranged for his wife and personal physician to administer LSD to him. It was thus, that on November 22, 1963, as he lay dying, Huxley received two intramuscular injections, one hundred micrograms each, of LSD. Along with the death of President Kennedy on that same day, the passing of Aldous Huxley presaged the end of an era.

The ability of psychedelics to generate instant mystical experiences intrigued spiritual seekers of all types. One of these was Aldous Huxley's wife, Laura, whose psychedelic experiences turned her life towards humanistic psychology and service to children. Manifesting her husband's intuition that psychedelics had inherent potential to enhance social cohesion and community mental health, Laura Huxley dedicated her career to developing novel and effective programs designed to help and inspire at-risk children and adolescents. Forty years after the death of her husband, she continues to work for the manifestation of their vision.

Another spiritual aspirant was Myron Stolaroff. Working as an electrical engineer, Stolaroff drastically altered his life's course after being given LSD. Along with the influential Canadian man of mystery, Al Hubbard, Stolaroff began to explore creative applications of the psychedelic experience. Their endeavors achieved fruition with the development in 1961 of the International Foundation for Advanced Study (IFAS) in Menlo Park, California. Under the direction of Stanford engineering professor Willis Harman and young psychologist (and later cofounder of the transpersonal psychology movement) James Fadiman, Stolaroff participated in cutting edge investigations on the use of psychedelics to catalyze creativity and problem solving. Until the federal government shut them down in 1965, the IFAS group contributed valuable information on the potential of psychedelics for human transformation and spiritual evolution.

By the late 1950s knowledge of these substances had already begun to escape the confines of academia and medicine. However, the course of psychedelic history was altered forever after the brilliant young Harvard psychologist, Timothy Leary, ingested "magic mushrooms" while traveling in Mexico. As the new decade of the 1960s dawned, Leary returned to Harvard intent on unlocking the mysteries of the mind with the help of these powerful psychoactive agents. He soon involved his colleague, fellow Harvard professor Richard Alpert (later to become Ram Dass), and their graduate student Ralph Metzner. Together, this trio of soon to be defrocked Harvard academics researched the mind-expanding, life-transforming and creativity-enhancing properties of the psychedelics. Indeed, the implications of many of their preliminary findings, unconventional research methodologies not withstanding, remain important enough to merit further scrutiny.

One rather daring study, led by the young Metzner, addressed the chronic dilemma of high recidivism rates for prisoners released from state prison. With the full sanction of prison authorities, inmate subjects were administered psilocybin, leading to dramatic restructuring of personality and, in some cases—after they had done their time—reduced reincarceration.

An early visitor to the rather informal research setting at Leary's house near the Harvard campus in Cambridge was an inquisitive religious studies professor from the neighboring Massachusetts Institute of Technology, Huston Smith. Inspired by Huxley's work on psychedelics, Smith enthusiastically agreed to be one of Leary's first subjects to receive psilocybin.

After many years engaged in scholarly examination of the mystical experience, Smith for the first time—as he describes later in this book—directly encountered transcendent visionary states that had previously been inaccessible to him.

Another of their many visitors during the early 1960s was a young and curious theologian, Rabbi Zalman Schachter. Seeking to deepen his own personal experience of the numinous, Rabbi Schachter was introduced to LSD by Leary, a story also told later in this book. As a result, Rabbi Schachter went on to influence many theologians, and cofounded the Jewish Renewal movement.

Inevitably, the forays into psychedelic experimentation by Leary and Alpert were more than staid Harvard could tolerate. Unwilling to reign in their explorations and conform to the academic research standards that they believed to be overly restrictive, the Harvard psychedelic psychology group engaged in an increasingly bitter dispute that resulted in their well-publicized firing in 1963. Far from dissuaded, they moved their research, both personal and professional, into the community.

Attempting to create psychedelically-fueled communities in various locales, including a donated mansion in Millbrook, New York, Leary and Alpert became lightning rods for an acrimonious debate on the potential value and risks of psychedelics. The ousted Harvard professors attracted growing criticism and harassment from politicians and a compliant media. In a futile search to find a setting where they could pursue their informal psychedelic investigations, they were forced on an odyssey around the United States, Central America, and the Caribbean.

Over time Tim Leary encountered a difficult path. In the years following his departure from Harvard and academia, his increasing identification with radical politics earned him several years in a high security prison and the dubious distinction of being identified by President Richard Nixon as "Public Enemy Number One."

Alpert followed an altogether different path. He traveled to India, where he experienced a religious conversion, changed his name to Baba Ram Dass, and returned to the West to share his tremendously influential story of transformation with a new generation of spiritual seekers.

The outlawing and demonization of psychedelics, beginning in the mid-1960s, ended most research. Ironically, at the same time psychedelics were essentially banned in medicine and prohibited in the culture at large, the historic role of psychedelic plant medicines in indigenous cultures around the world became the object of anthropological study.

Michael Harner was a graduate student who traveled to Peru to study the Shuar people of the Amazon. There he took the potent psychedelic plant brew, ayahuasca, as part of his immersion in their culture. The results of that experience had a profound effect on his perception of cross-cultural concepts of reality. Harner realized that he had vastly underestimated the importance of this drug to Shuar culture and their shamanism. He later trained to become a shaman himself, and went on to make landmark contributions to the field of shamanism.

Peter Furst was another young anthropologist who pioneered the academic study of psychedelic plants among different cultures. Over the years, Furst's efforts have been particularly critical to understanding the use of peyote among the Huichol people of Northern Mexico and in the Native American Church. Like Michael Harner, through using plant sacraments himself, Peter Furst gained an enhanced appreciation of the cultural sophistication of indigenous peoples and the central role that such sacraments played in native cultures. The work of these two contributors highlights the intrinsic value that traditions involving sacred plants have, with regard to understanding the effects and implications that psychedelics possess for our own time.

Although most psychedelic research subsided after the 1960s, interest was rekindled in the late 1970s by the rediscovery of MDMA (Ecstasy) by Alexander Shulgin. A former researcher at Dow Chemical, Shulgin established a successful second career as a prominent chemist with particular expertise developing and testing novel psychedelic drugs. Together with his wife, Ann, Shulgin introduced MDMA to a group of psychotherapists who successfully used this new medicine with a variety of difficult-to-treat patient populations. Unfortunately, the subsequent prohibition of therapeutic MDMA research also led to the rapid growth of the "rave" dance scene. At raves, young recreational users of Ecstasy and other drugs frequently did not take appropriate safety precautions, and drug misrepresentation by unscrupulous dealers reached a scale not previously seen. Recent surveys have shown that as much as half of all Ecstasy sold on the illicit drug market consists of drugs other than MDMA.

Through the last quarter of the twentieth century, it remained virtually impossible to legitimately study the healing potential of psychedelics as well as their inherent capacity to induce profound altered states of consciousness. The lingering acrimony aroused by the turbulent 1960s has only slowly receded. As a new century dawns, new opportunities present themselves. If, perhaps, we stand at the threshold of an era of sanctioned research, the lessons learned by veteran investigators of decades passed will be valuable guides for the road that lies ahead.

THE ELDERS PROJECT

The interviews presented in this book are an attempt to bring the wisdom of these pioneers to contemporary consciousness. While quiescent for much of the past few decades, interest in the healing and transformative potential of psychedelics persists. For new generations intent on exploring the myriad effects of this extraordinary class of compounds, the experiences and lessons learned by our predecessors are of no small value. Through their stories and their paths, our elders have much to teach us. If we are ever to fully unlock the potentials of psychedelics, or understand their mysteries, the lessons of the past should instruct our intentions for the future.

The genesis of this book traces back to the late 1980s, when we embarked upon the initial process of seeking out "elders" of the psychedelic research movement that seemingly ran out of steam almost two decades previous. After being the object of avid study and discussion during the 1950s and 1960s, the issue of psychedelics had become deeply repressed and virtually forgotten to mainstream medicine and psychiatry, other than as dangerous drugs with potential to induce serious mental injury. The legitimate exploration of psychedelics had become a remote memory, and rarely penetrated the veil of silence common to medical school and psychiatric residency programs.

Impressed by the remarkable capacity to facilitate healing when used under optimum conditions, we had read with fascination of the breakthroughs psychedelics had contributed to in the world of basic neuroscience research. And yet, we suspected there was far more to this phenomenon than we had observed during our experiences in medical school and psychiatric training in the 1970s and 1980s. At that time, to learn about this hidden history, one had to consult texts and older colleagues far outside the mainstream of our chosen profession.

Our plan was to methodically identify and interview the senior psychiatrists, psychologists, anthropologists, and theologians who had devoted their early careers to the rigorous investigation of psychedelics. What had they learned, and how were they introduced to and affected by their involvement in this field? Did they have any insights into the relevance this long-neglected area might hold for our own time? And what about safety and effectiveness? Did their novel, and now long-discarded, treatment models actually work? Were their patients healed, or were they harmed? What had they learned about the effects of culture and religion? What could they teach us from their experiences and wisdom accrued over the many intervening years? With *Higher Wisdom*, we hope to answer some of these questions.

Part One

Research

Consciousness, Creativity, and Chemistry

Research

Consciousness, Creativity, and Chemistry

But the man who comes back through the Door in the Wall will never be quite the same as the man who went out. He will be wiser but less cocksure, happier but less self-satisfied, humbler in acknowledging his ignorance yet better equipped to understand the relationship of words to things, of systematic reasoning to the unfathomable Mystery which it tries, forever vainly, to comprehend.

—Aldous Huxley[1]

Over fifty years have elapsed since Aldous Huxley received the "gratuitous grace" of perceiving, albeit fleetingly, the realms of transcendent consciousness from beyond the Door in the Wall. What he saw dramatically altered the final decade of his life, as he sought to envision a model of the salutary use of psychedelics in society. Though dismayed by the cultural disorder of his time, he held out hope that human evolution would eventually embrace these powerful compounds as essential for freedom and survival.

Psychedelics first became of interest to Western science more than one hundred years ago, when two German professors of pharmacology, Louis Lewin and Arthur Heffter, isolated mescaline from a sample of peyote (*Lophophora williamsii*) obtained from the American southwest. Through the 1920s and 1930s, steady progress was made in the study of the effects of mescaline, as well as initial investigations of *Banisteriopsis caapi*, one of the critical plants used to prepare the sacred Amazonian brew, ayahuasca. Cultural awareness of psychedelics mushroomed following Albert Hofmann's discovery in 1943 of the psychoactive effects of LSD, which he had synthesized from ergot fungus.

Hofmann's experience of psychic disintegration followed by psychospiritual rebirth laid the groundwork for the evolution of science and society's relationship with psychedelics. Three days after inadvertently absorbing a minute quantity of LSD, he deliberately measured and self-administered what he thought might be a low dose of the drug. Hofmann would later describe his frightening and beatific visions:

> My surroundings had now transformed themselves in more terrifying ways. Everything in the room spun around, and the familiar objects and pieces of furniture assumed grotesque, threatening forms. They were in continuous motion, animated, as if driven by an inner restlessness. . . . Even worse than these demonic transformations of the outer world, were the alterations that I perceived in myself, in my inner being. Every exertion of my will, every attempt to put an end to the disintegration of the outer world and the dissolution of my ego, seemed to be wasted effort. A demon had invaded me, had taken possession of my body, mind, and soul.

Shortly thereafter, Hofmann described:

> [T]he climax of my despondent condition had . . . passed. . . . The horror softened and gave way to a feeling of good fortune and gratitude. . . . Now, little by little I could begin to enjoy the unprecedented colors and plays of shapes that persisted behind my closed eyes. Kaleidoscopic, fantastic images surged in on me, alternating, variegated, opening and then closing themselves in circles and spirals, exploding in colored fountains. . . . Exhausted, I then slept, to awake next morning refreshed, with a clear head, though still somewhat tired physically. A sensation of well-being and renewed life flowed through me.[2]

Contemporary society has yet to explore the full implications of Dr. Hofmann's experience. In the 1960s, psychedelics exploded on the scene in pseudorevolutionary guise, preventing serious and sober scientific investigation. Since then, we have slowly yet steadily evolved to the point where it is now possible to conduct careful and well-controlled research studies looking into the effects of psychedelics on the human brain, consciousness, and healing.

Modern scientists have continued to elaborate on the structure and function of an increasing array of psychedelic compounds. Chemists such as Albert Hofmann and Alexander "Sasha" Shulgin have made important contributions to this evolving science. Emerging from both the natural world in their botanical form, or discovered through chemical synthesis in the laboratory, this unusual class of psychoactive compounds is attracting more and more attention. Important clues as to how they may optimally be utilized by a society in crisis can be found in the classic work of James Fadiman and Myron Stolaroff on the potential role of psychedelics in creativity and problem-solving. Given the critical issues facing our world today, we might listen to what these elders have to say.

NOTES

1. A. Huxley, *The Doors of Perception* (Middelsex, England: Penguin, 1954), 65.

2. A. Hofmann, *LSD: My Problem Child* (New York: McGraw-Hill, 1980), 17–19.

1

James Fadiman

Transpersonal Transitions:
The Higher Reaches of Psyche and Psychology

Born May 27, 1939 • James Fadiman graduated from Harvard and Stanford universities where he met and worked with Richard Alpert, who later became known as Ram Dass. It was Alpert who introduced Fadiman to psychedelics, with life-changing results. Fadiman's ideas about the mind, identity, spirituality, and society were transformed, and he set about reorienting his life accordingly.

Fadiman joined Myron Stolaroff and Willis Harman at the International Foundation for Advanced Study to investigate the effects of LSD on personality and creativity. From this work came his doctoral thesis and a series of important research papers.

After psychedelic research was banned, Fadiman directed his energy into a variety of projects. Seeing the need to expand psychology beyond its limited behavioral and psychoanalytic views, he helped inspire the birth of transpersonal psychology. This new field incorporated the best of conventional psychology with previously neglected arenas, such as spirituality and post-conventional growth, as well as Asian psychologies and wisdom. Fadiman was one of the founders of the Association of Transpersonal Psychology, the *Journal of Transpersonal Psychology*, and the Institute of Transpersonal Psychology, which is now an accredited doctoral graduate school. He served as president of both the Association of Transpersonal Psychology and the Institute of Noetic Sciences, he sits on the boards of several corporations, and has his own management consulting firm.

James Fadiman has also published widely. He has written the textbook *Personality and Personal Growth* (with Robert Frager); the self-help books *Unlimit Your Life: Setting and Getting Goals*, and *Be All That You Are*; an anthology, *Essential Sufism* (with Robert Frager); and a recent novel, *The*

Other Side of Haight. He is a popular teacher, consultant, and lecturer, with a delightful sense of humor, who has been called "the quickest wit in the west."

I'D HAVE TO SAY that I'm one of the inadvertent psychedelic pioneers. I was an undergraduate at Harvard, and ended up in a small tutorial with a young, dynamic professor named Richard Alpert. We became friends and ended up renting a house together for the summer at Stanford, where I worked for him on a large research project.

After my senior year at Harvard in 1960, I went off to live in Europe. The following spring, Dick showed up in Paris with Timothy Leary. They were on their way to Copenhagen to deliver the first paper on work with low-dose psilocybin. Dick was in great condition and said to me, "The most wonderful thing in the world has happened, and I want to share it with you." I replied, as anyone would, "Of course." Then he reached in his jacket pocket and took out a little bottle of pills.

My first reaction was "Pills? Drugs? What kind of weirdness is this?" I really had no idea what he was talking about. But that evening, I took some psilocybin from that little bottle, sitting in a cafe on a main street in Paris. After a while I said to Dick, "I'm feeling a bit awkward because the colors are so bright and sounds are so piercing." He hadn't taken anything himself, but he responded, "That's the way I feel just being in Paris." So we withdrew to my hotel room where he was basically a sitter for my session.

Out of that experience came my first realizations that the universe was larger than I thought, and my identity smaller than I thought, and there was something about human interaction that I had been missing. It was definitely a powerful bonding experience between us, and afterwards, a lot of my attachments seemed a little more tenuous. However, this session did not involve a dramatic stripping away of levels of reality. That came later.

One week later Dick was in Copenhagen and I followed him, somewhat like a dog that gets lost hundreds of miles away, and then finds his master. I showed up there, and we had another evening session. Out of that came the realization that when human beings are close to one another you can ask anything of each other, because you take into account the other's needs first. You would not ask anything that would be a true impo-sition. And so there was a kind of Three Musketeers consciousness that seemed to arise out of that.

Soon after, I returned to the United States, due to my draft board. I had received a letter from them basically saying, "Would you like to join us in Vietnam? Or might you consider the alternatives open to you by law?" One of these options was graduate school, and I'd been accepted to Stanford the year before. At the time I'd told myself, "I'll just put a hold on that because I would rather take some time to travel the world." But when my draft board wrote me, graduate school seemed to be the much lesser of two evils.

I showed up at Stanford as a first-year graduate student somewhat embittered, because I was truly there to dodge the draft. I felt that the United States government would make a terrible mistake having me as a soldier, due to a combination of my distaste for war, not wanting to kill people I didn't know, cowardice, and a number of deep philosophical truths which I didn't yet fully understand.

I started my graduate work feeling disappointed with psychology, because now I'd used psychedelics and I knew there was a lot more. I didn't know what that "more" was, but I sure knew that psychology was not teaching it. But hidden away in the back of the course catalog I found a "graduate special" called "The Human Potential" taught by Willis Harman who was, of all things, a professor of electrical engineering. The little write-up said, "What is the highest and best that human beings can aspire to?" and suggested various kinds of readings. As I read it I thought, "There is something about psychedelics in here. I don't know what it is, but this man knows something of what I know." At that point I was divid-ing the world into people who knew what I knew—which wasn't very much, but more than I'd known two months earlier—and those who didn't. For instance, I'd look at Impressionist paintings and I'd wonder, "Did this person see what they were painting, or were they copying other Impressionists?" And somehow, I knew. Whether I knew *correctly* or not was totally beside the point to me at that time.

Anyway, I wandered into Willis Harman's office, which was a typical associate professor of electrical engineering office in a building as drab as a hospital, and said, "I'd like to take your graduate special." He gently replied, "Well, it's full this quarter but I'll give it again. Perhaps you would be interested at a later date." I looked at him and said, "I've had psilocybin three times." He got up, walked across his office, and closed the door. And then we got down to business.

As it turned out, I had guessed correctly. This course was his way of dealing with the question, "How do you teach about psychedelics in a manner that doesn't get you either discovered or fired?" After talking for a while, we decided that not only would I take the class, but I would kind of coteach it, because unlike him, I was willing to be open with what was happening with me. I had much less to lose. So we taught it together, beginning with the question, "What is the best and highest a human being can be?" Gradually we moved from psychology to philosophy, then to the mystics, and eventually to personal experience.

Around that time I started to work with the International Foundation for Advanced Study. Funded by Myron Stolaroff, this foundation had been set up in Menlo Park, California to work with psychedelics. Willis Harman was involved, as were a few other people. They had no psychologist on their team, so I became their psychologist. This was a little ludicrous, since I was about two months into my first year of graduate work at the time, and hadn't studied psychology as an undergraduate. We began by working on a paper together, "The Psychedelic Experience," which described the results of the foundation's LSD therapy sessions.

While we were waiting for that paper to be published, Willis asked if I'd like to have a session with them. There I was, filled with my Dick Alpert-Tim Leary-human-closeness-low-dose-psilocybin-experience, and I said, "That would be great!" I showed up on October 19th, 1961 at the foundation's headquarters, two living room-like suites above a beauty shop looking out over a parking lot. I was offered the opportunity to take some LSD with Willis as a sitter, a lovely woman professor as a sitter, and a physician, Charlie Savage. Charlie basically did his physician-ness of giving me the material and then left to resume his psychoanalytic practice down the hall. I took the material and looked around and said to my sitters, "Well, aren't you folks taking something?"—because that had been the model with Dick and Tim in the other sessions I had before. I think Willis took a little amphetamine just to keep me cool. I put on eyeshades, lay down on a couch, and listened to music. This was the method that they had developed through the work of Al Hubbard and others.

And there in that room, my little mind washed away, much to my surprise. The day went on in classic high-dose psychedelic fashion. I discovered that my disinterest in spiritual things was as valid as a ten-year-old's disinterest in sex: it came out of a complete lack of awareness of what the world was built on.

I went to a place of total aloneness—the you've-got-to-walk-this-valley-by-yourself deep awareness of separation from the universe—the sense that there really was nothing at all you could hold onto. This, fortunately, is very close to the place next to it, in which there was only one thing and I was part of it. At that point there was what might be described as songs of jubilation throughout the heavens: "another jerk wakes up!" Not jubilation at the realization of who I, Jim Fadiman, was, but who I was *part* of. What a relief! I moved into a space of feeling that I was—not part of everything—but that *everything* was part of everything, and I was clearly part of that. Suddenly, it was obvious there is no death, and that the fundamental waveform of the universe is best described in human terms as love. This was all incredibly obvious. And for some peculiar reason, I, Jim Fadiman, was being given this awakening to my true self.

From that place I looked at various structures in my life and they were all, at best, amusing. It struck me that being a graduate student avoiding war seemed to be a perfectly plausible thing to do, since one had to do something in this incarnation, in this body. It was unclear to me whether I, Jim Fadiman, as a personality, had lived before. But it was also not very important, because the Jim Fadiman that was in that room on October 19th wasn't very important, but rather served as the box in which I found myself.

That evening, before going home with Willis, I went up to the top of Skyline, a glorious mountain ridge above Stanford. I looked out, and had an amazing feeling of identification with Creation. I walked around saying things like, "I've really done a splendid job at all of this." The "I" here was clearly not me, not Jim Fadiman, but the "I" was pleased with Creation, and pleased that part of me was observing other parts of me. Now, singing songs of praise to the Lord is an Old Testament notion, and you wonder from a "down-here" position why the Lord is at all interested in that, since He wrote the songs, and so forth. But when you're in the praising mode, it feels like a very nice way of congratulating yourself for jobs well done.

I went to Willis's house to come down for the evening, and looked into the eyes of his baby son, Dean. Dean was just crawling around at that point, and we shared one of those, "Hey man! Hey man! It's cool, right?" moments. I thought, "You're just in a little baby *body*." And he seemed to me to be thinking, "Yeah, that's what I'm doing now, but don't worry about it." He was an old soul, too.

Eventually I was dropped off back at my graduate student hovel. The next day I emerged, wondering what I should do, now that I knew what I knew, and given that I'd been reincarnated as a first-year graduate student at Stanford, in a world not hostile, but totally oblivious, to all of this.

I then began a rather delicate career as a graduate student, committed to making this psychedelic experience more available to everybody. At that point, there was no one I could see who wouldn't benefit from knowing what I called "the fundamental truth of existence." So I became a kind of dual agent. By day, I was an ordinary graduate student. I took to wearing a coat and tie to look as little like a hippie as possible. I thought, correctly, that the department would assume I was nothing other than what I appeared to be. At night, I read what I needed for my education, which was the *Bhagavad-Gita*, the *Tibetan Book of the Dead*, and so on. From time to time I'd stop reading and go out and sit in front of a small tree near my house, and watch it begin to vibrate and look like energy in the shape of a tree, to reunite me with what I was *really* about. There's a beautiful huge church at Stanford, with large stained glass windows, where I'd sit relaxing until the characters and colors seemed to be in motion, which reminded me of the psychedelics.

I began researching psychedelics as part of a team with Willis Harman, Myron Stolaroff, Charlie Savage, and others. But now I was looking at the work from a very different level than before, because *now*, finally, I understood what on earth we were doing. We were trying to discover whether—if you used psychedelics in a totally supportive, non-medical setting, with a high enough dose—you could facilitate an entheogenic experience. And if so, would that be beneficial?

For a few years this group had federal approval, because we cooperated with the government at whatever level seemed necessary. Our mentor was Al Hubbard, a mysterious character who was at various times a Canadian agent, as well as a United States federal agent. Because of his own transformative experiences, Al had decided that what he was going to do with his life was make psychedelic experiences and research possible. He was really the guiding light, and certainly the major disturber, in our little world.

The "advanced training," as it came to be called, was always done with Hubbard, usually in Death Valley. This was the most intense outdoor set and setting that existed, and it allowed a kind of opening that wasn't as easily achieved in any other place. You drove in from Lone Pine, and at some point you'd stop and take the material. Then you drove to several locations and spent time there, usually "eyes open," dealing with what was visible—or visible on the invisible planes there. You also dealt with your own life much more directly because of the harshness, enormous beauty, and enormous barrenness of the landscape. The advanced training was a major way of making sure you didn't get caught in your belief systems.

So part of the time I was doing government sanctioned research. Yet I was also involved on the other end of things, with the Ken Kesey world, because Dorothy, my wife, was friends with Ken. This made me one of the few people who was deeply involved in legal experimentation with high-dose religious experiences, and also hanging out with the primo group of psychedelic outlaws, total explorers with no restrictions on what they explored. They really did much more dangerous and exciting things.

At some point we discovered that morning glory seeds contained an analog of LSD, but I worried that they also might have terrible side effects or even be poisonous. So one morning Willis and I ground up a bunch of morning glory seeds that we bought from our local gardening store and ate them. Our intention was to see whether they were bad for you. As I look back, that's a kind of science I wouldn't practice anymore. But that day we walked up into the Biological Preserve above Stanford and lay around for the day. I did get a bit sick, but I also found that this analog of LSD absolutely took me toward the same place as LSD itself.

During that session I had one of those visions which colors forever the way you hold certain attitudes and ideas. In the vision, I was at this huge blackboard, writing a very complicated and sophisticated analysis of reality as I now understood it with the help of psychedelics. God came in and looked at this and said, "That was just wonderful!" Then he erased it all. And I asked, with a little bit of concern, "Why have you erased it?" He replied, "Well, that was just wonderful. I just loved that. And I certainly hope you'll do others."

I realized what I was being told was that the chances of you—in this body, in this lifetime, with these languages, in this civilization—*truly* understanding reality are zero. But also that it is extraordinarily entertaining, even nourishing, to invent these theoretical castles in the air. From that point on I was not committed to my deepest core beliefs, because I began to see that they were among the beliefs that I was changing. If I looked back a few years, I saw a real shift in the beliefs that I previously felt were core. So, since I was letting go of some every few years, I had no reason to assume that the ones I had at that time were going to last either. There was a certain relief in this, a letting go of pretentiousness.

How long were you able to work with psychedelics at Stanford, and how did it end?

It took me two years to get a committee that was willing to have their names on my dissertation, "The Effects of Psychedelics on Behavior Change"—a title I came up with so Stanford wouldn't throw me out. So I got my PhD, and therefore had learned a certain amount of research design and had some credibility, blah, blah, blah. The federal government then allowed us to do a study on the question of creativity, looking at whether psychedelics could facilitate problem-solving of a technical nature. Oscar Janiger and a lot of other people had done work with artists—but here was a real challenge: could we use these materials and get people to work on highly technical problems? The difficulty, we knew, was that if we upped the dose enough, they would all be much more interested in seeing God, and in letting go of their personal identities, time, and space. Obviously, we would need to use a low dose.

So, one night Myron, Willis, James Watt (our current physician), and I all got together and took twenty-five micrograms of LSD, a very low dose. We listened to music until the walls were breathing and we were in a reasonable state in the flow. Then we worked on the study. Our reasoning was that if we could *design* the study under a low dose, then it would be reasonable to run it, because we were doing exactly what we were asking the subjects in the study to do: namely to focus on the technical problems of research design, without getting caught up in the beauty and grandeur of the universe. Which we did. It was bootstrapping in its finest form.

We began to run this really gorgeous study with senior research scientists from a number of companies. We told them that we'd assist them in their most pressing technological problems, particularly if they were really stuck. Our criteria for admission to the study was that they had to bring at least three problems that they had worked on for at least three months. We had a range of people from the hard sciences, from theoretical mathematicians to architects. We took them in, four at a time. The mornings were the same as if we were doing a high-dose experience—have them relax, put on eyeshades, listen to music, try not to work on their problems. Then, around noon, we'd pull them out and ask them to work on their various technical problems until around four p.m. Then we'd let everyone review their work and assess its value.

A number of patents emerged out of that study. One of my favorite successes was an architect who had the task of designing a small shopping mall in Santa Cruz. It was a task with complicated architectural possibili-ties. At the end of the four hours, as he put it, "I saw the entire structure." He literally had seen it and walked around in it. It was designed; it existed as a kind of platonic form. For him this was just a total pleasure, because that was not the way he'd ever been able to do a project before.

But all good things come to an end. One morning in 1965, when we had four people doing the first, relaxing part of the experiment, we got a letter saying, in effect, "Hello, this is your federal government. We are now concerned that psychedelics are available, that people are misusing them, and that there are bad things happening in the youth culture. As far as we can tell, we can't do a thing about the problem that is bothering us. But we can stop somebody somewhere, which will make us feel better. So, we've decided this morning to stop all research in the United States."

Well, our little crew read this, then we thought about the four major scientists in the next room. And we all agreed that we had gotten this letter tomorrow. Nonetheless, that effectively ended our research.

We did however, publish those results, and there are a number of rather distinguished, very happy scientists who were involved in those studies. One became a vice president of Hewlett-Packard, another has won every major scientific award that the computer world offers. The irony of course, is that this was a totally acceptable way to bring psyche-delics into the culture. Not only was it acceptable to the culture, it was also acceptable to us as not denying people's spiritual values, because these were problems that people wanted to work on, things that mattered to them. Yet we were asked to not only stop the research, but to try and deny whatever we had already learned, and to keep society as ignorant as we could. We were asked to do this, while millions of people in the cul-ture at large were running around experimenting without knowledge, help, or support.

Given that you'd had such profound experiences yourself, what did you do next?

I really stepped back at that point. I felt more aware of the absurdity of this moment than I felt personally affected, because I was at a place where things didn't affect me much personally; they just happened and I did whatever I needed to do. So I stepped back and thought, "Well, what else is available?" At that time, because of the millions of people using psychedelics, enormous numbers of other spiritual pathways were starting to open up. Most came from existing traditions: meditation, fasting, vision quests, shamanistic practices, the peyote way. I couldn't use what seemed to be the cleanest, best, easiest way to work with myself and other people, so I said, "What else is there?"

I was a fresh PhD without employment, and I wasn't about to begin to sell life insurance. I was almost offered a position as a counselor at San Francisco State University, because they were desperate for someone who had experience with psychedelics, and who could work with students with these issues. But when they thought about it, they decided that if they hired me, or anybody like me, it would imply that there was some truth or legitimacy to what was going on. So, rather than have someone who really *knew* what was going on, they decided not to hire me.

This made me realize that my career was on rather shaky ground since my dissertation exposed me as one of "them," whoever "they" were. Sure, I had snuck through Stanford. But by the time I was done, Stanford's great terror was that they would be known as the "Harvard of the West," since Tim and Dick had been fired from Harvard by that time for doing research less controversial than mine.

So I tried to make use of my psychedelic vision in a very simple-minded way, which was to exhibit whatever I'd learned in my own life. There's a wonderful song by Bessie Smith, that says "if you got it, get it and bring it in here or else you've got to leave it out there."

One of the things I did was begin to work with what became the *Journal of Transpersonal Psychology*. This was a journal in which different religious and intellectual traditions could come together to talk, not about doctrine, but about experience. It allowed them to cooperate with each other in a way that hadn't previously been possible in either religious or psychological circles.

The *Journal* came out of a meeting at Esalen that we put together with the help of Esalen's founder, Michael Murphy. We brought together the best Catholics we could find (the most open, the most liberal, the most scholarly), and a number of us—not outlaws exactly, because there weren't too many laws, but people clearly beyond the fringe. We met for a weekend, and came away with the realization that a bridge between spiritual experience and psychology had to be built. However, these Catholics weren't going to lay a stone of it! So it was up to us.

One model that existed was the *Journal of Humanistic Psychology* and its association. So we began to form something similar. We wrote to the editorial board of the *Journal of Humanistic Psychology* and said, "We're moving on. There is more to the human condition than we have experienced with our humanistic orientation. We don't quite know where we're going, but here are some of the things that we're going to look at. . . . Would you like to join us?"

And the editors split, saying either, "I have some vague idea of where you're going and I'll go with you," or "Absolutely not." The major negative responses that come to mind are Victor Frankl, who said, "This is total nonsense," and Rollo May who, for various reasons, became a serious enemy of the spiritual and worked actively against it. Adding the spiritual back into psychology seemed to frighten him.

In many respects the humanistic movement was very progressive for its time. Why do you think the psychedelic issue, and the transpersonal movement, were so antithetical to their belief systems?

Well, having been on both sides, my thinking is that if you have been brought up with a world-view in which there is only this world, you've been brought up intellectually provincial. The only experiences you've had with religion have been with people who also have never had any *true* spiritual experience. What you have, perhaps, is formal religion, which gives you a community of people who speak in the metaphors of religion, because that's the best language they have. All this allows for is a rather impoverished vision of spirituality.

You then project onto others, people like me at the time, that if I'm speaking about being a divine agent of God, then I'm *clearly* a paranoid schizophrenic. Because paranoid schizophrenics also talk about being the divine agents or angels of God. Really what you have is a group of people who are dealing with the profound fear that their entire world-view is small. And when your world-view is small, and you're in a position of power, it seems neither unrealistic nor difficult, to say that the people who are attacking it must be wrong.

Psychology has a wonderful knack of turning disagreement into derangement, disability, or pathology. In the scientific world, "fear" is usually called "skepticism." Think about it this way: If you've had a little bit of biology, it seems highly unlikely that a duckbilled platypus exists. If you've never seen a giraffe or an elephant, it's easy to believe that they don't exist. So, if someone comes to you and says, "I would like you to meet my friend the elephant, who will carry us into the jungle," it is not surprising if you say, "I'd rather you go away, and I certainly don't want to hire you. And I most certainly don't want to publish your articles."

Would you say that this is also reflective of why the culture at large became so hostile to psychedelics, and why, after the initial enthusiasm, there was a wave of repression which included shutting down your program at Stanford?

Well, the way I look at it, psychedelics were a waveform growing in magnitude, and Vietnam was a stone wall. When psychedelics met Vietnam and the country split apart, the old guard who had created and maintained Vietnam, and were into war and so forth, were terribly, and correctly, threatened. Why? Because the psychedelic people were saying, "We are not really interested in any of your institutions. We're willing to do whatever's necessary to tear them down. We're willing to close down your university, not to add some courses. We're willing to eliminate your military, not improve training. We're willing to turn your churches into parks, because true religious experience does not work well inside walls."

So all the groups of the old guard said, "I don't know what you guys are up to, but I'm so deeply threatened that I will stop you to whatever extent I can." As a result, you had an amazing unity of the major institutions against the psychedelic wave. And what they said was, "We control the guns; we control the universities; we control medicine. And by God, we are at war with these people who are not content to let us live our lives, but are determined through the most vulnerable part of us, our children, to take away the love and respect and support of our institutions and ourselves." From that point of view, it's hard to know what else they could have done.

In the first six or seven years of the Journal of Transpersonal Psychology *there were a great number of articles addressing the psychedelic issue. Then, for about fourteen years, there wasn't a single article on psychedelics. What happened?*

Let's use that as a jumping off point to larger questions about the role of psychedelics in the culture. How and where did psychedelics really deeply influence parts of the culture? If you go down a list of the major people in transpersonal psychology, or spiritual psychologies in general, what you will find is that most everyone was deeply affected by their own personal psychedelic experiences, even if they didn't write about them in journals or discuss them openly with the outside world.

Computer programmers and hackers are a great parallel. If you were to go to a conference that featured the "breakthrough" computer minds from the first wave of computer companies, nearly all of them were deeply affected by psychedelics. But you won't find any mention of psychedelics in the history of computers, because it didn't serve them to mention it, except to one another. I suspect that at some point there will be a great "outing" of those people. But up until now, many of them have been asked to talk about their own psychedelic use, and they have said, "No thanks, we would rather not come out."

What you had in transpersonal psychology were people who were working with their own transpersonal and psychedelic experiences, and also trying to create and define this branch of psychology. We found that as we expanded, there were more and more people deeply concerned with a variety of aspects of spiritual traditions and how they affected consciousness. In a sense, while the major figures all were affected personally by psychedelics, the idea of what "transpersonal" *was* became much larger, and the explicit role of psychedelics was less important to filling in the puzzle.

People ask, "What is the difference between transpersonal psychology and conventional psychology?" I start by saying, "Well, conventional psychology is at least one hundred and fifty years old, and transpersonal psychology is forty-five thousand years old." What we quickly learned was that we were rediscovering things that many people had already found. We began to look to the Buddhists, and the Tibetans, and the Hindus—not only in order to explore our own personal experience, but also to see how a related world-view was discoverable through these much longer and more sophisticated lenses.

Remember my vision of standing at the blackboard with God? One of the things that event said to me was that my understanding of things was not very large. Perhaps I understood a fundamental truth of the universe, but if you asked me to describe it, I would fall into one metaphorical system or another, because I didn't have any choice. Those of us involved with the *Journal of Transpersonal Psychology* began to realize that rather than draw only on our own personal experience, which was initially naïve and wobbly, we could publish articles of incredible depth and sophistication, by drawing on thousands of years of other people's experiences.

Look at Castaneda's work as an example. In his first book, *The Teachings of Don Juan: A Yaqui Way of Knowledge*, he basically says, "I am a jerky graduate student. By chance I fell in with a bunch of people, some of whom were illiterate, but all of whom knew about a thousand times as much as I ever will. But at the end of my book I will throw in a little anthropological nonsense, just to prove that I am still a graduate student." He was working through a tradition unknown to the rest of us, a Native Mexican-American tradition. He was given psychedelics a lot because he had such a thick head and had so many conceptual boundaries, that the question for his teachers was, "What can we do to get him to understand anything at all?"

Basically we moved from our own self-congratulatory explorations to a much wider version of the world. I've given lectures and written books on certain religious traditions. Can I find psychedelics in those traditions? Of course. Do I need to mention it? Not particularly. Why not? For one, because psychedelics got increasingly worse press, and became less associated with fundamental religious experience, and more associated with whatever the federal government's dishonest take of the day happened to be.

In the last few years there seems to be a resurgence of interest in psychedelics. What's going on?

The culture is gently beginning to admit that—while the federal government has long since stopped research, the journals have stopped accepting articles, and funding for research has dried up—young people are still taking psychedelics. And these young people, who are mostly well educated, are beginning to admit to each other that the decades of misinformation haven't really held as well as the makers of that misinformation would like. It's another generation, some of whom are saying, "I've honestly looked at my own experience versus the walls of misinformation I've been fed, and my own experience seems to be more valid."

So now it's not so terrible to talk about psychedelics, because if you say in any public forum, "The government is both misinformed and misinforming," no one gets upset. You know, Hitler had a theory that the "big lie" would work. And it does, unless everyone has personal experience to the contrary. Well, twenty years of Grateful Dead concerts have left a culture of people who have had personal experience.

I did a series of films on psychedelics many years ago for KQED, San Francisco's Public Broadcasting System station. What we learned, in say 1967, was that young people assumed that if someone was introduced to them as a government official or a physician, then they were about to be lied to. That core understanding—that you cannot trust your government to tell you about your own inner experience—has been maintained since then. The reason that marijuana is now available for medical use, whether the federal government likes it or not, is because too many physicians were saying it was a good idea, in spite of all of the rules that prevent physicians, and psychologists too, from telling the truth.

There was a time when if you had cancer your physician wouldn't tell you. But now we're seeing another wave of people in positions of authority and knowledge and responsibility, who are being asked—particularly by their children, now the third generation—"What's the truth?"

So now psychedelics are coming out of the closet again. In what contexts might they become more accepted by society at large in the future?

I think you need to look at the use of psychedelic material in two contexts. One is entheogenic, and the other is psychotherapeutic. The entheogenic context says that religion is a private act, and that government suppression of private, internal events is fundamentally against humanity. President Clinton, on his first trip to China, said there are certain fundamental human freedoms. In the United States, one of these has been freedom of religion. That's the entheogenic path, the path that I am totally committed to. I now realize that the government did not just stop my research with that letter halting the creativity study in the next room. What it really did was say, "You may not practice your religion, or we will physically imprison you." That's a rather striking departure from what the United States has historically been about.

The other context—where my dissertation, for example, focused—is the use of psychedelics to help people live better lives by having less neurosis, less psychosis, less fixations, less perversions, and so forth. This is a very different realm, which should be in the hands of the people who historically administer interventions, which here have been called "medical."

Now I'm personally a lot more radical. In the United States around 1830 the laws were that anyone could practice any kind of healing or medicine they wished. If you hurt people you could be sued, but if you didn't hurt people then you wouldn't be sued. I like being free to help people. But now I am not a licensed psychologist, which means that I cannot legally help people and charge them. But I am a minister, so I can help people from a different angle if I wish. I have that freedom to be helpful. If I were a psychologist I would have an enormous set of restrictions on how I could help people. If I were a physician I would have a different set of restrictions. I've opted for the religious way, which gives me the maximum freedom to be of maximum use.

Looking ahead into the future, do you see a role for entheogens or psychedelics in these religious and healing areas?

Not until we get to the end of this current period of moral repression. This is a real Inquisition era that we've moved into, where the goal of an enormous number of people in this country is to prevent others from having the right to choose: the right to have children or not to have children, the right to have medicine or not to have medicine, the right to have religion or not to have religion. At the moment we're really reaching a pretty ugly place in terms of the decline of personal freedom. Hopefully we'll bottom out, and the next wave will not only allow psychedelics in the medical model, and entheogens in the spiritual model, but will really begin to set up structures for such uses that make sense.

For example, there are now a couple of religions coming out of Brazil that have found not only very sensible structures for the use of entheogens, but are remarkably middle class, not socially disruptive, and don't threaten to tear down the foundations of society's structures. That's what made our actions so difficult in the 1960s. It's not that our vision of what the world could be was incorrect. It's that by tearing down the buildings we happened to be standing in, we created a lot of problems. Hopefully that won't happen on this next round.

The nice thing about the medical profession's desire to alleviate human suffering is that everyone at some point needs to be helped. The entheogenic route is a little more difficult, but will probably occur as country after country stops buying into the United States' demands to have a drug policy that meets our morally conservative paranoia.

Medical marijuana is really the camel's nose under the tent here. We've got a substance that government says is unmitigated evil for all people at all times, no matter what, and refuses to learn anything about it. Well at some point grown-up nations started to say, "Golly, this really doesn't sound like the way an adult would behave." But most politicians feel they can't afford to admit that they were wrong.

Yet I think the future is basically bright, in cycles. In a sense I'd like it to get to the worst as soon as possible, so we could be done with it. Because, from a personal standpoint, this is a terrible time, where I don't have personal freedom. There's no freedom of speech anymore; it's called political correctness. Unless you're a right-wing fascist bigot you can't say what you want. And since I'm not, I can't say what I want in most public venues or I get attacked. I find this to be a terrible time. But from a slightly larger perspective, this is one of those "act two" events. Act one was the 1960s and act two is now when everything gets terrible. But when you work in fiction, you know that act three is where you either have a joyful exuberance of discovery and reunification and the evils get undone, or you have a tragedy. Either one is art, either one can have the same message, which is: No matter how great the darkness, there are still places of light.

So this is a call for people who are interested in being bold and brave and—as Ram Dass says—"standing up." This is a wonderful time to be a hero, because the forces of darkness are everywhere. As long as everyone is doing something, that's very encouraging." As Johann Wolfgang von Goethe said, "Let everyone sweep in front of his own door, and the whole world will be clean."

What would you say to young people about psychedelics?

I would basically give them my "1960s lecture" on set and setting, which is: If you're going to use psychedelics, do it with someone you love, and hopefully someone who has been there before you, and be aware that you may find out that the world is better than you ever thought. Beyond that, what I generally say to young people is to understand that the government has really misinformed you very badly, and that it would be an awful lot better if you knew what the truth was before you worked with psychedelics. Many people beginning to use psychedelics today may be a little too young. What I learned from my own research is that psychedelics take your life experience and compost it, so that something new can grow. If you don't have much experience, you don't get much out of it. I've always looked at psychedelics as learning tools. Even in the middle of a psychedelic experience, I would begin to think, "I wonder what I'm going to do with this?" In a sense I wanted it to be over so I could start to get to the digestion and assimilation phase, because the psychedelic experience itself wasn't my major interest.

Have you taken psychedelics in recent years? If so, have you found them useful?

I had a long period in which I didn't use them. Partly the problem was set and setting. Making things illegal really doesn't improve them. Most of my work was legal and legitimate, and when I took psychedelics near the end of that period, it was still basically an acceptable thing, which the "thought police" had not ruined.

But fairly recently I did have a major psychedelic experience. What I wanted to explore from that perspective was the question, "Had I lived my life within the framework of this larger vision which I'd had before, and now had again?" It was really like a precursor of the Last Judgment, where they get those scales and they weigh all those dirty things you did and all that groovy stuff you did, and you just watch the scale.

I was relieved to find out that my life's all right. On a higher level it couldn't matter less what my life was—had I been a mass murderer or a saint—at a high enough level that would just be the way the universe works. But the level I was looking at was conventional. In other words: Did I make use of what I'd learned in the way that I treated human beings, the way I treated myself, the way I loved, the way I expanded? It was a long self-evaluation session. I could have very comfortably gone to a more directly spiritual space where I could bypass all that. But I think what I got out of the experience was a reaffirmation that my personality doesn't hold my interest. It's a good tool; I like it. And it's a tool for the kinds of things I do in the world. But so is my car.

What do you think you would have been like without psychedelics?

Without psychedelics I would have been pretty boring. And I certainly couldn't have maintained a decent marriage. I have a decent idea of who I was as a Harvard undergraduate: silly, smart, clever, sarcastic, childish, arrogant, yech! I mean, I'm amused by who I was, but I certainly wouldn't have him for dinner. My world was very tiny, based on having a large vocabulary, a moderately high IQ, and little soul, so little that if you measured it in teaspoons you probably wouldn't have been able to taste me. So I am very clear that psychedelics are the fundamental resource upon which I have drawn to become a human being.

How have psychedelics affected your views about aging and death?

Well, those are really two separate questions. So, let's take death, because that's easy. My psychedelic experience has made it clear that for Jim Fadiman, death is going to end a lot of interesting anecdotal material. And, *as* Jim Fadiman, I certainly think that's terrible. But as I—this other I—big deal! I have the deep feeling that my personality is like my shirt, and when my shirt gets ragged enough I'll take it off. There are other shirts. So death is something that I don't particularly look forward to. But as someone said, "It will cure whatever ails you." As to aging, well I haven't found much going for it yet.

Shifting gears a bit, who do you think should take psychedelics? Say, if it was in your power to design policy?

If it was in my power to design policy I would probably design something the way adult literacy is designed, in which people are given this experience in a good setting, and those who are interested in helping other people are empowered to do so. Certainly it would be very useful for people who are trained in either mental health or physical health to be there as the primary guides, because sometimes there are problems with these powerful materials.

I feel strongly that we should return entheogen use to the context of a guided relationship, which has been the model in every traditional culture that I have studied. The idea that people should go off and trip with others their own age who don't know any more than they do, be they fifty or twenty or twelve, has never worked well in any culture, and it certainly doesn't work well in ours. So if I were the spiritual experience czar, and decreed that people would be allowed to have freedom of religion in the United States of America, I would start by saying that freedom of religion of an entheogenic sort will be done similarly to the way one flies a private plane. You don't start by going up alone. You first go up with someone who knows more than you do, and they drive until you're ready.

What advice would you have for those who are interested in making psychedelics available for healing or for religious experience?

A good bit of advice is: Never trust anyone in the media to give you a fair shake. But largely, I don't have any advice for you. I just kind of feel a combination of admiration and sorrow at the large rock you're pushing up a very stiff hill, because when you get it up to the top each time, somebody pushes it down.

In a sense, those involved with psychedelics in the healing arts are in a holding action; you are preventing the potential from being lost totally. But it's kind of like the Irish monks in the ninth and tenth centuries: You're holding the knowledge until it can be used. If you were allowed to do research I would be very happy for you. I just admire you, really, for being willing to do this work that I clearly have dropped out of. The medical-psychiatric approach might be the only door that was left open to you. All the others were closed. I watched them close a number of them in my face, and therefore took alternative routes to keeping the vision alive.

On the spiritual side, I encourage people to continue to let the divine wind blow through them, however that can be done, whether it's *satsang*, meditation, or whatever. As far as I can see, the national park system is a set of cathedrals designed for people to let go of their small self. So I'm very supportive of the national park system. You know, give me Bryce Canyon, Death Valley, Zion, Yellowstone. I think that's one thing that the government has not figured out: how much sedition is created by people falling in love with Nature.

From the long view, are you optimistic?

On the long view, I would say that there is no clear vision of history that shows us moving in one positive direction. Socrates is about as good as we get. We've now had a few thousand years, and there have been no improved models. So I'm neither optimistic nor pessimistic. If you've been in enough theater, what you realize is that the play will go on. But one of the things about the correct use of entheogens is that it engenders a core of optimism that no amount of "this world" can defeat. If you look through history with entheogenic eyes, you realize that, since the truth is always available, some people are going to discover it one way or another in every generation. In this generation a lot of us had a chance to discover it.

The potential problem with the transpersonal movement is the same one that confronts every wisdom tradition. Every spiritual tradition that is worth the name has at its origin somebody who had a breakthrough into the *true* reality. When they came back, they wondered, "How am I going to share this with anybody?" Somehow they found a way to do it, and eventually they had a lot of people who hung out around them, some of whom said, "I'll do the shit work. I'll arrange the meeting, I'll bring in the food, I'll handle things."

The handlers gradually—as they always do—got control of the situation. The original founder passed away, and the handlers started to make it easier for themselves, because it's easier to bring in the food if it's every Sunday, it's easier if everyone has a certain place to sit. So the bureaucrats always end up eating the spiritual food of the founder. Without a continual infusion of spiritual food you end up with what we would call a religion. The spiritual urge—the need to be part of your whole self—cannot be repressed any more than the sexual urge. But the expression of it always, inevitably—and I say that without any ill will—gets ossified. Inflexible bones lead to further inflexibility.

My concern, for instance, with humanistic and transpersonal psychology, is that they're still being run by people like me. I want to know who's going to get rid of me? Who's going to throw the old regime out? I am looking towards the next psychedelic generation to say to us, "What a bunch of tired old farts you are with this journal, this association, and this traditional psychology, when God is all around you!" And I want to say to them, "Carry me out of the palace. You win! Tear down the walls. Let's get back to basics." I mean, I'd appreciate it if you wouldn't *shoot* me. But please take my job!

2

Albert Hofmann

From Molecules to Mystery:
Psychedelic Science, the Natural World, and Beyond

Born January 11, 1906 • Albert Hofmann was born in Baden, Switzerland. After receiving his doctorate in medicinal chemistry from the University of Zurich in 1929, he went on to a long and successful career as the director of research for the Department of Natural Products at Sandoz Pharmaceutical in Basel. Specializing in the isolation of the active principles of known medicinal plants, during the 1930s Hofmann became the world's leading authority on the study of *Claviceps purpurea* (ergot) and ergot alkaloids. Methodically creating variations of one particular ergot derivative, lysergic acid, in 1938 he synthesized the twenty-fifth in the series—lysergic acid diethylamide—which he identified as LSD-25. After animal testing yielded no significant findings, Hofmann put aside his examination of this particular compound. Five years later, however, he experienced what he later described as a "peculiar presentiment," intuiting that there was more to LSD than he had initially suspected. In April of 1943, he resynthesized the compound, during which he inadvertently ingested a minute amount, precipitating a profound alteration of consciousness. Three days later, on April 19, he intentionally replicated the experience by ingesting 250 micrograms of LSD.

For the next three decades Hofmann played a pivotal role in the development of the nascent field of psychedelic research. Beyond his vital contributions to early LSD investigations, he also made another astounding discovery in the late 1950s, when he succeeded in isolating the active alkaloids of psychedelic mushrooms: psilocybin and psilocin. As the leading medicinal chemist of his day, his identification of these compounds from the legendary magic mushrooms was an extraordinary accomplishment, achieving a scientific breakthrough of far reaching implications.

Remaining vigorous and productive well into his ninth decade, Hofmann has had an inestimable impact on the development of psychedelic science and philosophy. Besides his many laboratory discoveries, he has written numerous scientific articles and a variety of books, most notably *LSD: My Problem Child; The Road to Eleusis* (with R. Gordon Wasson and Carl A.P. Ruck); *The Botany and Chemistry of Hallucinogens* (with Richard Evans Schultes); and *Plants of the Gods: Origins of Hallucinogenic Use* (with Richard Evans Schultes).

AFTER I HAD DISCOVERED the activity of lysergic acid diethylamide, and even before we had started our research, I knew that this substance would be important to psychiatry. I participated in one of the first experiments and took a small dose in the laboratory. For me, it was a terrible experience. With all of the lab equipment and people running around asking questions and giving tests, it was a hell. I was in the world of Hieronymous Bosch, with these terrible machines and people with white coats all around. I couldn't understand what they were doing there or what was going on in the laboratory.

I felt that there must be another approach to LSD. I had the feeling in this experiment, that there was something in me under the influence of the LSD that was trying to be happy but could not. It was a feeling, as in a dream, which could not come up because of the disturbance caused by the terrible testing environment.

I realized that I needed to try it again in a very different setting. Together with a friend of mine, a German writer, I had another LSD session in my home. My wife had prepared our home for this session with beautiful flowers and fruits, and some incense. I did not take a large dose, only fifty micrograms. I had a nice experience that was not very deep, but just fundamentally aesthetic. In my mind I was away in North Africa, in Morocco. I had not been there before, but I had the feeling that it was Morocco. I saw the camels and all the Bedouins and a really fantastic landscape. It was like a fairy tale that I lived. And from this experience, I learned how important one's surroundings are. I learned that when working with substances like LSD, one must always pay attention to the set and the setting.

Do you believe it is possible to reestablish psychedelic research as a respectable scientific field?

There are many good signs. After years of silence, there have finally been some new investigations in Switzerland and Germany, and also in the United States. The European College for the Study of Consciousness had a meeting in Heidelberg, and there were many good presentations. In Heidelberg I enjoyed meeting with Rick Doblin, of the Multidisciplinary

Association for Psychedelic Studies, and professor David Nichols, of the Heffter Research Institute. Both of their organizations are doing fine work. Their approach appears to be quite different than that of some of their predecessors from several decades ago.

Are you referring to Timothy Leary?

Yes. I was visited by Timothy Leary when he was living in Switzerland many years ago. He was an intelligent man, and quite charming. I enjoyed our conversations very much. However, he also had a need for too much attention. He enjoyed being provocative, and that shifted the focus from what should have been the essential issue. It is unfortunate, but for many years these drugs became taboo. Hopefully, these problems from the 1960s will not be repeated.

What implications do psychedelic drugs have for the field of psychiatry?

Shortly after LSD was discovered, it was recognized as being of great value to psychoanalysis and psychiatry. It was not considered to be an escape. It was a very important discovery at that time, and for fifteen years it could be used legally in psychiatric treatment and for scientific study in humans. During this time, Delysid®, the name I gave to LSD, was used safely and was the subject of thousands of publications in the professional literature. Actually, I recently had visitors from the Albert Hofmann Foundation, to whom I gave all of the original documentation, which had been stored at the Sandoz Laboratories.[1] This early work was extensively documented, and shows how well research with LSD went until it became part of the drug scene in the 1960s. So, from originally being part of the therapeutic pharmacopeia, LSD became a street drug and inevitably it was made illegal. Because of this reputation, it became unavailable to the medical field. And the research, which had previously been very open, was stopped. Now it appears that this research may start again. The importance of such investigations appears to be recognized by the health authorities, and so it is my hope that finally the prohibition is coming to an end, and the medical field can return to the explorations that were forced to stop over thirty years ago.

What recommendations would you give to researchers now who want to work with these substances?

When Delysid® was distributed legally by Sandoz, it came with a little brochure that explained how it could be used. As an aid to psychoanalysis and psychotherapy, and also as a means for psychiatrists themselves to experience these extraordinary states of mind. It was specifically stated on this package insert that the psychiatrist who was interested in using Delysid® should first test it on himself.

So you felt that it was important that the psychiatrist have firsthand knowledge of the psychedelic experience?

Absolutely! Before it can be used in clinical work, it most definitely must be taken by the psychiatrist. In the very first reports and guidelines written for LSD, this was clearly stated. And this remains of utmost importance today.

Are there lessons we can learn from the past that we should be attentive to, so that such mistakes are not repeated in the future?

Yes. If it is possible to stop the improper use of psychedelics, then I think it would be possible to dispense them for medical use. But as long as they continue to be misused, and as long as people misunderstand psychedelics—using them as pleasure drugs and failing to appreciate the very deep psychic experiences they can induce—then their medical use will be held back. Their use on the streets has been a problem for more than thirty years, as the drugs are misunderstood and accidents can occur. This makes it difficult for the health authorities to change their policies and allow for medical use. And although it should be possible to convince the health authorities that in responsible hands psychedelics could be used safely in the medical field, their use on the streets continues to make it very hard for the health authorities to agree.

It appears that teenagers are once again becoming interested in LSD, MDMA, and related drugs. Currently there is the rave phenomenon, where young people take psychedelics and dance all night. Why are such experiences attractive to teenagers, and how should we respond to what they are doing?

A very deep problem of our time is that we no longer have a spiritual basis in our lives. The churches are no longer convincing with their dogma. Yet people need a deep spiritual foundation for their lives. In the past, this foundation was built on accepted religious creeds, which people believed in. But today such beliefs have less power. We cannot believe things which we know are not possible, that are not real. We must go on the basis of that which we know—that which everybody can experience. On this basis, one must find the entrance to the spiritual world. Because many young people are looking for meaningful experiences, they are looking for this thing which is the opposite of the material world. Not all young people are looking for money and power. Some are looking for a happiness and satisfaction born of the spiritual world. They are looking, but there are very few credible sanctioned paths. And, of course, one path that still delivers for young people is that of the psychedelic drugs.

Such young people have a need to open their eyes. The doors of perception must be opened. That means these young people must learn by their own experience, to see the world as it was before human beings were on this planet. That is the real problem today, that people live in towns and cities where everything is dead. This material world, made by humans, has no real life. It will die and disappear.

I would advise young people to go out into the countryside, go to the meadow, go to the garden, go to the woods. Such places are of the world of nature, to which we fundamentally belong. It is the circle of life, of which we are an integral part. Young people must open their eyes and see the browns and greens of the earth, and the light which is the essence of nature. The young need to become aware of this circle of life, and realize that it is possible to experience the beauty and deep meaning, which is at the core of our relationship to nature.

When did you first acquire this visionary appreciation of nature?

When I was a young boy, I had many opportunities to walk through the countryside. I had profound visionary encounters with nature, and this was long before I conducted my initial experiments with LSD. Indeed, my first experiences with LSD were reminiscent of these early mystical encounters I had had as a child in nature. So, you see that it is quite possible to have these experiences without drugs. But many people are blocked, without an inborn faculty to realize beauty, and it is these people who may need a psychedelic in order to have a visionary experience of nature.

How do we reconcile this visionary experience with religion and with scientific truth?

It is important to have the experience directly. Aldous Huxley taught us not to simply believe the words, but to have the experience ourselves. This is why the different forms of religion are no longer adequate. They are simply words, words, words, without the direct experience of what it is the words represent. We are now at a phase of human development where we have accumulated an enormous amount of knowledge through scientific research in the material world. This is important knowledge, but it must be integrated. What science has brought to light is absolutely true. But this is only one part, only one side of our existence, that of the material world.

We have a body, and we know that matter gets older and changes. So therefore, since we have a body, we must die. On the other hand, the spiritual world is, of course, eternal—but only insofar as it exists in the moment. It is important that we realize this enormous difference between these two sides of our lives. The material world is the world of our body and it is where man has made all of these scientific and technological discoveries. But science and technology are based on natural laws, and the material world is only the manifestation of the spiritual world.

If we attempt to manifest something, we will have to make use of the material world. For you and I to speak with one another, we must have tongues, we must have air, and so forth. All of this is of the material world. If we were to read about spiritual things, it is only words. We must have the spiritual experience directly. And the experience occurs only by opening the mind and all of our senses. Those doors of perception must be cleansed. And if the experience does not come spontaneously, on its own, then we may make use of what Aldous Huxley called a "gratuitous grace." This may take the form of psychedelic drugs, or perhaps through disciplines like yoga or meditation. But what is of greatest importance, is that we have personal spiritual experience. Not words, not beliefs, but experience.

Projecting into the future, do you envision that there may be an accepted role within Euro-American culture for psychedelics?

Absolutely! I am convinced that the importance of psychedelics will be recognized. The pathway for this is through psychiatry, but not the psychoanalytic psychiatry of Freud, and not the limited scope of modern biological psychiatry. Rather, it will occur through the field of transpersonal psychiatry. This transpersonal view takes into account the material world *and* the spiritual world. It recognizes that we are simultaneously part of both worlds. What fits with the concept of transpersonal psychiatry is that we open our doors of perception. What transpersonal psychiatry tries to give us is a recipe for gaining entrance into the spiritual world. This fits exactly with the results of psychedelics. It stimulates your senses. It opens your perception for your own experience. How this phenomenon affects our existence in the material world can be understood through scientific research, and how we can integrate this knowledge with our spiritual selves can be achieved through the transpersonal path.

You have lived through two World Wars and a Cold War. When you look ahead into humanity's future, are you hopeful, or not?

I am hopeful for the long distant future, but for the near future I am terribly pessimistic. I believe that what is occurring in the material world is a reflection of the spiritual state of humankind. I fear that many terrible things will occur around the world, because humankind is in spiritual crisis. But I hope that over time humankind will finally learn what it needs to learn. I recently reread the compilation of lectures that Aldous Huxley gave in San Francisco in 1959, called *The Human Situation.* Everything that we are concerned with today, about the ego, consciousness, and the survival of humankind, can all be read in this book. I would like to recommend it.

What can we learn from the so-called primitive cultures who use psychedelic substances as part of their religious practices?

The most important thing is that they use psychedelics in a spiritual framework and we don't. We must learn from them, we must identify the right structures, we must find new uses. I could imagine that it may be possible to create meditation centers for psychedelic use in natural surroundings, where teachers could have experiences and train to become adepts. I perceive this as being possible, but first psychedelics will have to become available to medicine and psychiatry. And then it should be made available for such spiritual centers. Basically, all that we need to know we can learn from how the primitive people use psychedelics as sacraments, in a spiritual framework. We need such centers, but we also need the psychiatrists. These psychiatrists must become the shamans of our times. Then I think we will be ready to move towards this kind of psychopharmacopeia.

Back in the 1960s many people became frightened of LSD and other psychedelics, including many psychiatrists. Why did this happen?

They did not use psychedelics the right way, and they did not have the right conditions. So, they were not adequately prepared. Psychedelics enable a delicate and deep experience, if used in the right way. But remember, the more powerful the instrument, the more the chance of damage occurring if it is not used properly. Back in the 1960s, there were unfortunately many occasions where psychedelics were used in the wrong way, and consequently they caused injury. The great tragedy is that these valuable medicines were not always respected and not always understood. So, the psychedelics came to be feared, and were taken out of the hands of responsible investigators and psychiatrists. It was a great loss for medicine and psychiatry, and for humankind. Hopefully, it is not too late to learn from these mistakes, and to demonstrate the proper and respectful way psychedelics should be used.

NOTE

1.   In the early 1950s, Sandoz began collecting LSD- and psilocybin-related articles as part of Albert Hofmann's work with these substances. For nearly thirty-five years, Sandoz gathered over four thousand documents: LSD and psilocybin journal articles from the late 1940s through the early 1980s, a few student theses, newspaper clippings, and other unique items. In the mid-1990s, the collection was given to the Albert Hofmann Foundation, and during the late 1990s, along with the Multidisciplinary Association for Psychedelic Studies and the Heffter Research Institute, they collaborated to create a digital index of the papers. In 2002, largely due to the efforts of representatives from the Erowid web site, a digital index of this entire collection was created. It can be found online at www.erowid.org/ references/hofmann_collection.php.

3

Myron Stolaroff

How Much Can People Change?

Born August 20, 1920 • Myron Stolaroff was a Stanford University trained engineer who directed long range planning for Ampex Corporation for many years. In the early 1960s, he retired from his industrial career to cofound (along with Willis Harman and James Fadiman) the International Foundation for Advanced Study (IFAS) in Menlo Park, California. Between 1961 and 1965 the IFAS conducted groundbreaking studies on the effects of LSD and mescaline on creativity and problem solving. After the Food and Drug Administration (FDA) revoked permission to conduct investigations with psychedelics, Stolaroff continued to experiment with a variety of unscheduled substances, until the imposition of the Controlled Substance Analog Act of 1986. Since that time he has devoted himself to studying how the knowledge he acquired through the use of psychedelics can be utilized to deepen meditation practice and to catalyze personal growth and development. Stolaroff published two well-received books on this topic during the 1990s, *Thanatos To Eros: Thirty-five Years of Psychedelic Exploration* and *The Secret Chief: Conversations with a Pioneer of the Underground Psychedelic Therapy Movement*.

MY BACKGROUND IS IN ELECTRICAL ENGINEERING, but my spiritual path was responsible for introducing me to psychedelics. In 1955, I belonged to a spiritual group called the Sequoia Seminar, which sponsored a lecture by Gerald Heard, and I was astounded by his brilliant mind and prodigious memory. Gerald told me about a Canadian who had administered LSD to him and Aldous Huxley. I was quite amazed by what he said about his experiences, particularly since I considered him to be a great natural mystic. So I got in touch with the Canadian, who turned out to be Al Hubbard.

How did you come to research psychedelics?

I had my first LSD experience with Al in 1956. Afterwards, I introduced him to members of the Sequoia Seminar, and a number of those people then had experiences. Eventually we decided to set up a group to do research with Al's guidance, but we immediately got into conflicts because Hubbard was not popular. He was a strange character, and these were pretty quiet, contemplative people. They all thought he had a tremendous ego, and in those days we were all desperately trying to get rid of our egos. The group created a protocol that I thought was ridiculous, because they ignored all the things that Al had taught us. It was like starting over from scratch. I ended up losing interest, so I left the group and continued to work with Al.

Eventually, we began to feel that this work was important enough that we should start setting up centers, and in 1961 we established one in Menlo Park: the International Foundation for Advanced Study. I resigned from Ampex, where I was in charge of long range planning, to work full-time with this foundation.

We simply wanted to make the experience available under appropriate conditions. We charged a fee, which they were doing up in Canada. We conducted interviews to ensure that those who came were appropriate candidates, and we worked out procedures for preparing them. We incorporated the pretreatment that Al had developed, which used Meduna's mixture of carbon dioxide and oxygen, which was an excellent means of preparation.

Al persuaded Charles Savage, a psychiatrist at the National Institute of Mental Health, to be our medical director. Charles interviewed every candidate first to determine the person's suitability for the program. We had people fill out very complete biographies that went into all aspects of their life: relationships, problem areas, aspirations, and so on. We set up offices, constructed beautifully appointed session rooms, and we were in business. Then we put together a research team. Willis Harman and James Fadiman joined us, as did Bob Mogar—a psychologist who was an assistant professor at San Francisco State College. Within just a few months we began to put people through various protocols and tests.

One test excited Mogar very much. He was quite an expert in the Minnesota Multiphasic Personality Inventory test, which he considered to be largely impervious to the changes that people underwent in psychotherapy. He was astounded when he saw some of the scales that he thought were quite stable making significant shifts after a psychedelic session. Not only that, but when these individuals were retested, the shift continued—sometimes for a year or perhaps two years.

Charles Savage was convinced—this the first real argument I had with him—that mescaline was an emetic. I said, "No, it's not an emetic. It's just that people get into things that make them sick. But if the experience is conducted right, that can be avoided and those things resolved without their throwing up." Well, he didn't agree with me, but I don't think we ever had a person throw up, in all our foundation's work.

How many years did this work continue in Menlo Park?

We started in March 1961 and closed in August 1965 when the FDA withdrew our Investigational New Drug (IND) approval. It wasn't just with us—they took away everybody's IND throughout the nation. I think there were some 75 investigations, and they withdrew all but five, which were involved with animal work—no human work at all.

What was the source of your funding for the foundation?

I personally financed the whole thing, and we always operated independently. Fortunately, I had made out quite well with Ampex. I acquired stock at 13¢ a share, which I sold for $40 a share. I only wish I'd had more. [laughs]

Over the four and a half years you did this work, how many subjects did you work with, and how many sessions did they have?

There were 350 people, and mostly they just had one session each. Some had two, and then a few had psilocybin follow-ups. We primarily used LSD and mescaline. Especially with alcoholics, we felt that mescaline helped them break down their resistances and go deeper inside.

What was the purpose with using Meduna's mixture during this research?

People would visit the therapist and review their autobiography. Then we would administer carbogen: Meduna's mixture of carbon dioxide and oxygen. We usually gave them about three inhalations. They'd have an inhalation, share what they experienced, and then they'd have another one. It usually took about two or three. One woman I worked with personally, a nurse, said she got as much out of the two preparatory sessions as she got out of the LSD experience. And she had a great LSD experience.

I once claimed that if I ever had to go back to work, I could make a living as a CO_2 therapist. I enjoyed doing it, and felt I helped people through it quite well. But after it was all over, I'm not so sure. It's pretty traumatic.

I worked for two years with it myself, with a physician friend, and had a lot of tremendous experiences. But he stopped working with me because he said, "Myron, we're just recycling." I'd have a great experience, a good discharge, a lot of anger and stuff, and feel really wonderful for several days. Then I'd begin to load up again. We did this once a week.

I'd have another discharge and feel great, and then I'd be back sort of in the same place. After a couple of years, he said, "Myron, we're not getting anywhere."

If I could remember everything that happened in those experiences, I'd be the smartest man in the world. But they fade, the CO_2 experiences usually fade rapidly. However, a few of them really stuck and were very significant.

What was the purpose of that as an introduction to the LSD?

There were several. First, it taught people how to let go to the experience. Second, it was a great abreactor or emotional releaser. If you have repressed stuff, when that CO_2 hits you, it really releases. People experience unconscious material for the first time in their life. It's strange, but you talk about the unconscious and you read about it, and then you think you know what it is. But you can't know what's unconscious. By definition, it's unconscious! So people are always shocked when real unconscious material comes up, and a lot of unconscious material came up in these preparatory sessions. This made people realize how much more there was to be learned and gained. It gave them a lot of enthusiasm for the subsequent LSD session, because they often felt a lot better after abreacting. So it had a number of advantages as a preparation.

Sometimes when people were psychologically "stuck" in LSD sessions, we'd bring in the carbogen tank. It would only take a few breaths while on LSD to break through a barrier. We didn't do that very often, because we preferred that the individual work through any psychological obstacles that came up. But every once in a while it seemed to be very helpful to push a person through.

What effects did this research have been on you personally, and on your career?

I thought it was the most exciting work that one could possibly do. I mean, watching these people come to life, watching them deal with very difficult, painful situations and resolve them. I was convinced early on— even before we set up the clinic—that LSD was the greatest discovery that humankind has ever made, and this conviction was repeatedly reinforced. Even though we learned that it's not the panacea that we originally hoped for, and that it required a lot of preparation and follow-up work, it was still a remarkable discovery.

By the time we set up the clinic, I had already decided I was going to spend my life in this work. My experience at the clinic simply reinforced this decision and kept revealing further possibilities. Toward the end we began researching creativity, which showed enormous promise. Eventually—since I had come from industry—I wanted to go back to working in industry. Because I could see how you could help such people—managers or designers—become more creative. All their work could be enhanced. I'd hoped that this would open up, but now we see that this is quite a ways down the path.

How did this research alter your beliefs about the nature of mind?

One of the amazing things about these substances is that you can see levels inside yourself that you never before suspected. I think what you learn is that there's something basic that we all yearn for. I think our deepest yearning is to be intimately related to each other. Actually, it's to be intimately related to God. That's our deepest need. I think the breaking of those initial bonds is the most painful thing that we experience.

If people weren't wanted as children, or if they had parents who did not really nurture the child, this is where real crippling of human beings takes place—in the breaking of those initial intimacies. I think a lot of our energy is funneled into the quest to restore that initial intimacy. We keep searching. I think that a lot of *men,* in particular, have enormous defenses against real intimacy. It's a major human problem.

Do you think that psychedelics help one push beyond those barriers?

It makes them clearer, which is how you identify the problem. Then you learn how to push beyond your own private barriers to open yourself to intimacy. It's still hard, but if you keep going on this path, you reach the point where you have no doubts that this is the goal. Ultimately, true liberation in the Buddhist sense is reaching wholeness, where you are totally at peace and intimate with everything that exists. If you leave out even one person, you've left out part of yourself; you can't be really whole until you've absolutely accepted every living creature.

What have psychedelics taught you about human potential?

It's infinite. It's absolutely infinite. I don't see how there can be any end. We're going to learn more and more, we're going to become increasingly creative, we're going to create better technology. We're going to learn how to get along with each other. Whether on this planet or somewhere else; whether this planet even *survives,* I don't know.

The world's great thinkers don't know whether this planet will survive. In *Voices on the Threshold of Tomorrow* by Georg Feuerstein, 145 of the world's great thinkers share their views of the future. None of them are willing to say that the future is assured. But most of them seem to agree that if we do have a future, it will be because we've learned compassion, and because we've learned the spiritual basis of life.

To what degree did your experience with psychedelics cause you to reevaluate the different schools of psychology?

Every school is based on some values and principles that are correct. The trouble starts when you think your way is the *only* way. You see this even in some of our best teachers, but that's so crude!

We're all different, and different people respond to different paths. There's a place for all of them. But when you get invested in any of them you have a problem, and then you need to look at what the others have to offer. There may be a stage in one's development where the approach taken by some specific school of thought is very helpful. Then when you resolve particular conflicts, some other approach may be helpful.

Through your work with psychedelics did you find yourself changing allegiance from one school to another?

I recognized early on that Jung had a profound understanding of the mind, and I still think that Jung was the greatest and bravest psychologist who ever lived. I don't know of anyone else who was as courageous in exploring the unconscious as Jung was.

Tibetan Buddhism has a great deal to offer. But it suffers from lacking a full psychology, as the meditation teacher Jack Kornfield has pointed out. I think Jack has done a great service in showing how therapy can help on the Buddhist path. The Buddhists have tried to do it without a full understanding of psychology, and this can make it much more difficult and less rewarding. Ken Wilber comments that you can have enlightened beings from the Buddhist standpoint and still have poor personalities. One always has to remain open to new possibilities and considerations.

How did your work with psychedelics alter your understanding of reality?

Taking psychedelics is like having films removed; they remove obstacles to awareness. They point out where I've lost touch with the real intimacy of my surroundings. They allow me to recognize those walls that I have built up between myself and reality, and can dissolves those walls. When these are removed, you are "there." Then the trick is to learn how to *stay* there, and that's where some kind of spiritual discipline is essential. I find meditation to be the best tool for maintaining that clarity.

In the end, I think we really *do* have to learn to get "there" without chemical help. We have to grow a "God muscle." Humans are here to develop and grow. We keep developing our skills and our wisdom, our athletes perform better, we keep getting more virtuosos. As a species, we keep expanding our capacity.

But we have to take responsibility for ensuring that everyone advances. If you are advanced enough, perhaps you can just meditate and reach higher levels of awareness, and that is good for *you*. But I look at it as a partnership where we each have to do the practice to develop the muscle, to develop the skills, and then we have to share what we have learned.

How has your research influenced your views on death?

I've come to accept reincarnation, but I don't like some of the Buddhist concepts which don't acknowledge individual survival. I really have a strong sense of a survival of individuals. From what I have seen and experienced, individuals mean a great deal. It's one of the real mysteries of creation: how do we become individuals, and acquire this type of consciousness? Does that individuality disappear when we die? Frances Vaughan, in her interview in William Elliott's book *Tying Rocks to Clouds*, expressed her feeling that when you go back, you're like the drop that goes back to the ocean and you no longer exist as an individual.

But I have a very comfortable feeling that between reincarnations we move into a higher consciousness and contemplate the whole thing: what we've done, what we've developed, where we missed the boat. We prepare ourselves for the next incarnation. I can't say that's *really* true. All I can say is that it *feels* right to me. But I don't have any doubt about the survival of consciousness in some form or another.

How would you sum up the benefits of the research and the clinical work you did with psychedelics? And what were the costs—the negative side?

The greatest benefit was finding out what's *truly* real. That's the greatest prize that anyone could possibly want. While that prize is *available* to us, it's not guaranteed, and I don't think we get it unless we really want it. The bottom line is intention. For those who really want it, I think it's available.

The greatest cost? In order to *really* achieve in life, I think the primary requirement is honesty. I think we pay the biggest price for dishonesty, and dishonesty comes about in many ways. For example, suppose you have one of those great, blessed visions and see how wonderful everything is. And then suppose you come back and ignore that, and just continue life as usual. Maybe you have some bad habits, you're very judgmental and caustic and so on, and you come back and continue with these. I think you pay a price for that, and your situation becomes worse. So perhaps the biggest cost is trying to reach out for the best without being willing to pay the price, in terms of accepting the responsibility to change.

What strikes you most about the people who you have been able to follow up on over the years, formally or informally? Are they just like anybody else, or does something set them apart?

I think that the most distinguishing mark is accepting spirituality in their lives, a conviction that life has a spiritual basis. They fashioned their lives to live in harmony with that idea as much as they could, and because of this, they really stand apart from most folks. You can tell it when you get together with them; there's an immediate harmony. It's just different from getting together with other people who haven't had psychedelic experiences.

Those people who have had psychedelics are more accepting and less judgmental. They're easier going, more relaxed, have better senses of humor. They have greater clarity that they use in their work, in their profession. A lot of them found they get along better in their marriages and with their kids.

You published reports indicating long-term positive change in those people who took part in your studies, right?

Yes. The subjects filled out questionnaires at various times after their experiences: three months, six months, a year. A lot of those scales kept going up. The further away they were from their initial experience, the higher the rating was. For example, "belief in God" and "less anger" kept growing over time. With a few items, there was some fall-back, but predominantly, as I recall, they continued to be favorable.

What effects did you observe in people who had gone through your program in terms of their psychological adjustment?

Well, let me start with engineers. Because I'm an engineer and one of our major therapists was an engineer, we attracted a lot of engineers into our program. I concluded that engineers in general are very sensitive people who have been so injured in the area of intimacy that they found a vocation in which they wouldn't have to deal in human relationships. Instead they deal with objects. When they went through our program they discovered the feeling part of their nature, which they had pretty much repressed. Psychedelics opened tremendous doors for them. All of a sudden they got along better with their wives and children, and they began to appreciate art and music.

Of course, I don't think anybody could go through the program without leaving with a far greater appreciation of music, because listening to music is a remarkable experience under psychedelics. We had a number of people who came to us who were only interested in popular music, and had no interest in classical music. We always asked, "Well, would it be okay if we feed in a little classical music here and there?" And they'd respond, "Well, okay." They left *loving* classical music—much preferring it to popular music! I think that was true with almost 100 percent of them, although we didn't keep statistics on it.

Looking back on the 1960s, do you think psychedelics had some role in the anti-Vietnam War movement?

Oh, I'm sure! I think most psychedelic people immediately see the ridiculousness of war, that it's a stupid way to resolve human differences. Of course, it's based on the fact that we can't communicate. One thing you really learn under psychedelics is the value of communication and how to communicate more effectively; for example, being more honest and getting over our own judgments.

I know one of the tremendous gains I made; I suddenly woke up one day and realized that I never *really* listened to anybody. I do think we can become better listeners, but we have a long way to go.

Another thing that individuals need to do is to learn how to *be* a learner. It's so important to learn how to learn. Once you learn how to be a learner, then life is just a tremendous, continual opening. And psychedelics can help with that. But some people begin to lose their ability to stay open, because they haven't recognized or been willing to put in the effort that it takes to maintain a new state of being.

One of the great lessons I learned was that the amount of work, determination, and depth of intention required for enduring transformation was a lot greater than I had thought. I originally felt that once you had seen these vistas, you had it made. But you lose them. You really need ways of maintaining this awareness and better state of being. Charles Tart says, "We're living in mass hypnotism." Our culture and all that impinges on us, mitigate against the kinds of things you learn with psychedelics. You've got to develop a really sound foundation to be impervious to those kinds of influences.

Do you think there are people who are naturally open to these better states of being?

Oh, no question about it. Some people don't need psychedelics at all, they are real naturals.

We've heard the positive side. Do you feel that psychedelics have any deleterious side effects on health or memory or cognitive ability?

I'm not aware of any. However, one thing I've noticed is that older people stop taking psychedelics, because they find the experiences increasingly uncomfortable. Why this happens would be a wonderful research project for someone. One psychologist friend is convinced that the body doesn't process them properly any more.

But I'm convinced that if you're going to keep using psychedelics, you have to raise your level of responsibility—and if you don't, maybe you get into more trouble. I think that's the problem. Your potential keeps growing, and if you lived up to your potential, you'd be functioning at quite an enormous level. But if you're not prepared to do that, then I think you're caught.

What do you mean by uncomfortable?

The experiences are not pleasant. Instead of getting into a wonderful, universal space, into euphoria or bliss, one becomes quite uncomfortable—body discomforts of various kinds. No insight occurs and no particular learning happens.

Is this because these people are really dropping the ball with regard to integrating their experiences and working on the insights?

That's what I feel, but it's just a feeling, and I don't know how justified it is. The main reason I feel that way is because I have encountered those same discomforts. There have been times when I thought, "Jesus Christ! Why in the hell am I doing this?" But I find that as I face the discomfort and work through it, I always end up in a better place. With very few exceptions, every experience I have is better than the last one—and that's saying a lot! It could be because some areas of my life are now better resolved than they were before. There's less anxiety, less self-interest, more compassion for others.

Have you known people for whom psychedelics were actually harmful?

Very definitely! There are some people for whom the experience is clearly harmful. Hopefully, one learns not to work with such people, as you do begin to develop a sense of what it takes to have a successful experience.

To what do you attribute society's reaction to psychedelics and the current repression of them?

I think the bottom line is honesty. This is a point that has not been made enough. I think it's a point that all of us in this field should really emphasize. Psychedelics are for honest people. If you're really honest, you're going to get rewarded. It's the dishonest ones that suffer and have the bad trips, because they don't want to accept the painful psychological material that comes up, which can be very difficult to accept and acknowledge.

I think one reason that psychedelics have become illegal is because they bring into awareness more than most people are willing to face up to. They require admitting a lot—admitting greed, admitting self-interest, and repressed hostility in the psyche.

Historically, Hitler was someone who understood this. He recognized the anger that people suppress, so he gave them a target: the Jews. Having a common target made people feel good, and they mobilized around him. Our politicians are doing something similar, only it's "druggies." Everybody wants to hate "druggies." That allows us as a society to overlook our own shortcomings and responsibilities, and to project our inner anger.

Governments will mobilize the people against a common enemy, which causes the people to lose sight of the fact that our own leaders and systems are corrupt. And your feeling is that psychedelics force the user to really examine just how flawed our personal lives, our relationships, and our collective mind sets are.

Our government, our leadership. Oh my God! Five trillion dollars in debt! What does that say? What does that say about *morality*? What about kids being brought up in a nation where our "morality" allows us to run up five trillion dollars in debt? Good God!

Looking back over the course of the last half-century and all that has happened with psychedelics—how interest has risen and fallen, how antagonism has increased—what is your vision of the future?

I think there are some positive signs. The Food and Drug Administration is taking a somewhat more liberal view, and television documentaries increasingly present psychedelics in a more favorable light, or at least with less of a dogmatic political agenda.

What have we learned from the past fifty years that might help us to set up a process that doesn't just replicate what happened in the 1960s?

Unfortunately, some young kids have an opening and then they see how awful things are, and then they've got to cuss out everybody, and play the "we're right and you're wrong" game. We have to be open and see where people are, instead of taking a rebellious attitude. We have to learn how to communicate, and you can't communicate with someone who isn't listening to you. Flaunting drug use turns people off and makes it hard for them to listen. We've got to learn how to help put people at ease, get them to relax, get them to be willing to listen, and get them to look at the facts. We have to learn to communicate.

If it were up to you, how would you propose regulating psychedelics?

There has to be training for facilitators of psychedelic therapy. But the hardest problem to solve is that no matter how much training you give, the person has to have heart. How are you going to select for that? Compassion is such an essential ingredient a facilitator.

Do you think that compassion is something inborn? Or is it something that people can learn?

It depends on how you define learning. You can't learn it out of a text-book, although such a book might be helpful. Rather, it's something you have to learn through experience. You learn to have compassion for people by learning to like yourself, and for a lot of people that is very difficult.

How do you think psychedelics should be regulated? What if prohibition collapses and everyone has access? Should psychedelics then be regulated like alcohol or cigarettes?

If these substances were accessible, I suspect things would equal out over time. Look what happened with recreational use of MDMA. After people use it two or three years—particularly if they're only using it recre-ationally—it gets to be where it's not interesting anymore, and use peters out. I think that would happen with most of these things if they were used in less appropriate manners, but I don't think our society is going to allow this to happen.

One of the best approaches is that which Bob Jesse of the Council on Spiritual Practices has taken. He has published the requirements for a guide—those things that should be known and honored by someone who fulfills that role. So a guide may have to have a particular set of creden-tials. The big problem is that this seems to argue that you need a review board. But who's going to be on the review board? Certainly people who haven't had some psychedelic experiences can't be on the review board. But then such people might argue that anybody who's *had* a psychedelic expe-rience is prejudiced and biased. I haven't really thought this thing through, because I figure we are a long way from that, as yet.

The point is that psychedelics can be used in any particular field for creativity and for learning skills. For example, musicians can learn to play their instruments better if they're playing under the influence. A relative of mine improved her guitar-playing and singing enormously just by play-ing under the influence. At the Hofmann Foundation we're supporting research, because in this country science is God. If the scientists don't accept it, nobody else has a chance. So we've got to prove that psychedelics have some efficacy in therapy. Once that's done, then hopefully we can broaden into other areas.

Should legitimacy and efficacy be established via medical or psychiatric research, before attempting to establish its value in other areas of society?

That's the most practical path. But I can see that it might fail, and the *real* path—the path of fostering spiritual growth—is what Bob Jesse's trying to do with the Council on Spiritual Practices. It's more honest, in a way, because psychedelics are inherently spiritual tools. At the same time,

I think it would be a tragedy to overlook the potential benefits of psychedelics in therapy and other applications.

You've been referred to as one of the "great elders" of the psychedelic community. How do you define such a position?

An elder is one who's lived a long time, who has accumulated quite a bit of life experience. Have you heard Jay Stevens talk about the "happy grays?" When he was writing *Storming Heaven,* his book on the history of psychedelics, he interviewed a lot of people, some of whom he eventually nicknamed the "happy grays." These are the people who began taking psychedelics in their thirties or later, who incorporated psychedelics into their lives after they had already had a bit of life experience, and their lives flourished and were made richer. Stevens puts people like the Shulgins, myself, and a number of others into that category.

On the other hand, Stevens also interviewed people in their early twenties, and he couldn't wait to get away from some of them. They had an arrogance, a kind of know-it-all attitude, and they obviously hadn't really resolved things in their life. Stevens became convinced that having some life experience and maturity under one's belt before consuming psychedelics made a big difference. That might be another definition of an elder—letting the young ones age enough to see the folly of their youth.

Perhaps the appropriate time to introduce these experiences would be when somebody is already pretty secure in their adult identity.

If they are going to be used indiscriminately, I think that's true. On the other hand, I'd hate to set a rule that you must be a certain age, because I know that some young people have benefitted enormously from early experiences. I was asked to give LSD to two young people who were the children of a Stanford philosopher. The father was a fascinating man who felt he was at the end of his life, but he got a renewal by taking MDMA. Anyway, I provided an LSD session for his children. One of them didn't do much with it, but the other had some very real and important life changes.

Looking back over your experiences of the last forty years, are there things that you know now that you wish you had known then? And would you have done things differently?

Lord, yes! Prepare better. Make better rapport with subjects. Know their intentions, and provide better support without interference.

4

Alexander T. "Sasha" Shulgin and Ann Shulgin

Frontiers of Pharmacology: Chemistry and Consciousness

Born June 17, 1925 • Alexander "Sasha" Shulgin is a pharmacologist and chemist renowned for his discovery of many new psychoactive compounds. Born to a Russian émigré father and American mother in Berkeley, California, he began his education at Harvard University, where he stayed only two years before enlisting in the U.S. Navy. Discharged following the end of World War II, he resumed his studies at the University of California Berkeley, where he received both his bachelor's and doctorate degrees.

After receiving his PhD in 1954, Shulgin engaged in postdoctorate work in pharmacology at the University of California San Francisco before embarking upon a career as a research scientist in industry. During the early 1960s he eventually reached the position of senior research chemist at the Dow Chemical Company.

In 1960, Shulgin took mescaline for the first time. Fascinated with the subjective response, he went on to develop expertise in the synthesis of chemicals similar in structure to mescaline. Subsequent to his departure from private industry and Dow Chemical in 1965, he went on to teach pharmacology and public health at the University of California Berkeley and San Francisco General Hospital.

In the late 1960s he was first introduced to MDMA, which he believed held great potential in psychiatric treatment. In 1976, some years after developing an improved synthesis of MDMA, Shulgin provided the compound to a psychotherapist friend and colleague, Leo Zeff. From that point in time, hundreds of psychotherapists were introduced to the MDMA treatment model developed by Zeff before the drug was scheduled in 1985.

Over the span of his long career, Shulgin has discovered a variety of novel psychoactive compounds. As well, he has synthesized and tested hundreds of additional compounds, meticulously catalogued in over two hundred articles in professional journals and four books. Shulgin has also published detailed descriptions of his rigorous experimental methodology for human self-administration.

Born March 22, 1931 • Ann Shulgin worked extensively as a lay therapist with psychedelics such as MDMA and 2C-B while they were still legal, as well as with hypnotherapy. With her husband Sasha, she has coauthored the highly influential books *PIHKAL* (*Phenethylamines I Have Known And Loved*) and *TIHKAL* (*Tryptamines I Have Known And Loved*), which summarize their extensive research. She is currently working with Sasha on their forthcoming book in this series, tentatively titled *Book 3*.

SASHA: TAKING 400 MILLIGRAMS of mescaline got me involved in studying psychedelics, and the magic has not left me yet. Interestingly, for Ann it happened almost at the same time, with the same compound and the same guide, which is quite a coincidence. We didn't know each other, and we didn't know our guide knew the other.

Ann: I was in my twenties at the time, and although I hadn't had any experiences with extrasensory perception, I'd had the spiritual experience that I detailed in our book *PIHKAL*. That experience convinced me that there was a nonphysical world of some kind. I read Aldous Huxley's books, *The Doors of Perception* and *Heaven and Hell*, which convinced me that psychedelics could open up an entrance into this nonphysical world. At the time, I felt that ESP functioning was repressed in most people, because they're taught that no such thing exists. Therefore, they think that they're nuts if they find themselves experiencing these weird things. So I suspected that the psychedelic experience might take away this sort of defensiveness.

Might a particular class of psychedelics be better at facilitating telepathic phenomena? For example, what about the empathogens—those phenethylamines, such as MDMA (Ecstasy), where individuals experience a profound emotional connection? Would these substances be interesting to test ESP?

Sasha: Absolutely! Those are heart to heart, or head to head, person to person.

Ann: You have to have a drug and a dosage strong enough to allow the subject to overcome the conditioning that says "this can't happen," and "if it does, this is chaos, weirdness, and frightening." The subject has to be able to move into another reality and accept it.

Sasha: If you begin by denying that this can happen, you create a situation in which it can't happen.

Ayahuasca has traditionally had an association with telepathy. When the Germans isolated one of the active ingredients from ayahuasca, harmine, they originally called it "telepathine." But other than that kind of folklore, is there any evidence of harmala alkaloids fostering telepathy?

Sasha: I'm hesitant to emphasize a single compound, because different people have different responses.

How has your work with psychedelics affected your lives and your careers?

Sasha: In essence, it has shaped my career. I've taken it as an intriguing challenge to try to find some synthesis between chemistry as a discipline and brain chemistry as a mysterious unknown, and to discover chemicals that can be used as tools to help explain that interrelationship.

I hold a very firm belief that we give too much power to the drug. The drug is a facilitator or a catalyst at most, but the real power lies inside us. The drug merely lets us see or do with more ease.

Ann: But you don't want to go to the other extreme, saying that it doesn't matter what drug you take. The fact is that if you take DMT, you will not open the door that mescaline will open. They open different doors, and offer different experiences. But the experience is still part of your own interior condition, it is not contained in the drug. Because what you get is what your psyche or your inner teacher thinks it's time for you to get.

Sasha: The doors are in your own mind.

How have your experiences with psychedelics affected your beliefs about the nature of mind?

Sasha: Well, I've abandoned any confidence that you can learn much abut the mind from the brain. So, I moved from researching the brain to exploring the mind quite intentionally, quite to the offense of the scientific community, who like to think the brain holds all the answers. They think you can take a section of rat brain, make it radioactive, photographic it, and know how psychedelics work. I don't think you know at all. You might learn where the radioactive tracer in some compound went, but not how the compound worked. I've been asked time and again: "How do psychedelics work?" I don't know how they work. The whole picture doesn't hang together yet.

The search for explanations of psychedelic experiences quite often leads to the use of words which are most often associated with religion or spirituality. If one keeps the search for explanations for psychedelic activity restricted to the brain, the terms encountered involve receptor sites, synapses, and neurotransmitter concentrations. But when one explores a bit further, into the dynamics of the *mind*, the words become harder to find. The medical dictionary doesn't help when there are unanswered questions involving telepathy, reincarnation, or the eternity of the soul! I believe that many of these phenomena are real, and I hope some day to catch a glimmer of understanding.

Why do you feel there has been so much resistance to these drugs and to researching their effects on the mind?

Ann: The general populace of our country has been encouraged by the government to be afraid of all mind-altering drugs, except perhaps alcohol. Spokespersons for the War on Drugs have encouraged the public to believe that psychedelics and MDMA are addictive, like heroin and cocaine, while the voices of people who truly understand psychedelics have been too few, or too afraid of retaliation, to be loud and persistent.

The main reason for the prejudice against psychedelics in the scientific and academic communities is, I believe, the same as that which motivates the lawmakers, and that is a deep-seated fear of their own unconscious psyches. An unconscious fear of the unconscious, you might say. This fear relates to the shadow parts of themselves, of which they are usually unaware. Any drug that opens doors to the shadowland is seen as a threat, because these people have not explored this inner territory, and they associate it with psychosis and chaos. Since they do not dare unearth what they unconsciously dread in the depths of themselves—the hidden axe-murderer or uncontrolled monster—they project this danger onto anyone using a psychedelic. Fearsome laws and legal punishments are the result.

The rest is, of course, a simple matter of power. Governments do not easily tolerate challenges to their pronouncements, and once a drug has been officially declared "harmful" by a government agency, the voice of a dissenter becomes the voice of an enemy.

Sasha: I'm of the position that no government, politician, nor head of the justice department, nor DEA should practice medicine and say what drugs you can or cannot use. Here I get into trouble with some physicians, but I don't even believe *physicians* have the right to say what you can and cannot use. I think the individual has that right. Now, the individual is an idiot if he doesn't ask a physician for advice. But the final decision should be the individual's. Sadly, the ability to *make* such decisions was taken from the individual in 1912 and put into the hands of the Food and Drug Administration. From there it was put into the hands of the government, which began dictating what drugs can and cannot be used. It's been taken out of our hands, and we've been left with an absurd "war" on some drugs.

What are your views of the War on Drugs?

Sasha: I wrote a chapter in our book *TIHKAL* called "Cui Bono?" Literally: "To whose benefit?" For example, if you were investigating a crime, you would ask: who might benefit from that crime? And the whole War on Drugs is dedicated—though I don't think this is a thought-out process—to moneymaking, power, and control.

Politicians think, "If we only increase the penalties by another 10 percent, I'll be reelected." Then consider the amount of money that goes into prisons as opposed to schools. So, it's all reinforcing! The only way you're going to undo it is to deprive the people who benefit from it. And they're not about to let you! So I don't see it being undone at all. Oh, there may be slight moves toward liberalization of medical marijuana, or slight moves toward research with psilocybin, but probably not much more.

Ann: I think that the cure for this entire problem can come from only two directions. One is the media, and the other is the religious community. If psychedelic use is going to be allowed, I think it will have to come through people asking that they be allowed as spiritual tools.

What led you to introduce MDMA to the psychotherapy community?

Sasha: Several things. First, while on it I experienced a state in which I was able to be attentive without much stimulation, and able to hear and respond to someone else's comments and questions without imposing my own ego upon them. I was especially able to search out a problem within my own internal world and openly admit to myself that it really existed and could be addressed. Some of these events have been sketched in the MDMA chapter in our book *PIHKAL*.

With a modest dose, I felt as though I had access to the help of a gentle psychotherapist with whom I could openly share private feelings and worries. And I had total confidence that I could drop any inhibitions I might have about sharing my private life. To my continued fascination, I *myself* was that gentle therapist. I could talk to myself quite honestly, trust myself with some disturbing personal problem, and then allow myself to search for a solution. Amazingly, there was total and accurate recall of the entire experience. This inspired me to share it with a dear friend who was an intuitively gifted therapist, and the rest is history!

Were you surprised when MDMA was outlawed?

Ann: I was, mostly because it was such an unbearable thought, I hadn't given it any room or energy. Along with many others, I wept the day I heard this dreadful thing had happened.

Sasha: I too was very saddened, but not surprised. The wave of popular use, under the name of "Ecstasy," was seen by government authorities as a resurgence of the out-of-control mania that accompanied the popularization of LSD in the 1960s and cocaine in the 1970s.

The youth were seen to be acting up without any social responsibility, and something would have to be done about it. It seems to be part of our embedded philosophy, that if something is so out-of-hand, it must be brought under control by prohibition. This has never worked before, and it isn't working now.

By the mid-1980s was recreational MDMA use, particularly by young people, actually a serious problem?

Sasha: I'm not sure of your definition of a "serious problem." Every one of us has been a teenager. And most of us went through a stage that might be described by the phrases, "I'll do what I want to do," and "Don't trust anyone over thirty," and "I am immortal." That "youth phase" can involve music, sex, drugs, and other related forms of rebellion. It has happened in the past and it will happen in the future. Is this a serious problem? Not necessarily. I see it as a fact of life. It is an expression of divine independence that is sadly forgotten by many of us as we mature into serious and responsible adults. Would most of us want to relive it? Probably not. But do most of us regret having lived through it? Probably not.

Do you think the "rave" phenomenon would have become so widespread if MDMA had not been scheduled in the mid-1980s?

Sasha: That's a hard one to answer. I feel compelled to judge this type of activity—from the distant past right up to today's problems—by saying that prohibition does indeed play a very important role. The disallowing of unwanted behavior, be it in areas of religion, economics, private relationships, or public opinion, has never withstood the passage of time. The scheduling of MDMA in the mid-1980s brought the flavor of criminality to its use, thus providing a tangible symbol for the definition of illegal behavior. It gave wide publicity to a compound that was formerly not too well known. A negative action of those in authority against something often provokes young people to suspect that there might be some reward there that they had been unaware of! "They wouldn't be opposed to it unless there was something worth while there."

Ann, how did you become an MDMA psychotherapist?

Ann: In stages. I became a lay therapist using MDMA in the early 1980s when it was still legal. In the first stage, one or another of our friends would ask to spend an afternoon with Sasha and me, making it clear that he or she wanted to use MDMA to help sort out some personal problems. At first, Sasha and I would both spend time with such a friend, but we discovered that I was more able to handle the psychological insight process than Sasha. Very quickly it became my job, and he happily retired to his study after greeting the friend/client, leaving the rest to me.

At this early stage, the average number of clients was somewhere around one per month, and I was still doing what most beginning MDMA therapists did at that time: taking MDMA with the client. After a few sessions, I realized that it was counterproductive for me to take the drug along with the client, because it was essential for me to concentrate intently on what was happening with the patient. It also dawned on me that I didn't *need* to take MDMA to increase my empathy or understanding of what was going on in the client, and that I was not dependent on the drug for opening up whatever abilities I might have as a therapist.

Gradually, the number of patients increased. One dear friend, a psychiatrist who was ready to retire, did some work with me, and after this he sent me two of his most difficult patients, both of whom he described as his "failures." He added, "Let's see what *you* can do with them." It was a challenge, and I learned a tremendous amount from both people.

One of these patients was a man who was psychologically addicted to the use of nitrous oxide, also known as "laughing gas," which is used by dentists as an anesthetic. After months of work, and good bonding with me, he was still occasionally using nitrous.

Then, one day, he tucked himself into bed with his nitrous bottle, and pulled the sheet over himself for privacy. Needless to say, he was found dead shortly afterwards. I was surprised, briefly angry, then simply sorrowful at the inevitability of the death. Neither I nor the magical drug, MDMA, had made a serious dent in this gentleman's devotion to nitrous oxide, and neither of us had created in him a strong enough interest in living. From this case I learned, for the first time, that MDMA couldn't solve everyone's problems. I also learned that, no matter how hard I might try, I couldn't, either.

The second patient was a classic borderline personality, which I was not experienced enough to recognize for quite a while. When I finally understood, I also had to admit to myself that there wasn't much I could do to change his very old and ingrained habits of distorted thinking and behavior. He was in his sixties, and he was unconsciously determined to keep his world just the way it was, since he knew the rules of his game and how to manipulate the people close to him sufficiently well to stay safe and—in a strange sense—contented.

It was a new experience for me, having a client who lived in a very dark castle, complete with imaginary moat, whose major effort was, not to make his way out of his darkness, but to draw his therapist into it to keep him company. When I fully realized what was going on, and what would undoubtedly continue going on forever if I worked further with him, I found him a new therapist. He seemed perfectly happy to make the change, and the last thing I heard was that all was going very well. I spent a good deal of time thinking about what this man had taught me, on many levels, and what the term "borderline" meant. Again, MDMA had changed nothing, and neither had I. But I had learned a lot.

After about a year—during which I didn't charge for my services—I met a hypnotherapist. She was mentioned in our second book, *TIHKAL*, where we called her "Audrey." This was my first work with the shadow, and my first use of hypnotic trance along with MDMA. The combination worked extremely well, and after six months of intense work on both our parts, Audrey's shadow problem was successfully resolved.

A few months after that, she asked me to work with her. We worked with carefully selected patients who had completed their hypnotherapy with her, and were now ready to continue with spiritual growth work, using MDMA and some other psychedelics such as 2C-B. Both drugs were legal—or, as Sasha says, "not illegal"—at that time. I spent two years working with Audrey, and the experience was extraordinary. Again, I have written about this time and what I learned from it in *TIHKAL*, in a chapter titled "The Intensive."

When MDMA was made illegal in the mid-1980s, Sasha and I decided to write our first book, and I left the practice of psychotherapy with deep regret. I knew that I could not possibly do both writing and therapy, since each demanded full concentration and tremendous mental energy. As well, the continuation of MDMA therapy would necessitate going underground, involving Audrey, myself, and every client in the deliberate performance of a felony, which I was not willing to do.

Could you describe a case that exemplifies the healing potential of MDMA psychotherapy?

Ann: Before I describe such cases, I want to say a few things about MDMA, which is known as an "insight" drug. Taken at the psychotherapeutic dosage level of 100 mg to 125 mg, MDMA does two things simultaneously: it allow the patient insight into himself, while—in some manner we don't understand—putting him into a state of peaceful acceptance of whatever he may unearth. Along with this feeling of acceptance, there is usually a strong sense of appreciation, even love, for himself as a total human being, warts and all, and often a deep compassion for his helpless, traumatized childhood self. This ability to employ insight without fear or defensiveness usually takes six months or more in standard psychotherapy; yet it can be accomplished in one day with the help of MDMA. MDMA can be the great penicillin for the soul. MDMA therapy allows for clarity, a dropping of defenses, and a reestablishment of trust. It is tremendous for marital therapy. Sometimes the outcome of a couple's therapy is a firm decision that divorce is better than staying together. Of course, when we used MDMA or any other psychoactive material, the sessions were no longer fifty-five minutes; they'd become six hours minimum.

Let me describe two successful therapy cases. One of these was early on, during the first year of learning how to use this drug to help people. Or, to be more precise, how to help people help themselves.

This case involved a married couple who were good friends of ours. Their marriage had been in trouble for some time, with each of them attempting to prove the other wrong, in matters both great and minuscule. Hostility and defensiveness had made communication between them stilted and painful. In response to the tension in the home, their two boys were beginning to act out, adding to their parents feelings of guilt, shame, and anger.

These two much-loved friends came to Sasha and me for an MDMA session, both of them expressing hope for some way out of their entanglement. They sat facing us, at opposite ends of our long couch, and didn't look at each other for quite a while. After they consumed the MDMA, neither Sasha nor I did much work that afternoon. Our friends started talking to each other and they continued, gradually moving closer to each other, until—at the two-hour point—they were sitting side by side, holding hands.

MDMA is also known as the empathy drug. Along with acceptance of oneself and compassion for one's own past and present bewilderment and pain, there comes an equally intense empathy and compassion for other human beings. Our friends rediscovered each other. Their defensiveness disappeared, and they remembered why they had fallen in love.

Within a month of this session, one of their sons was stricken with a fatal illness. The two parents later told us that without the healing of their relationship that day, they would not have had the strength and courage they needed for the struggle that faced them for more than two years, trying to save their son.

There was a second case I remember with some satisfaction—a woman in her thirties named Sheila, who suffered from chronic depression. Her parents lived half a continent away, but now and then, Sheila had to go home for the holidays. Whenever she did so, arguments erupted, and she became aware of a deep anger directed at her parents. She came to me, having heard about MDMA, because she had become worried about hurting her parents emotionally, without having any apparent reason for doing so. She could not understand her depression, since her life was reasonably fulfilling, and she could see that there were many pleasant things going on which should—she felt—make her happy. She told me that she knew several people whose lives were dreadfully difficult in comparison with her own yet, as she said, "They seem to be a lot more content than I am; they laugh more than I do. They aren't depressed! With all the good things I have in my life, why am I in such a sad state?"

We worked together for several months. Then one day, recalling her childhood, she said, "You know, I remember being happy. I remember being really happy, before I was eight years old. What could have happened to change me so much? After my eighth birthday, I wasn't happy any more." I asked some questions about memories of her parents when she was seven or eight, and after telling me that she couldn't remember anything in particular, she went silent for a moment, using the MDMA to open herself to impressions of that time. I kept quiet and waited.

Sheila sat up in her chair and said, "I do remember one thing my father said to me around that time. I guess I was running around like I usually did, having fun, maybe making too much noise. I don't know. Dad took me by the shoulders and told me that the only people who were *really* happy in this world were people who were going to die soon. He said the world was full of pain and sorrow, and the only happiness was in heaven, if you had been a good person. So if I felt happy all the time, maybe it meant I was going to die."

I could only respond, "Oh, my God!"

"Yeah," said Sheila, "He was a Catholic, and he believed in hell, and maybe he thought that would scare me into being quiet for a while. I don't know. But he shouldn't have said that, I really think he shouldn't have said it."

"You're damned right he shouldn't have said it!" I fumed, "That's child abuse, honey! No wonder you stopped being happy!"

She told me she still wasn't sure there was any connection. But she thought about the words, remembered the sudden fear, and slowly it all moved together into a certainty, and she began to cry.

For certain patients, MDMA can be a key to repressed memories. Sheila was unusual, in that she had been able to retrieve the actual words which had turned her young life dark and fearful. Most people have to pull strands of incomplete images from their unconscious: a mother's face shouting anger, a brother's malice, the damp hands of an uncle, none of them quite sufficient to explain what had gone wrong in their lives.

For Sheila, this session was the turning point. It took another two or three months of work before she was able to feel some pity for her now elderly father, instead of the customary anger. Very gradually, she allowed herself enjoyment, and even moments of real pleasure, without the old terror descending on her. The insight gained in her MDMA sessions served her well, and when we said good-bye, she was a lovely woman who smiled easily. Within six months, I heard that she was engaged to be married.

What are some basic "dos" and "don'ts" of how to structure an MDMA psychotherapy session?

Ann: If MDMA were legalized tomorrow, I would suggest that future therapists should keep in mind certain rules in conducting their sessions. I'll describe what I consider the most vital of these.

As the therapist, you should know as much as possible about your patient, before considering giving him (or her, of course) MDMA. You should ask for copies of his medical records. You must be familiar with all the published information on MDMA, and you should have taken the drug yourself, at least once.

A contract must be explained to the patient, and the patient must agree to it. The contract has three rules.

The first rule is that, although any and all feelings of hostility can be freely expressed in the session, the anger may not be physically acted out against me or my possessions. If the acting out of a traumatic event is needed, I will supply both the opportunity and the means. Otherwise,

anger and hate will not cross the line into physical action. (Many therapists have a room or space in which a patient can act out rage, tearing
apart old sheets or pillows supplied by the therapist.)

The second rule is similar to the first, but it applies to sexual feelings.
No matter what the fantasy or urges, you can and should talk about them,
but no physical acting out is allowed.

Finally, you must agree that if an opportunity to go over the threshold into death presents itself in the trance state, and you are tempted for
any reason to go, you are not to do so. To put it another way, you will not
die on my time, in my house or my office, because your death would cause
me harm, and you will not cause me harm, as I will not cause you harm.
(The patient's unconscious mind will register the fact that, no matter what
might happen during the session, there are rules that must be followed.
There is a fuller explanation of this rule in our book *TIHKAL* on pages
225–26.)

A minimum of six hours should be set aside for a session with
MDMA. This will allow sufficient time for either a single dose (usually
125 mg), or an initial dose followed ninety minutes later, by a supplement
(usually 40 mg), if the patient so chooses. When the patient believes he
has returned to baseline, his vision should be tested in a dark room, with
a flashlight, to see if there are any tracers of light remaining. Such light
tracers are indicative of the visual distortions that can accompany many
psychedelics. He should not be allowed to drive himself home until there
are no tracers seen. Ideally, the patient should stay overnight in the place
where he had the MDMA, or he should take a taxi home, because there is
always a possibility of his being distracted by post-session thoughts and
reminiscences while driving.

The patient must be told that he has the right to change his mind at
any time about taking the MDMA. If his intuition tells him that this is
not, after all, the right time to use the drug, he must understand that his
change of mind will be honored and respected.

Shifting the subject slightly, there are certain people who I think
should never be given psychedelics, including MDMA, especially people
who are psychotic. I think that the loss of the sense of self, or core self,
which happens in psychosis, is a contraindication to these drugs. Psychedelics are not for people who are trying to *find* mental health. Rather, they
are for people who are basically healthy and have strong cores. They are
for people who are eager to explore themselves emotionally and spiritually,

and to explore further than ordinary psychotherapy is going to take them. That, of course, is not for everyone.

What other psychedelics do you think may be of potential value to psychiatry and medicine?

Sasha: Many psychedelics will be valuable as research tools. There are a number of compounds that effect subtle changes in the thought process or within the sensory system. And there are illnesses that have these changes as part of their symptomatology. An increased understanding of brain function could come from investigating how these drugs do their thing. Labeling them with radioactive tracers, and following their travels in the intact brain with tools such as the PET scanner, could eventually lead to creating medicines to relieve pathological symptoms—and from this, to eventual cures for mental illness.

Are there any compounds that you have not investigated, which you would like to subject to rigorous examination?

Sasha: Oh my, yes! Many of them. I have synthesized a form of an interesting tryptamine with fourteen deuterium atoms (heavy hydrogen atoms) on it. Will it be different than the nondeuterated counterpart?

There are tempting locations in several active compounds where a perfluorinated methyl or ethyl group could be easily placed, with totally unpredictable consequences. There are also several cacti that I have explored that are rich in new alkaloids, none of them known to be psychoactive in man, and yet the total plant extracts are indeed active! Is there a minor component that is tremendously potent, or is it some combination of components that does the job? There are many unanswered questions and, as is usually the case, finding the answers will lead to yet more questions.

Have you examined salvinorin A, the active diterpenoid compound from the plant Salvia divinorum? *Is there anything particularly intriguing about this compound?*

Sasha: My experience with salvinorin A has been quite limited. I observed a session when the isolate was being smoked, and its potency and the rapidity of action were most impressive. Less than one milligram of the pure white chemical was quite sufficient to produce an intense experience. To me, what is most intriguing about this compound is its complex and potentially fragile structure. It is not an alkaloid (there is no nitrogen atom present), and it has a three-dimensional structure that is a treasure of asymmetry. Seven of its two dozen or so carbon atoms are chiral and so there are, in theory, 128 isomers that could exist. And just one of them is the actual salvinorin A itself. What a rich area for future exploration!

What are your views on plant psychedelics versus their isolated or synthesized alkaloids? For example, "magic mushrooms" versus pure psilocybin? Are the experiences they induce identical or are there substantial differences?

Sasha: No two experiences are really ever the same. That holds whether the chemicals are from an intact plant, its isolate, or a synthesized chemical that is presumed to be responsible for the activity.

With the whole plant, there may also be questions about properly identifying it. And certainly there would be questions related to potency and stability, which in turn could be related to whatever manner of preparation it went through before it was consumed. Even though a mushroom or a cactus closely resembles some prototype model, it may actually be a subtle botanical variation that is new to you. And even when you have accurately identified the plant, its alkaloid composition can vary depending on the season or the growing conditions. Thus, what is consumed may be a mixture of many compounds in unknown proportions.

The purified isolate, or even better a synthetic sample, has the intrinsic virtue of being of known identity and purity. However, your physical and mental state today is going to be different from what it was the last time you tried this compound, and hence the experience will be different. There is truth in the old saying, that you cannot cross the same river two times.

Is there anything particularly interesting or unique about ayahuasca?

Sasha: Ayahuasca adds yet further complications to the "plant versus compound" question, in that it is usually not made from just a single plant, but from a combination of plants. The components used in the preparation are variable, and the recipe followed can be quite different from one cook to another. Although the active ingredients are classically assumed to be plants that provide a mixture of N,N-dimethyltryptamine (DMT) and harmaline, I have seen active ayahuasca drinks that do not contain either compound. So it is not surprising that one's experiences can be quite variable. But even on occasions where a single, uniform brew is shared amongst several individuals, responses can vary from the dull and boring to the extreme and frightening.

In all of your years of laboratory and personal explorations, what is the most interesting compound you have examined?

Sasha: I would put 2,5–dimethoxy-4–ethylphenethylamine (2C-E) very high on this list. It allowed two opposite energies to blend together in, for me, a new and unique way. On one hand, it took complete control over me, in that it presented visions, or thought trails, or memories, that could not be ignored. "Do not move on from this place until you have resolved the questions that have come up or resolved the problem now at hand." Once this was all completed, I could move on to the next scene. And yet, at the same time, I had complete control over it. The answers and conclusions were totally my own. It was a rich day, although exhausting, as it seemed as if it would never end. But I did not want it to end. There were many facets, many nuances, and a totally clear recall of all that went on. An interesting compound.

Projecting into the future, are you optimistic or pessimistic that MDMA and psychedelics may be accepted in the future as sanctioned treatments for psychiatric and medical illness?

Sasha: For the near future my pessimism outweighs my optimism. The outrageous War on Drugs has become firmly ensconced in our political and economic world, and there is no incentive to soften it. In fact, all prospective changes are directed to making it more encompassing and more penalizing. It has now been conjoined with another unwinnable war, the War on Terrorism, into an Orwellian structure that seems pretty permanent.

Ann: I, on the other hand, remain optimistic. Perhaps positive change will not occur soon in the United States, as Sasha points out. But I believe there may be a greater chance of making progress in Europe and elsewhere.

Do you have any final statements you'd like to pass down to the younger generation?

Sasha: Stay curious.

Ann: And know yourself as well as you possibly can, by whatever means you choose.

Part Two

Psychotherapy

Personal and Transpersonal

Psychotherapy

Personal and Transpersonal

In the history of the collective as in the history of the individual, everything depends on the development of consciousness.

—Carl Jung[1]

Probably the greatest challenge facing each of us individually and all of us collectively is how to change painful and pathological behavior. How well we answer this challenge may determine our individual and collective fate, as well as the fate of our species and our planet. Historically, there have been three kinds of answers, but their success and the speed of their success have been modest.

The first approach has been moral exhortation. From time immemorial we have been urged to "fight the good fight" against our self, or at least against our baser self. But as we all know, our baser self turns out to be a worthy adversary, and as the Christian Saint Paul lamented, "I can know what is right, but I cannot do it."[2]

The second approach has been spiritual practice. Fasting, prayer, contemplation, and yoga are some of the time honored methods. These can certainly be transformative, but progress is usually measured in years or even decades.

The newest addition has been psychotherapy, which can clearly help some people and some conditions. However, once again the process can be painfully slow. Freud wrung his hands over "therapy terminable and interminable," and therapists speak of breakthroughs and regressions, and lament the " false hope syndrome," whereby people underestimate the difficulty of changing ingrained habits.[3]

Because of this, the quest in psychotherapy has always been for faster and more effective methods, and the dream has been of finding ways to induce "quantum change"—long-lasting transformation following a powerful but relatively brief experience.[4] Consequently, reports that psychedelics could dramatically accelerate therapy were startling. Extraordinary claims poured from clinics and consulting rooms; claims of profound openings, deep insights, dramatic catharses of long buried traumas, and rapid healings of chronic intractable problems. Over the next few years therapists worked to assess such claims and find optimal ways to work with these powerful new tools, experimenting with different drugs, doses, settings, and techniques.

Numerous case histories and personal reports document dramatic breakthroughs and benefits. However, the careful long-term research needed to assess these claims was cut short by the government's clampdown. Therefore, we still do not know the full range of possibilities and limitations of psychotherapy with psychedelics, and we are still trying to grasp the profound implications of these chemicals for our understanding of mind, pathology, therapy, and human potential.

NOTES

1. C. G. Jung, *The Collected Works of C. G. Jung,* 2nd ed., vol. 4, pt. I. Four archetypes. (Princeton, NJ: Princeton University Press, 1969).

2. Saint Paul, *Romans* 7:18–19 (Revised Standard Version).

3. J. Polivy and C. Herman, "If at first you don't succeed: False hopes of self-change," *American Psychologist* 57 (2002): 677–89.

4. W. Miller and J. C'de Baca, *Quantum Change: When Epiphanies and Sudden Insights Transform Ordinary Lives.* (New York: Guilford, 2001).

5

Betty Eisner

The Birth and Death of Psychedelic Therapy

September 29, 1915–July 1, 2004 • Betty Eisner was a psychologist who worked at the University of California at Los Angeles School of Medicine in the 1950s and 1960s with physician Sidney Cohen, a leading researcher during the early era of investigation into psychedelics. Eisner has been recognized in particular for the contributions she made in developing the use of LSD for the treatment of alcoholism. She and Cohen were active participants, along with such luminaries as Aldous Huxley, Gerald Heard, Alan Watts, and Anais Nin, in discussions focused on socially acceptable uses of LSD.

Eisner also made contributions pioneering the use of Ritalin and carbogen with patients undergoing treatment with psychedelics. In particular, she became known for group psychotherapy models utilizing experimental combinations of psychoactive drugs and bodywork. She wrote a dozen scientific papers related to psychedelics and consciousness, and also penned the 1970 book *The Unused Potential of Marriage and Sex.*

AT AGE 35, I was doing my doctorate in psychology at the University of California at Los Angeles, and I saw a posting on a bulletin board that simply said: "Wanted: A psychology student to help with a drug that's unusual." I had a feeling that it was LSD, because there had been an article on it in *Look* magazine, and I wanted to take LSD because it sounded so fascinating.

I couldn't help immediately, as I would have liked to do, because I was too far along with my own dissertation. So I told a friend that I'd tell him about this opportunity if he promised to let me be the first subject of their study. He agreed, so I took him to meet the researcher, Sidney Cohen. After they had taken LSD themselves, they made me their first subject in the first research study that Sid did.

It was November 10th, 1955. The study was actually very frustrating, because just as the LSD experience would start, the facilitators would pull me back and have me draw or complete tests—that's what that study was about. But in between the prescribed activities, I could feel how incredible the drug was, and afterwards I said to Sid, "It seems to me this drug has therapeutic potential."

After my experience, I met with Sid when I had time off, and we read reports on LSD research. We also met with Al Hubbard, Humphry Osmond, and other researchers who told us what they had done. We worked for about a year getting ready to try to discover what the possible therapeutic benefits of LSD might be.

In early January of 1957 I had my second session, this time to investigate the therapeutic potential. In the first session with Sid, they kept pulling me back for psychological testing. It was as though I was in a great, lovely, green pasture—which was reality—and they kept bringing me back to the fence and asking me questions about the fence, which seemed totally irrelevant. [laughs]

After my first experience, we had decided that somebody should always be with the subject, and consequently I had been sitting in on other people's sessions since that time. So a friend sat with me for my second session. This friend had experience with psychoanalysis, and she said I went through the equivalent of five to six hundred hours of analysis during this session.

During this second session I encountered my psychological defense patterns and I had an awful experience. It's hard to describe, but the session left me profoundly depressed. Sid was gone, and my friend was asleep, but I was up all night, and what I went through was dreadful. So I went to the library in our house and read Saint John of the Cross, which was the one thing that helped bring me out of it. I'm not normally subject to depressions, but this depression persisted until the next session. I had taken a very low dose of twenty-five gamma [micrograms], and ten days later, I again took twenty-five. And that time I broke through to the mystical experience, which ended the depression. It was as though all of the necessary preparation work had been done in the earlier session.

This convinced me that using low doses was the correct method. I swore I'd never do to a patient what was done to me—to generate such an enormous influx of so much psychological material. I would do it gently. So in our studies, we gave subjects twenty-five gamma the first session, fifty the next week, and then seventy-five the third week. After completion of the initial psychotherapeutic study, Sid and I wanted to do a study with cancer patients, but the money didn't come through. So then I took psychedelic therapy into private practice

Overall, I worked with Sidney Cohen for about a year and a half. It wasn't a long period of time, but it was very productive. Sid was a clear-headed researcher with an incredibly sharp mind. But Timothy Leary's antics eventually turned Sid against LSD, which was a tragedy. Before Tim died, I went to visit him, and he apologized, saying that he was sorry he had messed up our work. I was amazed that he said so.

How would psychedelics be viewed if Timothy Leary hadn't played a part in their history?

Very differently. They would have taken a scientific path. We were planning things like clinics where people could go to have LSD experiences, supervised by doctors. This would have been run by people who were familiar firsthand with LSD—because you have to *know* LSD or you can't do anything. It's ridiculous to say LSD is this, that, or the other, if you haven't had it.

Early on you found that the way to go was to start with low doses, gradually build up, and always have a sitter present. Was there anything else that proved to be valuable?

We also found that music was terribly important[1], and of course preparation. But the basic element of LSD therapy is *trust*. Trust enables the person to let go to the drug, so that it works. With our approach, we had no situations in which the drug didn't work, but Sid did a study with psychoanalysts, and it didn't work for them! One of them said, "Oh, it's just like a martini. It's nothing." But he and the other analysts didn't really let go.

One of the problems at Harvard was that they began using LSD in unsupervised settings, creating almost a kind of cocktail party environment. Did that go on among the researchers at UCLA?

No, not at all. At first I did the sessions with Sid at the veteran's hospital, and later—after I went into private practice—we did them in my office. But then the psychological associations got spooked, so we had to do them in a hospital under medical supervision. It was very important to me to hold the sessions in a safe environment. Eventually we had group sessions, sometimes with as many as twenty-two people. But I never took the drug myself in the group sessions.

The use of group sessions actually started with Bill Wilson, of Alcoholics Anonymous fame. Bill Wilson took LSD along with Tom Powers, who handled the publicity for AA, and Sid Cohen and me. That was the first group session. Strangely, for Tom and me the drug didn't work for four hours while we were doing therapy with Bill Wilson. [laughs] Then it hit the moment we got out of the hospital environment! Interesting.

What were Sid Cohen's LSD experiences like?

He would never talk about them, even in the early years. Now I know that in his 1964 book *The Beyond Within: The LSD Story,* one of the reports presented is his own. But he was very chary about personal things, and he never shared his own experiences.

Could you tell us about Bill Wilson and your experiences with him? Perhaps give us some background to his session, and what followed.

Alcoholics Anonymous was actually considering using LSD. Alcoholics get to a point in the program where they need a spiritual experience, but not all of them are able to have one. Tom Powers was Bill Wilson's right-hand man in this. Tom had been through hell with alcoholism, so he brought Bill Wilson out to meet us. Sid and I thought it might be a good idea to try a low dose together, but when I met Bill, I thought, "Uh-oh, this is going to be *his* therapy session." And that's one of the things it turned out to be. We each took twenty-five gamma, except for Bill. Sid offered him several pills, and Bill said, "Don't ever do that to a drunk," and he took two. But the rest of us just took one.

He was supposed to come back again, but things changed. I think that the board that ran Alcoholics Anonymous got scared, and they pulled back. They were going to do an LSD experiment and Sid went to talk to them about how to set it up. But I think they got scared and shut it down. As you know, Alcoholics Anonymous is formally against *any* kind of drug. They're even against aspirin!

After his session Bill Wilson thought that LSD could be a powerful facilitator of alcoholism treatment?

That was what I thought. He certainly was better, and Tom Powers said he'd never *seen* him in such good shape. He was wonderful, and later we received a letter from him, thanking us and saying he felt better than he had for a long time.

Were Humphry Osmond and Abram Hoffer using LSD for alcoholics in Canada by this time?

That was a little later. But Humphry came down to see us, and eventually he and Hoffer did their study. Later Keith Ditman, of the Neuropsychiatric Clinic at UCLA Medical School, replicated their work.

All of these people used higher doses?

There are two techniques: the low dose, and the high "mystical experience" dose. Al Hubbard was a proponent of high doses, and he felt that it was important to give people life-changing mystical experiences. And that's what Humphry and Hoffer also found in Canada, as did Keith Ditman.

In our therapeutic approach, we started with low doses a week apart. However, Hubbard used preliminary sessions with, for example, nitrous oxide to "blow off stuff" and get people's problems out of the way. That way, during the LSD session the person would be more likely to have a mystical experience. But the beauty of the low-dose LSD was that it enabled a person to let go as much as he or she wanted. Perhaps just a little bit at first, then a little more the next time, and finally they would allow it to happen completely.

How often did that incremental progression actually produce mystical experiences?

In our study, people got through to this resolution in all cases. We kept giving them sessions until they did—five or six sessions at most. Let me present a specific case—an alcoholic who we started at fifty gamma, and later we gave him seventy-five gamma. During one session, he uncovered a traumatic war experience where he had killed two Germans in order to get free. Uncovering that experience made the difference. He'd had twenty-eight hospitalizations for alcoholism, but following the LSD sessions he didn't return to the hospital for alcoholism. He still had problems, but alcohol was no longer one of them.

Who originally had the idea that LSD would be good for alcoholism? Where did that come from?

I think it came from several places simultaneously. Of course, the main source was Humphry Osmond and Abram Hoffer. But I think anybody who studied LSD recognized that it would be effective with alcoholics.

I used LSD from 1957 until 1964, when they took it away. By then, I had read about the UCLA alcohol clinic, where they gave a drug called Ritalin and the alcoholics abreacted a lot. We decided to try it, and found that it worked fantastically. We gave Ritalin sessions before the LSD sessions, and that would save some of the expense of going into the hospital.

With some sessions we gave intravenous Ritalin on top of the LSD. If somebody got to a point in their trip where he or she was really stuck, the Ritalin would blow the defenses away. It was incredible.

Would you say that ketamine did the same thing?

Yes, it's very hard to maintain defences against ketamine. But Ritalin is much better because it's more controllable. You can start it orally or you can use it intramuscularly or intravenously, and use it with LSD.

What amount of an oral dose of Ritalin was used for these sessions?

We used fifty to one hundred mg orally, a pretty high dose. We also did bodywork, since we found that this worked well in conjunction with Ritalin.

Did you yourself use Ritalin when you were exploring it, before LSD was taken away?

Yes, because I always tried drugs myself if I was using them on patients. When I first tried Ritalin, I had planned a two-hour hiatus before seeing my next patient. But at the end of the two hours I was still very out of it, and I could barely deal with my patient. I could see how strong a drug it was, and that it was very good for reducing defensiveness.

So using the Ritalin helped make an LSD session more manageable? Were many other groups of psychedelic therapists or researchers using Ritalin in combination with psychedelics?

If you hit a barrier, Ritalin would blow you through the barrier. But it wasn't exactly *manageable*; it was explosive. But no, this was not in common use. Virginia Johnson used very high doses of Ritalin, but she didn't use LSD. Another therapist, Tom Ling, who heard about it from me, wrote some papers on Ritalin in combination with LSD. At first, he used methamphetamine, because that's what Al Hubbard had told us would be good to prepare for LSD. Then we found the Ritalin was better.

How did Sid get along with Al Hubbard? They seem to be very different types.

There was something about Al Hubbard that was quite sincere, and you had to accept him on that basis. I think Sid accepted that, but he thought it was bad that Al didn't get proper training—because Al got a mail-order PhD, to be called doctor. But I don't think it mattered. He did so much good, and in such a marvelous way, that he was very valuable.

Al established several clinics, the first one in Canada. Later he was instrumental in founding the clinic in Palo Alto that Myron Stolaroff, Willis Harman, and Jim Fadiman worked at. After the late 1960s, when the mainstream became increasingly hostile to psychedelics, Al moved back to Canada. Al should get enormous credit for the work he did. We called him the "Johnny Appleseed of LSD," and he really inspired the researchers. We might not have agreed with all his methods, but we had to recognize what a good job he did. He died in 1982.

How many patients did you treat with LSD during your career?

My study at the hospital involved only 22 patients, but in private practice I saw a lot over twenty-two years. People came from long distances to see me. The results of these studies were, quite frankly, incredible.

Tell us more about your work with ketamine?

We started out with intramuscular shots of ketamine, around seventy-five to eighty-five milligrams, but it took too much time for it to work, and if you had several people in a group session, the timeline got all messed up. So we tried it intravenously, as I remember around twenty or twenty-five mg. Then, wham! Bam! You can't defend against ketamine, if you're taking it in a therapeutic setting.

My husband Bill found out about ketamine at a group session in a Mexico City clinic. They offered him a shot of something they had just recently found out about, without telling him what it was. Everybody who worked at that clinic thought it was a great thing to have this special new drug. So he took an intramuscular shot of one hundred milligrams, and had quite a trip. The next day, he took pains to look at the bottle, and it was ketamine. So he walked across the street to the farmacia, bought some over the counter, and brought it back to the United States in his shaving kit. Then we came across an article—I think it was published in Iran—which talked about the therapeutic aspects of ketamine. That enabled us to use it, so we applied for and got the ketamine around 1970.

How have your experiences with psychedelics changed your world-view, your view of spirituality, and how you understand the mind?

They had a profound effect. They change you so much psychologically, and when mystical experiences come, you see the true fabric of the universe. I think that psychedelics are the most profoundly important drugs that we could have, and I think our culture handled them really badly. I hope we have another chance to use them properly.

What do you feel went wrong?

I think Tim Leary was mainly responsible for things going wrong. His "turn on, tune in, and drop out," message came at a time when young people wanted something else to latch onto, I guess.

I heard Aldous Huxley and Humphry Osmond talking to Timmy and saying, "Please, this is not the way to do it." Sid warned him too, saying, "This is going to be a mess. This is not the way to do it." But Tim wouldn't listen—he was rather hardheaded.

Did you have any non-drug-induced mystical experiences prior to taking LSD?

Yes. But my own LSD use has mostly been psychological and therapeutic in nature. From time to time I broke through into the mystical
realm, but not very often.

*After LSD therapy was banned, did you stop your involvement with psy-
chedelics altogether? Or did you continue to work with them informally?*

No, we had Ritalin, so we used the Ritalin instead. I tried to stay
within the law the whole time.

*So, you stayed with what was legal: Ritalin and ketamine. Did you use
anything else?*

Yes, carbogen—also known as Meduna's mixture (30 percent carbon
dioxide, 70 percent oxygen). That's another marvelous drug for blowing
people through problems. It produced a lot of strange experiences, and
sometimes very difficult experiences, but despite that, it could really help.

*What was the response from other psychiatrists and psychologists? How did
they respond?*

Badly. Particularly the psychologists, who went after me relentlessly
until they finally got my license. They were scared. But before they succeeded, I did twenty-two years of psychedelic therapy, just with LSD, then
Ritalin and ketamine.

*Do you feel you were under even greater attack than some of the psychia-
trists?*

Sure, I was a woman. At that time there were very few women in this
field—the field was totally male dominated. The psychiatrist I worked
with who did the ketamine shots had his license suspended for one day.
Mine was taken away entirely!

Could you talk about the possible social benefits of psychedelic therapy?

I think that our civilization is going downhill rapidly. It's becoming
increasingly materialistic, more individualistic, more selfish, more hard-
core. I think it's tragic that this has happened. Richard Alpert and I have
discussed this, and he feels the same way. LSD brings us back to our inner
reality, and our inner reality is connected to the cosmic center—that
which *is*, we could say. LSD helps people touch that center and change.

*You said you focused mainly on therapeutic applications, but did you find
that psychedelics have a place in a spiritual practice? Perhaps for someone who
isn't working on psychological issues but more on spiritual growth?*

I'm not spiritually inclined. If someone wants a mystical experience,
that's great. But can one work on religious problems? I think I'd have to
be a religious healer to be able to answer that.

What do you think about the term entheogen*?*

It bugs me. "Psychedelic" has a lovely history. It was invented, through a dialogue between Humphry Osmond and Aldous Huxley. In a little poem, Osmond suggested:

"To fathom Hell or soar angelic, Just take a pinch of psychedelic."

What about your own use of psychedelics these days? Are they still personally valuable?

I haven't used any for a while, as I've had so many physical difficulties. To tell the truth, I've been scared that I might have one of those awful experiences. I'm not up to it.

Any thoughts on MDMA? Have you had any experience with MDMA?

I had one, and it really was nice and relaxing, and my defensiveness was released. I'd like to try it with my husband Bill, only I don't know where to get it.

How about ayahuasca? Have you ever had that?

I haven't. But I did try ibogaine, although I didn't have much of a reaction. In the past, when these sort of drugs became available, I'd try them to see if we could use them therapeutically.

Did you do any follow-up with the people you treated using LSD, or hear how they fared?

Not much, but we ought to do a follow-up study.

Let's say our society allowed you to design public policy concerning psychedelics. How would you like to see them used and controlled?

Having clinics is a very good idea, so that's the first thing. But the political situation related to drugs is such a bleeping mess that to set up such clinics you'd almost have to change the thinking of the whole country. But good heavens, that's not anywhere in the near future.

Through the ages these drugs have helped humanity. Why should we be denied them, for goodness' sake?

What would you say about young people using psychedelics?

My kids were initiated as teenagers. Well, I guess they'd have to have been, what with me so involved in it. It was a positive thing. I think the psychedelics helped with adolescent rebellion. They made it a little clearer what was going on.

That's what the Brazilians say about the use of ayahuasca among adolescents. In fact, they say that ayahuasca is a prophylactic against drug abuse.

My kids never abused drugs. Never! The rebellion of teenagers occurs because they see no way out. But if they have a transcendental experience that allows them to see through and beyond that, then they are obviously helped.

Do you see a down side to psychedelics, and what sort of cautionary advice might you give to people?

If the people who are giving them don't know what they're doing, it's disastrous. That's obvious. I'm curious about how psychedelics would fare in a world where people had legal unlimited access. Would people's experiences get better and better, or would the positive effects wear off in time?

Is there anything that you know now that you wish you had known back when you started working in this area?

I wish I'd had the energy to do more and that there had been more time. That's my only regret. I think it's important to remember that the drug is its own teacher. One of the main things I would say to a patient is, "The deep unconscious knows better than we do." If the person had a question, I would wait for the answer to come out of the patient, because that person's unconscious is what is involved, and the deep unconscious knows much more than we do.

How would you characterize what psychedelics actually do?

Don't they peel levels off, like one can do with an onion? You can sit there and watch the Freudian or Jungian principles manifest themselves. Then you can go deeper and deeper and deeper, until finally the ego cracks completely and you transcend it, or so it seems to me. Don't you think so?

Absolutely. Some say they are magnifiers of the unconscious, microscopes into the unconscious.

Well, they allow access to it. I would think they could be marvelous teaching drugs for a psychiatrist.

Have you encountered many psychiatrists who would agree with that?

I haven't really known many. I think people got scared off by the antidrug war, scared of dealing with the illegality of it. Everything got tainted.

What was the impact on the careers of those professionals who continued to be involved with LSD work?

Well, I personally don't know any people who were, although I heard that there were some who continued surreptitiously. I don't think that's a good thing to do, because it's not a surreptitious drug. At a certain point it was no longer even possible to talk publicly about this topic. Well, one didn't, anyway. I'm glad at least that has changed in recent years.

NOTE

1. For a discussion of the importance of music in the psychedelic therapy session, see B. Eisner, "Set, setting and matrix," *Journal of Psychoactive Drugs* 29, no. 2 (1997): 213–16. Betty Eisner is thankful for the contributions of her daughter Maleah Grover and her son David Eisner in helping to complete work on her chapter.

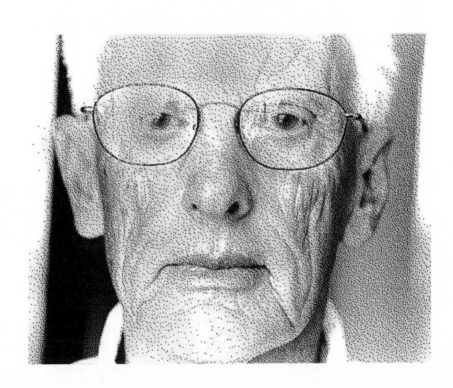

6

Gary Fisher

Treating the Untreatable

Born June 2, 1931• Gary Fisher was born in Winnipeg, Manitoba, Canada and received his bachelor's degree at the University of Manitoba and doctoral degree in research psychology at the University of Utah in 1958. He has held faculty positions in the Department of International Relations at the University of Hawaii and in the Department of International Health Education at the University of California at Los Angeles School of Medicine.

In the late 1950s and early 1960s, Fisher conducted pioneering research on the use of psychedelic drugs in autistic and schizophrenic children. He subsequently explored the role of psychedelics in adults with major mental illness and in patients with terminal cancer. He has contributed a number of pivotal articles in the literature on the application of psychedelics with a variety of seriously ill subjects. Fisher was also a collaborator of Timothy Leary in Mexico, the Caribbean, and at Millbrook in New York. He has written several relevant papers, including "Some comments concerning dosage levels of psychedelic compounds for psychotherapeutic experiences," published in a 1963 issue of the *Psychedelic Review*, and "The psycholytic treatment of a childhood schizophrenic girl," published in a 1970 issue of the *International Journal of Social Psychiatry* (London).

I FIRST HEARD ABOUT PSYCHEDELICS from my wife's brother Nick, a psychiatrist who had been tutored by Al Hubbard and worked under Humphry Osmond and Abram Hoffer in Saskatchewan. He came to visit us and told me about the work they were doing. So I went there and had my first psychedelic experience in Canada in 1959.

At the time, I was a very tight-assed psychologist, a psychologically and emotionally constricted person. I had done a PhD in both research psychology and clinical psychology, and had trained as a psychoanalyst. But I didn't like psychology, I didn't like the training I'd had, and I felt misplaced in the program I was in. The only way I survived was by being academically exceptional.

What were your expectations of your first psychedelic experience, and how was the actual experience?

I had no expectations whatsoever. In fact, I didn't have a clue what I was getting myself into. Nick tried to explain what it was all about, but I clearly didn't understand a word of what he said! [laughs]

What happened in that experience was that I got to see God, and then I was totally transported into a new world. What was so interesting is that the effects of that first session lasted between six and eight months. I didn't start coming down until about the seventh month.

Did you take time off?

No. At that time I was employed at a hospital in Southern California, working with psychotic children. I don't want to identify the hospital, because when they finally discovered what we were doing, they just freaked. They got rid of all the files related to our work.

The administration at the hospital had not known what LSD was. Nobody knew what it was at that time. So I was able to work with the most violent children in the hospital. We were blessed with having a special psychiatrist in charge of the ward—he was a charming man. He never took LSD, as he was afraid of it, but he was intrigued with the possibilities, and he trusted me. When we started to work with the children, he saw the results and was fascinated. So I was left alone to do my work. At that time they didn't have research review committees. I was only twenty-nine years old, and not sophisticated enough to be frightened of the unknown.

You could do research without a lot of restrictions or oversight, but the administration did know about your work, and you published papers, right?

Since I was so low in the pecking order, I didn't ever know the administration. I suppose that the ward doctor just considered it "trying out a new drug." Nothing was published until long after I left.

But, it wasn't secret. You told anyone who asked what you were doing, right?

When I told one fellow we were trying LSD with psychotic children, his eyes popped, his eyebrows raised, and he said, "You're trying to convert psychotic children to Mormonism?" Mormons refer to themselves as Latter Day Saints or L.D.S.

No, the psychedelic studies weren't hidden. At the time we didn't have any reason to think it should be. Sandoz Laboratories was sending LSD in the mail, directly to physicians, and the drug wasn't illegal or regulated.

Could you describe your initial work using psychedelics with these children?

The first patient we treated was an eleven-year-old girl who was dying of something akin to marasmus. Marasmus is a condition of wasting away of the body, where nutrients are not assimilated. It occurs in infants who have no human contact. They go into such an isolated mental state that not even intravenous feeding is effective.

The girl was actively suicidal and would make every attempt to destroy herself. She was in twenty-four-hour restraint. When let loose, she would batter herself: smash her eyes, smash her head against the rails. She looked like an old, wizened lady—nothing but skin and bones, and battered black and blue. So the psychiatrist said, "Why don't you start with this girl. She's going to die anyway, so there is nothing to lose." It was quite a challenge to take as my first patient someone who was in such a terrible situation. I was afraid that maybe she would die during the session. But I didn't have any alternative, because this was who I was given.

What dose of LSD did you give her? A low dose, or a high dose?

We didn't use low doses with any of the patients. My guess is that she got 300 or 400 micrograms, and she weighed maybe fifty-five pounds. She was just skin and bones, and was totally incoherent. She screamed, babbled, and spat if you got near her. She was not in contact with anybody, nor had she ever been since she was hospitalized.

During the session she started wailing like a wounded animal—it was the most chilling sound. Then she started screaming, and the pitch would increase and increase. We tried everything to make contact with her, to no avail.

After about seven or eight hours I was exhausted, and so frustrated that I just yelled at her, "Nancy! When are you going to stop screaming! I can't stand it anymore!" [laughs] She stopped and looked at me. This was the first time she had made eye contact with anybody, and said, "I have a long way to go, so just stay out of my way." That was the first thing she ever said to anybody. Then she went back to screaming. That was our session.

How did she do after that? I assume you had subsequent sessions.

Hers was an amazing story, which we subsequently published. Once she started speaking, it was possible to work with her more effectively. She was a very intelligent girl, perhaps an ancient soul. She was a challenge—conniving and manipulative—and she gave us a run for our money. Her bottom line was always that she had control over hurting herself; this became her ace in the hole. As she improved, she would eventually just carry a Kleenex around, put it on her hand, and say that the Kleenex was stopping her from hitting herself. So we would grab the Kleenex and hide it, and she'd say: "Damn you! Damn you! Give me that napkin!" There was a whole power struggle that went on for months.

Of course, during this time she was no longer in restraints, and she could move about on the ward. She struck up a companionship with one of the other girls in the program, and she was in constant contact with the staff.

She must have had eighteen or nineteen sessions spaced apart by two or three weeks, and every session was productive. Between these sessions, we had to develop a whole treatment program for managing her, as she was extremely bright and incredibly manipulative. One time she said to me, "Well, I can't fool the day staff, but I can still fool the night staff." Then as soon as she said it, I could tell that she was thinking, "Oh my God! I've given myself away!" I looked at her and said, "That's not going to last very long, is it?" And she said, "Damn you!" So, that night I got together with the evening staff and clued them in on what to do, because she was still manipulating the hell out of them. Talk about a tough patient! But she was no longer hurting herself. And although she remained in the hospital, she got well enough to attend school.

How many children did you end up treating with psychedelics?

We started with twelve, and after a period of time we narrowed it down to only those six who were the most responsive, and continued with them. There was no way that we could continue with all twelve of them, as we just didn't have the time. We did a total of eighty-seven sessions. One girl had three treatments and didn't need anymore; she was going to a regular school outside the hospital during the day, while still living at the hospital at night. But she was completely functional and was just waiting for a placement.

What gave you the rationale for doing this?

My rationale was this: If LSD could bring about the miracle it did for me, it could work for anyone—even schizophrenic children.

Was this the first experiment using psychedelics with psychotic or autistic children, or was there prior work that you had heard about?

No, this was in 1959 or 1960, and I hadn't heard of anything. Then by late 1962, we could no longer legally obtain LSD, and all these projects were shut down.

I wrote a long paper on the treatment of one girl, and it was read at the International Association for Social Psychiatry in London by my friend Dr. Joyce Martin. Joyce was a psychoanalyst, and one of the early people who worked with outpatients using LSD in low doses. The editor of the *International Journal of Social Psychiatry* was in the audience and wanted to publish the paper, so that was my first publication.

The paper was about a girl named Patty. When I told her that we couldn't continue this work, she asked, "Why?" I said, "Well, we can't get LSD anymore." And she asked, "Don't you know where it is?" I replied, "Sandoz still has it but they won't give it to us because we're not allowed to use it anymore." She asked, "What's the man's name who has it?" So I told her the Sandoz representative's name, and she took my hand and said, "Gary, this is what I think you should do. You go up to San Francisco and find this man, and you tell him that Patty Simpson sent you to see him. And tell him that Patty Simpson says, 'Please give Gary some LSD because Patty Simpson really needs it.'" We cried for two days. This was a girl who, when we started, was completely psychotic, totally out of contact, destructive, violent, and entirely unmanageable.

So your results with these kids who were not responding to any conventional treatment were excellent. Most of these kids came back to life, right?

Yes. Older schizophrenic children, ages seven to nine, had the most successful response. The least responsive children were very young and had primary autism. Although one girl who was three years old did have a successful response.

We weren't much focused on diagnoses, as these kids were all totally dysfunctional—incredibly disturbed, violent, and noncommunicative. However, their behavior changed somewhat, even with the young children who were nonverbal and who didn't have as much response. One three-year-old girl initially would not let anyone touch her or allow any interaction. After the LSD treatments, she would want to come and touch you and be with you, and sit on your knee and stroke you. Totally opposite from before, when if you got near her she would screech.

So behavior changed, even in kids who had no verbal ability and no interaction, which is amazing. Remember that the ward was total bedlam—forty or fifty kids who were destructive to themselves and others, or curled up in beds in corners. There was debris, feces, vomit, and urine everywhere—just the housekeeping duties were ominous.

After LSD became unavailable, did this kind of work stop? Was there any way for you to follow up, or to use the principles to do other work?

Well, Timothy Leary had set up an organization, the International Federation for Internal Freedom. After Tim came back from his experience in Mexico, he visited me and sat in on part of a session, and he was blown away. When we were shut down at the hospital, he asked me if I would help train his staff. So I went down to Mexico and we tried to set up a research center there.

But not necessarily for really sick people?

No, the people that came were usually contacts that the Harvard people had. As I recall, the Mexican government wanted payoffs, and Timothy refused to do that, so we were evicted. Then we went to Antigua, and tried to set something up there. But that didn't work out, so we went to Guadalupe.

Peggy Hitchcock had bought an island in the Grenadines, and the New York people decided to send supplies there. I had my wife and three small children with me, and one of the other women was pregnant. We were supposed to go over and be the Swiss Family Robinson and start our own community on the island.

Eventually, after being kicked out of the Caribbean, we got to Millbrook, New York. It became pretty apparent that we weren't going to be able to do LSD research, so we decided that we would become an ashram and learn how to do whatever we needed to do without the drugs.

It sounds like you spent quite a few years traveling around with Timothy.

It was not that long. It was all very truncated, because we kept getting evicted rather quickly. Anyway, Timothy then agreed that we would establish an ashram. But he never really honored his word. He'd go into New York for something or other, and then he'd be on television saying outrageous things about the government, politics, and LSD, and the whole revolutionary trip he wanted to lead. Then he'd come back to Millbrook and we'd all dump on him about his TV appearance. For a while he would be contrite and good, and then he'd get bored at Millbrook and he'd leave again, and repeat the whole process.

Timothy and I were on totally different pages. I wanted to assist people in achieving their own internal revolution, while Tim wanted to lead the young to overthrow the established order. I quite believe that he never understood what psychedelics are all about. One time when Tim was going to do a huge rally at the Santa Monica Civic Auditorium, he was pondering what the marquee should read, and Alan Watts said, "Oh Tim, just say it like it is—Timothy Leary: The Second Coming."

You knew then that he was going to cause trouble for LSD?

Oh yeah, I knew it! I was the first to leave! I could tell that it was going to be chaos there, because he was not on the same frequency as the rest of us. He should have been in show business.

Where did you go after Millbrook?

I went to visit Dr. Joyce Martin, my friend in London. As I mentioned, she was one of the original LSD therapists in Europe. She used the method that has been termed "psycholytic"—with small doses of fifty to seventy-five micrograms.

She bought a place in Malta to set up an LSD research center there. The Maltese government agreed to allow LSD research at her clinic as long as there were no Maltese citizens involved in the sessions! [laughs] That would have been easy to comply with because most of our clients would have been from England and America. So she built a hospital clinic in Malta with LSD rooms, and housing there for us and the other staff. I was headed to London to pick her up on our way to Malta, when she died in her sleep. She had cancer, and I had no idea she was ill. She was in her seventies when she died.

After the job in Malta didn't work out, where did you go next?

I went to Hawaii, looking for adventure and lots of nature. While at the University of Hawaii, I did community development work for the Peace Corps and the Agency for International Development—even some training of the military brass for community development work in Southeast Asia. That was a wonderful experience. When I came back to the mainland, I taught at UCLA and was also on the psychiatry staff at Cedars-Sinai Medical Center.

There were many cancer patients at Cedars who had intractable pain. The head of the psychiatry department asked me if I would conduct some LSD sessions to see if this would be effective in pain management. And of course I did. I didn't really tell them my rationale, because it wouldn't have made sense to the oncologists. I suspect they thought that LSD would simply reduce the pain. But I thought that if the patients had some insight into what their cancer was all about, and made peace with themselves and with their world, then the overlay of pain—which is psychic pain—would be reduced and they would have an easier death. And that's exactly what happened.

How many people did you treat in this context?

Not too many, because the head of oncology was very disturbed by the results. To give you an example, one of the first people we treated was a neurotic and demanding lady who had invasive cancer. She had an amazing LSD experience. She got into all her internal conflict and her dysfunctional relationship with her family. When we saw her the next day, she had refused her pain medication. The head of oncology came to see why and she said, "Well, I'm not *having* any pain." He got quite flustered and said, "Well, you must be having pain. I can show you on your X-rays where your cancer is, and it causes pain. You're lying to me." She replied, "I don't need pain medication right now. Maybe I'll need it down the line, but right now I don't need it, and I don't want to take it because of the side effects. Why should I take it if I don't need it? I'm handling everything okay." He said, "You either take this pain medication or I'll discharge you." She wouldn't take it and so he discharged her.

The physician thought we were making these people psychotic, because they didn't believe they had pain. [laughs] It was a real mess. I continued to see and treat other people, but he was very obstreperous about my treating his patients. He couldn't understand what was happening, but he didn't want to know.

When people are confronted by something that doesn't fit into their model of reality (e.g., a patient not having pain when she's supposed to be having pain), for their *own* sanity, they have to come up with an explanation. The easiest in our society is the insanity explanation. If you dissect the insanity explanation, it always reduces to "I don't understand this phenomenon because it doesn't fit into my model of reality."

Was it unusual for another professional to be so hostile toward the use of psychedelics in treatment?

You've got to remember that after LSD was in the streets and people began taking it indiscriminately, a lot of people became very disturbed and psychotic. As a result, many psychiatrists revisited the earlier idea that LSD was a psychotomimetic. That's where it all began; when LSD was first introduced they thought it mimicked psychosis.

By the late 1960s, you found the environment to be unreceptive for this work?

It was probably the late 1960s when we were working with cancer patients. The paper, "Psychotherapy for the Dying: Principles and Illustrations with Special Reference to the Utilization of LSD," was published in 1970 in the journal *Omega*.

We also did work during the late 1950s and early 1960s with other kinds of people in the community. For example, my brother-in-law would come down from Canada and we would go to people's homes to treat alcoholics.

I also gave LSD to a number of psychiatrists, trying to train them how to use it. There were about five people in our own core group at the hospital, and we used to sit for each other for this sort of work. We also had sessions with people in the artistic community. There was a network of people doing this sort of psychedelic work at that time.

I gave LSD to some Buddhist monks from Thailand. That was fascinating! One night a fellow appeared on my doorstep. He had heard about my work at the hospital while he was living in a monastery in Thailand, and he specifically came over to visit me. Because he was interested in children, he ended up working with kids at the hospital. And then a friend of his from Thailand also came over, and I gave him an LSD session too.

How did they compare it to Buddhist meditation?

One man who had been in the monastery for about sixteen years came for a session, and I gave him twenty or twenty-five milligrams of psilocybin. For about two hours he was totally silent, then this beatific smile appeared on his face, and he quietly said, "Ah! This is what my teacher has been trying to tell me for the last sixteen years."

The experience with the other monk was also wondrous. The fellow's name was Carl, and when he first arrived at my house, he had a couple pair of pants, two shirts, and his bicycle—that was it. He had a wooden leg, because his leg had been blown off in the war. As a teenager he had been in the Nazi army on the Russian front, but he walked away from the war. Then he went to Sri Lanka, and he eventually ended up in Thailand, where he had been in a monastery for many years. So I kept saying to Carl, "Don't you want to have a session someday?" And he'd say "Oh yes, that would be nice." But then I'd wait for him to ask, which never happened. Finally I said to him, "Carl, don't you really want to take this?" He asked, "Do you want me to take it?" And I said, "Well, yeah, I'd really like you to take it."

So he took it, and I waited and waited and waited. We had our usual ritual—music, a red rose, photographs—and I kept asking, "Has anything changed yet, Carl? Anything changing?" Always he said, "No." Finally I laid down on the floor, and away *I* went. I had the most incredible experience, where he took me back from the beginning of his life, up to where he was in my living room. He took me on his whole life's journey, through the Nazi army in Russia, walking all the way through Saudi Arabia, and finally ending up in my living room. He was a remarkable man, and I experienced his life.

Nonverbally?

Nonverbally. I really lived his life. He took me there! After many hours I sat up and exclaimed, "My God, Carl!" He just smiled. It never affected him one iota; it didn't touch him. It affected *me!* I experienced oneness with Carl's consciousness—and it was "the peace that passeth all understanding." The roads to Nirvana are so unknown and always so surprising and unexpected. You can never fully prepare a person for an LSD experience—it simply can't be done.

Your work at Cedars with psychedelics stopped around the early 1970s. Have you had any personal experiences since then?

No. It was many months following my first session before I approached the consciousness of "ordinary" reality. Fortunately, after a successful psychedelic experience, you never go back to your previous state of consciousness—that's the whole point of taking psychedelics. If you don't integrate the higher levels of consciousness into your daily life, then the trip has been irrelevant. In statistics, the maxim is "a difference, to be a difference, has to make a difference." If a psychedelic experience doesn't result in your becoming a being who is more human, then psychedelics are meaningless and don't make a difference. I have never known anyone who had a profound transcendental experience who wasn't significantly changed in his or her daily life by that experience.

After my first session, I realized that I had to learn how to get into altered mind states without drugs. So that became my agenda. It didn't seem to me to be a reasonable assumption that you had to depend on a drug for these kinds of mind states. So I started studying Agni Yoga, and then Zen and Buddhism. I read material from various schools of thought regarding altered states of consciousness. Castaneda's books came out, and of course I read those. And then Jane Roberts' books on the Seth material. The Seth material in Roberts' book *The Nature of Personal Reality* is as close as I've ever read to what I was beginning to understand about the creation of "actuality." That book nails down in nice detail how our universe works. It's incredible: Roberts just took dictation from Seth, whom she was channeling.

I don't know if I believe that I can discover things *with* psychedelics that I can't discover *without* them. I think that if I got to the point where I felt as though I couldn't learn any more without them, then I would take them again. But so far, I'm still learning daily. So, I haven't yet come to a point where I've run out of things to learn.

Giving up psychedelics was a very conscious decision on my part. When I was doing LSD therapy treatments every other day or so, I was in a contact high state. I didn't need drugs.

At one point we were experimenting with dosage levels, and I decided that I would take the smallest amount of psilocybin that could be titrated to see if I would get any results. My co-workers groaned, "Oh, God, here's the scientist again! Now he wants to do this!" They tried to talk me out of it. But I said, "No, I want to see what's the least amount to give me a full trip." The smallest amount you could give was two milligrams, so I said, "I'm going to do a session with two milligrams." They said, "Okay, if that's what you want to do." I had one of the most profound experiences I'd ever had on drugs, on merely two milligrams of psilocybin, and it lasted for two days. After that I figured, "I probably don't even need two milligrams."

In an article you wrote on dosing in the Psychedelic Review, *you said you would introduce people with psilocybin, and then maybe a couple hours later give them LSD, right?*

If I were working with people today who were really blocked and really disturbed, I would still use 600 to 800 micrograms of LSD, because I think it requires that much to demolish that kind of rigid ego. If working with people who have done a lot of internal work, my drug of choice would be psilocybin. But we used hefty amounts of psilocybin. Of course, to be on the safe side, using 400 micrograms of LSD after the psilocybin gives you more assurance that the necessary "boost" is there.

If you had never come across psychedelics, where do you think your life would have gone?

I'd have been dead years ago. I wasn't even up to the point of being unhappy back then, because I didn't even have that much consciousness. You have to have certain smarts to know you're unhappy. I didn't even have that.

To what do you attribute the resistance to psychedelics in our culture? Why have they become such an anathema to the mainstream?

That's an enormous question, which has to do with power, money, and politics. It's power politics. With psychedelics, if you're fortunate and break through, you understand what is truly of value in life. Material, power, dominance, and territory have no value. People wouldn't fight wars, and the whole system we have currently would fall apart. People would become peaceful, loving citizens, not robots marching around in the dark with all their lights off.

What is your understanding about the evolution of consciousness in our society; are you optimistic?

Humankind has progressed over many hundreds of years, and I expect it will continue to progress, LSD or no LSD. There are thousands of psychedelic substances on the planet, and humankind has always used them. The human condition is of a divine nature. We are spirits in human form having human experiences. I think that the process of learning to become "a complete human being" is what reincarnation is all about. I've had a few thousand lifetimes in the human form, and find I'm still somewhere in preparation for preschool.

Do you feel that psychedelics may still have some value in facilitating human evolution, or has their value run its course?

I don't think it's ever been tapped. It's only just beginning. Only a very select few people have ever had the opportunity to take these substances in appropriate environments and with noble intentions.

If psychedelics were sanctioned and people had access to settings where they could be used optimally, what might they accomplish?

I don't know how you could institutionalize psychedelics in the culture as it exists. I think that idea may be an oxymoron. The functional way is in a very informal manner, through one human to another; just as one might read a wonderful insightful book and then want to share it with a friend, I think maybe that's the way the psychedelic experience will spread in an optimal fashion. I don't think I would start with trying to train psychiatrists or psychologists in the use of psychedelics. I can't see how putting them into a medical school or a psychology department would work. I would just go around looking for people who are naturally kind.

So you don't feel that psychedelics hold unique potential as treatment tools or for training programs in psychiatry and psychology?

They could be used as training tools in *any* sort of investigation on the planet! If you're focused on something, have an intention, and go into an expanded state of consciousness, you're going to understand what you're working with in a totally new perspective. It doesn't matter what area of inquiry you are looking into. Psychedelics could be useful in any form of inquiry.

How would people be trained in the use of psychedelics?

In the 1950s we all had wonderful aspirations for where this was going to go. After someone had an LSD experience, one comment, which now seems a bit funny, that some people would make was, "Soon there will be more of us than there are of them—more converted people." Having been around since the beginning of the research with psychedelics, and having lived so many years and seen what has happened, I just don't know anymore. That's why, in the practical sense, I think it has to be spread via a brotherhood and sisterhood network where people bring others who are seekers, and it unfolds in that manner.

What are the dangers of psychedelics?

Training therapists how to use psychedelics can be a dangerous process. I'll give you an example. The social worker from the hospital where I was running sessions was a big guy—six foot four, 250 pounds, and sort of passive-aggressive. He was unhappy because he wasn't included in our LSD treatment program. I didn't think he was the right kind of person to be part of the group. But he kept bugging me: "Why can't I be a sitter?" I explained, "As you know, you have to go through the experience first." We did the traditional Saskatchewan-model training, where people have their own sessions, and then sit in on a few sessions with us, and then eventually become sitters themselves. Finally the psychiatrist came to me and said, "The social worker says that you won't give him LSD, and he feels real bad. He feels excluded, and he's really bugging me. Why don't you give him a session? Get off the criterion stick."

I reluctantly agreed and said to the social worker, "Okay, let's have a session." I knew that this guy was not put together all that well, so I said to the group, "Everybody's going to have to come to this session." He was a big guy, and if he got out of hand, I wanted everyone there—all six of us. Sometimes a person on psychedelics can get combative out of fear, based in paranoia or mania, and there should be a few people available to simply sit on the person until he or she moves on from that state.

So the social worker came to the session and took the drug. After a while he said, "I think I'll lie down, because I'm feeling a little woozy." Then he closed his eyes, and listened to the music, and seemed to be doing fine. One of the sitters decided to get some food, one of them got a telephone call, one had to go to the bathroom, and the others had to go somewhere else. Everybody disappeared and I was left alone with him. I'm sitting there thinking, "Boy, the best laid plans of mice and men. Here I am with this guy and all the other sitters have disappeared."

I was listening to the music, when all of a sudden: Boom! It was like being hit by a truck! I opened my eyes, and he was sitting up looking at me and he was stark raving mad. He was just totally psychotic. Holy shit!

And he was terrified. He had red hair, and his face was just as brilliantly red. Slowly he got up, walked toward me, and put his hands around my neck.

He's choking me, and there's nothing I can do. There's no phone in the room, there's nobody I can call for help. The door's locked and I can't get out. I don't know where the hell my keys are, and he's going to kill me. I think, "Well, I'm going to go peacefully. I'm not going to struggle. You sometimes learn in the hardest ways."

He was squeezing my throat, and I remember seeing my hand turning blue. But I was doing pretty well; I was centered. If I started gagging, I'd think, "No, don't gag." I began going unconscious, when all of a sudden I felt him stop. I felt him pick me up, and I started coming to. He was holding and comforting me.

In postsession meetings, I didn't bring up episodes from the session until the subject brought them up. Memories will arise into the consciousness when they are ready to be integrated. It took him nearly a year to *remember* that episode. When he finally did, he told me this: "When I came out of wherever I was, I saw you as the devil. I had to kill the devil for me to live and for the world to live. I was terrified that I would die, and so I was killing you. But then as you were dying, I looked at you, and you changed. You turned into the infant Jesus. I took you in my arms and held you."

Did the session have any long-term impact on this man?

For the first eight months, he couldn't recall anything from the session. Then, after he remembered, he was totally changed. So in answer to your question asking how people need to be trained to do this; the answer is: The trainer has to be willing to die! [laughs]

Do you feel that you would have been better off if you had held to your original intuition about not giving him a session?

Absolutely not. Because the final result was very positive. But more than that, I learned another lesson the hard way. I was coming from a place of fear, and whenever you make decisions out of fear, you just get exactly what you feared you would get. I was trying to protect myself from being hurt by this large man, so I surrounded myself with all these "body guards," but then they all disappeared and this guy behaved exactly as I feared he would. So again, I learned about what happens when you make a choice out of fear.

How have your experiences with psychedelics affected your understanding of death?

Death is a transitional state. There's nothing magical about dying. You don't get an automatic free ride or the golden ring, just because you die. Some people think that when we die then somehow we get peace, or some goodie, or some particular bonus just for the event. But that's not my experience.

What would you say to young people about psychedelics?

Is this a child who's been raised with love, acceptance, and understanding, surrounded by Nature? Have they, at some wonderful time, been introduced to other levels of actualities and realities through ritual within their family? If so, then an introduction to psychedelics could be an incredibly beautiful experience at the any age, if the setting was right and the motivation noble.

Is there anything that you know now that you wish you had known back in the 1950s and 1960s, when you were first working with psychedelics?

If you were a Zen student and I were a Zen master, I would get out my stick and smack you. It's not a question. Just think about it. I don't mean to be sarcastic, nor do I mean to be down-putting. But it isn't a question. Do you understand why it isn't a question? Because one can't change the past and who would want to anyway, if you embrace that past and use it meaningfully in the now. All Maya is an illusion. It's just a distraction from being in the now. I wish I'd never had an ego. [laughs] I wish I didn't have one now. What else do you want to know?

7

Stanislav Grof

The Great Awakening: Psychology, Philosophy, and Spirituality in LSD Psychotherapy

Born July 1, 1931 • Stanislav Grof is widely regarded as the world's foremost researcher of psychedelics. Beginning at Charles University in Prague and continuing later in the United States at the Maryland Psychiatric Research Center, he supervised several thousand clinical and research sessions with psychedelics, considerably more than any other researcher. He has therefore perhaps seen a vaster panoply of human experience than anyone else in history.

From his analyses of these experiences, Grof developed groundbreaking, comprehensive, and systematic psychologies and metaphysics. His contributions in these areas are remarkably multifaceted, encompassing psychodynamic perspectives such as those of Freud, Jung, and Rank, Asian approaches such as those of yoga and Buddhism, as well as his own unique insights. The great humanistic psychologist, Abraham Maslow, evaluated Grof's work as "the most important contribution to personality theory in several decades."

Drawing on the deepest experiences of his subjects, Grof constructed a vast metaphysical vision, which he summarized in his book *The Cosmic Game*. This vision has major overlaps with the Perennial Philosophy or what we might call the *sophia commmonalis*: the common core of wisdom and understanding at the heart of the world's great religious traditions.

In addition to psychedelics, he has also researched a wide array of related topics in the fields of transpersonal psychology, psychotherapy, and consciousness studies. With his wife Christina, he instituted the study of spiritual emergencies and cofounded the Spiritual Emergence Network. Together they also devised a powerful nondrug consciousness modifying technique, holotropic breathwork, which is now widely used around the world.

Grof's many professional positions have included researcher at Charles University in Prague, assistant professor of psychiatry at John Hopkins University School of Medicine, chief of psychiatric research at the Maryland Psychiatric Research Center, and scholar in residence at Esalen Institute. He is also the founding president of the International Transpersonal Association and cofounder with Christina Grof of Grof Transpersonal Training in Mill Valley, California.

Stanislav Grof's publications include the books: *Realms of the Human Unconscious, Beyond the Brain, The Holotropic Mind, The Adventure of Self-Discovery, LSD Psychotherapy, The Cosmic Game,* and *Psychology of the Future: Lessons from Modern Consciousness Research.*

I WAS BORN IN PRAGUE, CZECHOSLOVAKIA, where I received an MD degree from the School of Medicine of Charles University and later a PhD from the Czechoslovakian Academy of Sciences. I decided to study medicine after reading Freud's *Introductory Lectures to Psychoanalysis,* which made a deep impression on me, and then I specialized in psychiatry and completed a Freudian training.

However, as I got more involved in my field, I reached a point where I experienced a conflict regarding the relationship between psychoanalytic theory and its practice. As time went by, I became increasingly excited about the theoretical achievements of psychoanalysis. In many different areas psychoanalysts offered seemingly brilliant explanations for a variety of mysterious problems—the symbolism of dreams, neurotic symptoms, psychopathology of everyday life, insights into religion, sociopolitical movements, art, and many others. This aspect of psychoanalysis was exciting.

However, I was also becoming increasingly aware of what you can achieve with psychoanalysis as a clinical tool, and that was a different story. Psychoanalysis had a very narrow spectrum of indications, and patients had to meet specific criteria to be considered good candidates for this form of therapy. Those who met the criteria had to commit themselves to spend exorbitant amounts of time in therapy: three to five sessions a week for many years. And in a lot of cases, even after years, the results were not exactly breathtaking!

I had great difficulty coming to terms with this situation. To become a psychoanalyst, one had to study medicine. And in medicine, if we really understand a problem, we are usually able to do something pretty dramatic about it. In those diseases with which we have limited success, we understand the reasons for our failures. In the case of diseases such as cancer or AIDS, we have a good idea where the problem is and what would have to change for us to be more successful. Yet here I was told that psychoanalysis provided a solid theoretical understanding of the problems we were dealing with, and nevertheless so little could be done over such a long period of time. It did not make any sense.

I found this situation disappointing, and I started to regret that I had chosen psychiatry as my profession. I like to draw and paint, and my original intention was to work in the Barrandov Film Studios in Prague in the department of animated movies. When I first encountered Freud's writings, I had already been interviewed and accepted by Jiri Trnka, the leading creative artist in the field of animation. So, at the time of my painful conflict about psychoanalysis, I started nostalgically thinking about my old passion of animated movies, and recalling my original plans. I strongly felt that choosing psychoanalysis as my life's work was a major error. But then something important happened in my life.

In the mid-1950s, while I was experiencing this conflict, I worked in the psychiatry department of the school of medicine in Prague. This was the time of the golden era of psychopharmacology: the discovery of the first tranquilizers, reserpine and chlorpromazine, and their introduction into laboratory and clinical practice of psychiatry. Chemistry would soon solve most of the problems in psychiatry, right?

One day, the psychiatry department received by mail a large box full of ampoules. It came with a letter explaining that the enclosed substance was LSD-25. Its powerful psychoactive properties had been discovered in April of 1943 by Dr. Albert Hofmann, a chemist working for the Sandoz Pharmaceutical Company in Switzerland. He had accidentally become inebriated while synthesizing it. The letter described a pilot study that had been conducted with this substance in a group of psychiatric patients and normal volunteers. The preliminary results strongly suggested that this substance might provide fascinating insights into psychoses. On the basis of their observations, the Sandoz representatives suggested two possibilities.

One was that the drug could be used to induce a condition similar to naturally-occurring psychoses, but lasting only a few hours. This experimental "model psychosis" would make it possible to study various parameters before, during, and after the LSD session, and get some important insights about what was happening physiologically and biochemically in the body of the patients at the time when their mental functioning was so profoundly changed. The idea was that this might provide some insights that could be then applied to understanding schizophrenia or other naturally-occurring psychoses.

But the Sandoz letter also proposed another possibility, one that profoundly influenced the destiny of my personal and professional life. It suggested that LSD might be useful as a kind of unconventional training tool that would provide psychiatrists, psychologists, students, and nurses the opportunity to spend a few hours in the world of their patients. As a result of this experience, they would be able to understand them better, to communicate with them more effectively, and hopefully to have better therapeutic results. I got very excited; I would not have missed this opportunity for anything in the world.

Before you administered LSD to a patient, you took it yourself?

Yes. All through my years of psychedelic research, I have always personally experienced the psychoactive substances before I administered them to others. So I took LSD myself as one of the early Czech volunteers. I was given 150 micrograms, and this happened on November 13, 1956. It was Saint Stanislav's Day, my name's day—something we celebrate in Czechoslovakia in addition to birthdays, and certainly a memorable one.

My first LSD experience had an unusual twist to it. My preceptor was interested in electroencephalography (EEG) and wanted to find out how LSD would affect the brain waves. So a condition for having a session with him was to have one's EEG recorded before, during, and after the session. At the time of my session, he was particularly interested in what is called "driving" or "entraining of the brain waves"—trying to change their frequencies by some external input, either acoustic or visual. So I had to agree not only to have my EEG taken, but also to have my brain waves driven in the middle of this experiment.

About two and a half hours into the session, when the drug effect was culminating, a research assistant came to do this experiment. She asked me to lie down, and pasted EEG electrodes on my skull. Then she brought in a giant strobe light, put it above my head, had me close my eyes, and turned it on. The next thing I knew, there was this incredible flash of light, beyond anything that I could even imagine.

At the time, I thought this was what it must have been like in Hiroshima at the epicenter of the atomic explosion. Today I think about it more in terms of the *dharmakaya*—the timeless experience of nonduality that appears when one dies, as described in the *Tibetan Book of the Dead*. In any case, what happened as a result of the strobe flash was that my consciousness was catapulted out of my body. I lost the research assistant, I lost the clinic, I lost Prague, and then I lost the planet. I had a sense that my consciousness had absolutely no boundaries, and I had become all of existence.

Then the experience took an astronomical form. For what seemed like eternity, it appeared as though the whole universe became the playground of my consciousness. There were all kinds of incredible astronomical processes happening, for which I did not have any concepts, let alone names. (This was before I had read about things like the Big Bang, black holes, white holes, worm holes, quasars, or pulsars.)

While this was happening, the research assistant was meticulously following the protocol. She started with two frequencies, brought one of them slowly to sixty hertz, and then took it back and put it for a while in the middle of the alpha range, then the theta ranges, and finally delta range. I found this effort to capture the enormity of my experience with the use of these scientific gizmos utterly futile and ridiculous. When she finally turned the strobe off, my consciousness—and with it the universe—started to shrink rather rapidly. I was able to find our planet, Prague, the clinic, and finally my body. There was no doubt in my mind that my consciousness was independent from my body, since it took me some time to realign it with my body, and finally reconnect the two. Needless to say, I was very impressed by what had just happened to me.

What happened to me was enormous and seemed like the beginning of a new life. I had played with the stroboscopic light before, but all I had experienced was a beautiful display of geometrical patterns and colors. I had not experienced anything like what happened during the combination with LSD. So I knew the drug was somehow the key to my fantastic experience. My interest in psychiatry, which was at an all time low just before this experience, got an enormous boost. I decided to dedicate my life to the study of nonordinary states of consciousness.

I joined a group of researchers working in Prague, who had access to several psychedelics and were conducting a comparative study of psychoactive substances. We had a group of about forty subjects, mostly professionals, who were willing to participate in this study. They would come to the research institute for a day at a time to experience each of the psychedelics we were studying.

We worked with LSD, LAE, psilocybin, psilocin, DMT, DET, and DPT. We had contact with the Canadian researchers Humphry Osmond and Abe Hoffer, and included in our study the chemicals adrenochrome and adrenolutine that they provided. Our group also received a prestigious Purkyne Award from the Czechoslovakian Academy of Science for the discovery of psychedelic properties of benactyzine.

The days of these experiments had a full and comprehensive schedule. Every hour on the hour we collected samples of blood and urine. We also used a battery of psychological tests and physiological examinations—pulse, blood pressure, EEG, galvanic skin response, flicker fusion, and so on. This was done on a double-blind basis; neither the subject nor the researcher knew which of the drugs was administered on any particular day and the series included one day when an inactive substance—placebo—was administered in lieu of one of the psychedelic substances.

Were these tests conducted on normal subjects, or on patients?

The substances were administered to "normal" people—psychiatrists, psychologists, physiologists, and biologists, along with some lay volunteers. We were our own guinea pigs. Since this research was done in the spirit of the "experimental psychosis" model—searching for possible biochemical causes of psychoses—the study also included psychiatric patients, diagnosed as psychotic or schizophrenic. But these individuals were not given any psychedelics; they functioned as a control group.

We matched them with the subjects in our experimental group by a variety of parameters—age, sex, IQ, and others. They were brought into the research institute for a day and they would go through the same tests as the subjects in the experimental group, only no active substances were given, only the placebo. We were trying to establish if our findings in normal subjects, at the time when they received psychedelics, would converge with the values observed in schizophrenic patients.

It was thought that LSD produced a "toxic psychosis." The experiences we were having and observing in others were believed to somehow be artificially produced by the interaction between the drug and the neurophysiological and biochemical processes in the brain. But then I started noticing something interesting: an incredible interindividual variability of the reaction to the administration of psychedelics. If we gave these substances in the same dosage and under the same circumstances to a number of people, each of them had a completely different experience.

Sometimes, the session was primarily an aesthetic experience characterized by unbelievably colorful visions resembling kaleidoscopic displays, stained glass windows of Gothic cathedrals, or arabesques from Moslem mosques. These were similar to what we now know as fractals—computer-generated graphic representations of nonlinear equations. For some individuals, the session took the form of a deepened personal psychoanalysis, with regression to childhood and even infancy, reliving of various traumas, interesting insights, and so on. Somebody else would have an experience that was primarily somatic—breathing difficulties, headaches, nausea, or even throwing up. On occasion during the sessions, people got very depressed, manic, or paranoid. Others felt angry or guilty. And some experienced ecstatic rapture or total bliss and peace.

We found out that there was an equally amazing intraindividual variability. When we repeated the sessions with the same subjects, same substances, same dosages, and in the same set and setting, each of their subsequent sessions was very different from the previous ones. Moreover, there actually was a progression from more superficial layers of the unconscious to deeper ones. One of my clients later called this process of chemical archaeology the "onion-peeling of the unconscious." At that point, I realized that psychedelics were not causing "toxic psychoses," but were catalysts of psychological and psychosomatic processes. They were not producing artificial experiences by interacting with the brain. Rather, by increasing the energetic level in the psyche, they were bringing into consciousness the contents from the depth of the unconscious.

In view of these observations, it did not seem far-fetched to see LSD as a tool comparable to a microscope or a telescope. Like these devices, LSD made it possible to observe and study processes that were normally not part of our everyday experience. At that point, I became interested in LSD as something that could accelerate psychotherapy. I knew from Freudian psychoanalysis that if you can get to unconscious sources of various symptoms and interpersonal problems, this should have therapeutic implications. And here we had a tool that could take us there faster and reach deeper than verbal approaches. With this realization, I took my experimentation back into clinical work. I started a study with a group of clients who had serious emotional and psychosomatic problems, and in whom all the traditional forms of treatment had failed.

You had also lost interest in your conventional psychoanalytic practice by this time, right?

Pretty much so. I remember a few early LSD sessions when I still had the patient in a reclining position on a couch and I was sitting in an armchair behind the patient's head, the way I was used to doing it in psychoanalysis. I expected that I would get the descriptions of their experiences and would give them interpretations. But I soon realized that I understood only a very small range of their experiences—those that fell into the biographical domain, which I was prepared for by my psychiatric and psychoanalytic training. One after another, my LSD psychotherapy clients started moving far beyond the limited experiential territory of postnatal biography and the individual unconscious. Suddenly I started seeing many things that one does not read about in psychoanalysis.

Initially, this made me uncomfortable; my clients were going through these intense experiences and I did not have a clue what was happening to them. They were convinced that they were dying, losing control, or going crazy, and were afraid of never coming back to ordinary reality. Several of them also experienced their biological birth with very extreme physiological manifestations. I was confused and not quite sure where the experimentation with this mysterious substance was taking us.

I therefore decided to have a few sessions with higher dosages myself, to get some insight into what was happening. These sessions were extremely challenging and taxing, and took me to the realm of my unconscious that I today call perinatal. Although these sessions were difficult for me, I also found them to be healing and transforming. As a result, I became increasingly comfortable with these states in other people. I became capable of guiding and supporting my clients wherever their inner journeys took them.

Did your early experiences rekindle any memories of previous experiences with mystical or nonordinary states of consciousness that you may have had when you were younger?

In the late 1940s when I was a student, seventeen years old, I spent four months in a Communist prison. This was a year after the armed *putsch* that led to the Communist takeover of Czechoslovakia and subsequent Soviet hegemony over our country. A schoolmate of mine had brought to school one of those chain letters that you are supposed to copy and send to ten of your friends. It asked Czech people to write to the American Embassy in Prague and request intervention at the United Nations that would lead to free elections in Czechoslovakia, which were prevented by the Communists. One of the students who received a copy of this leaflet reported it to the police. The police arrested and interrogated the initiator of this action and, within two hours, they obtained the names of all of us to whom this leaflet was given. Early that afternoon, two men in leather coats collected me at my apartment and I spent four months in prison.

The first part of my stay there involved pretty rough interrogations. We were kept in a cell and never knew when the prison guards would come to fetch us, but this usually happened during night hours. They would take us to a small room where we had to face bright lights shining directly into our eyes. Two men whom we could not see kept asking questions about various areas of our personal history. And then, after a period of time that varied from one interrogation to another, they let us go. We did not know if they would come again in twenty minutes or two hours, or if they would let us sleep for the rest of the night.

This interrogation continued for about ten days, during which time, I was sleep-deprived and under stress. As a result, I started slipping into nonordinary states of consciousness. And I remember that, in spite of the precariousness of the situation, something in me was fascinated by those states. I had a sense that this was not just a disturbance of my usual state of mind, but an opening into another dimension of existence that harbored undreamt of possibilities. I see now that this was my introduction into a realm that I have been exploring my entire life.

I managed to insist during this entire time that I had not read the leaflet, since I received it at the end of a break between classes and put it into my pocket to look at it later. After four months of incarceration, I finally had a trial and was acquitted for "lack of evidence." When my American friends hear this story, they find it unbelievable that it is possible to spend four months in prison just for receiving a leaflet, but that was the reality of our life at the time.

Had you had any previous experience with or interest in spirituality?

I did not have any formal exposure to religion in my youth. This was related to a little drama in the history of our family. My mother's family was Catholic and my father's family had no religious affiliation. When my parents wanted to get married, my mother's parents insisted on a church wedding, but their church refused to marry my parents, because my father was a pagan by their definition. For a while there was a lot of commotion, and it seemed that the wedding would not happen at all.

Then my mother's parents found a brilliant solution: they made a major financial donation to the church, and the church decided to relax its standards and marry a pagan. So the dream of my mother's parents came true and the wedding was a very ostentatious event. They lived just across the street from the church, and they were able to stop the traffic and roll carpets from the altar to the house, so that the guests could walk directly from the altar to the wedding banquet. My parents were so disenchanted by this whole affair that they decided not to commit me or my brother to any religion. They wanted us to make our own decision when we came of age.

As a result, when we had classes in religion at school, my brother and I had a free hour. We could go for a walk, read something, or play. So I had absolutely no formal exposure to religion. From this background, I went to medical school, which certainly is not something that cultivates mystical awareness. I studied medicine at a time when our country was controlled by the Soviet Union and had a Marxist regime, and they exerted great effort to protect our minds from being polluted by what they considered to be the "opium of the masses." Everything that even remotely smacked of mysticism and idealism was either ridiculed or censored.

But there was one thing that was important for my spiritual development. My mother was a follower of Paul Brunton. He was an English philosopher who had spent some time with Sri Ramana Maharshi in India, and who had written many popular books about his spiritual adventures. He traveled all around the world and had groups of followers in many different countries, who would attend his talks and meditate with him. When I was about twelve or thirteen years old, my mother took me to a couple of such meetings. I became fascinated by what Brunton had to say and started reading a lot of Indian literature.

The problem for me was that these people were not just talking about Indian philosophy and religions, but they were also meditating. And there was no way I could meditate. I just sat there bored to death, and felt that it was a colossal loss of time—there seemed to be so many more interesting things to do. But the interest in India stayed with me. Paradoxically, my real spiritual awakening came where one would least expect it—from my laboratory and clinical research. After I had experienced psychedelic sessions, meditation became easy for me and seemed to be a natural activity.

When you started observing mystical experiences, what kind of reception did you receive from your colleagues who were not directly involved in psychedelic experimentation?

Initially, in my excitement and enthusiasm, I made some attempts to share these observations. But I quickly learned that it was not wise to talk about them. Those who were not directly involved did not believe that something like this was possible or that it had any heuristic relevance. There was a tendency to dismiss these experiences as toxically-induced phantasmagoria.

So there were just a few people, all of whom were actively experimenting with psychedelics, with whom I could discuss these phenomena. Even many colleagues experimenting with psychedelics were not open to the fact that they were ontologically relevant—that they revealed revolutionary new information about the human psyche and new dimensions of reality. There was definitely a strong tendency in academic circles to dismiss psychedelic experiences by using traditional reductionistic explanations, and to see them as manifestations of "toxic psychosis" or as derivatives of personal biography.

Here was this remarkable new tool, which opened a whole new understanding of the mind, and yet you ran into a wall of resistance, even very early on. How do you understand that resistance from your colleagues?

People were committed to the theoretical frameworks, philosophical world-views, and ways of thinking that they had absorbed from their education and from living in Western technological culture. I have a lot of understanding and sympathy for this resistance, since I experienced it myself.

It is not easy to question established authorities. Imagine that you are this greenhorn, just a couple of years out of medical school, and you are surrounded by these academic authorities with impressive titles and credentials. And they present certain perspectives as proven scientific truths that are obvious and beyond any reasonable doubt. Under these circumstances, it is not easy to trust the findings of fledgling researchers, including your own.

During my medical studies I attended a lecture by William Laufberger, a world-famous Czech professor of endocrinology and neurophysiology. The subject of his talk was the nature of memory. During the discussion period—as if anticipating the findings of my own later research—I asked, "How far does our memory reach? Can we, for example, remember our birth?" I got this scathing and condescending look from the renowned professor as he answered in a tone that suggested that an idiotic question like that was unworthy of a medical student, "Of course not; the cortex of the neonate is not myelinized. How could there be a record of birth?" So, something in me was already anticipating my future interests. But I certainly got a poor reception for that question.

Today I see that his response was unworthy of a university professor. Memory is a phenomenon that exists in organisms that have no cerebral cortex at all. It is a fundamental property of living matter. Several years ago, neurobiologist Eric Kandel received a Nobel Prize for studying memory processes in a sea slug, and now biologists talk about primitive "protoplasmatic memory" found even in unicellular organisms. There is also increasing research evidence of sensitivity and memory capacity of fetuses in the womb.

*Returning to the reaction of the Marxist regime to psychedelic substances.
How is it possible that you were allowed to do this sort of research?*

Well, if you live in that kind of regime you learn how to talk—what
you can say and what you should not say. You learn the right strategy for
presenting things to the public. Needless to say, this sort of discrimination
was essential with regard to psychedelic research. So, for example, we
knew that we could not mention that during the sessions our patients
regressed to childhood, and that some of the material that came up had
Freudian elements in it, because psychoanalysis was banned at the time,
and Freud's books were on the list of forbidden literature.

Marxism, with its ultra materialistic world-view, is violently opposed
to anything spiritual, and considers religion of any kind to be dangerous
to the world revolution. We could not mention that some people had
mystical experiences, as we knew that would stop the research. So the
strategy of presenting the results to political ideologists was identical to
that of protecting this work from academic attacks. We presented what we
were doing as basically chemotherapy: these were the diagnoses of the
patients, these were the dosages, these were the numbers of sessions, and
these were the results. We simply did not discuss the mechanisms involved
in the results.

If we needed to go a little farther, we could make a good case for psychedelic research as a source of important evidence supporting the materialistic world-view. You administer a known substance in minuscule
dosages and it profoundly changes consciousness for several hours. Can
there be a better proof of the primacy of matter over consciousness?
Dialectical materialism, the philosophy underlying Marxism-Leninism
that all of us were force-fed at that time, has profound implication for
strategy and tactics, as shown by Lenin. It teaches you how to twist facts
and present your case in a way that best serves your purpose.

I did not talk about the most fundamental theoretical implications of
psychedelic research until I came to the United States. Initially, there was
no resistance against psychedelics in Czechoslovakia. At the time when I
was leaving Czechoslovakia in March 1967, LSD was listed in our official
pharmacopeia, together with insulin, tetracycline antibiotics, and other
respectable medicines, complete with indications and contraindications.
Any professional, psychiatrist or psychologist, who wanted to work with
LSD had to have five guided personal LSD sessions and conduct thirty
sessions with patients under supervision. And then he or she could start
practicing LSD psychotherapy.

—

What happened when you took LSD yourself in higher doses?

What made a difference in my experience was not only the increase of the dosage, but also the change of set and setting. My early sessions were conducted in a laboratory atmosphere, where there were many interferences and interruptions due to the different procedures we had to undergo—psychological testing, physiological examinations, collection of urine and blood, etc. This did not leave much time for systematic introspection. When I started working with patients in a psychotherapeutic setting, the primary focus was on their inner world. To my surprise, they had experiences that were quite different from mine. So one day when I was alone at home, I decided to take LSD on my own, increase the dosage, and focus exclusively on introspection to get a good sense of what the LSD experience was all about.

I took 300 micrograms and, within an hour, I was in a claustrophobic nightmare—a hellish no-exit situation associated with the ultimate existential crisis. I felt that my existence was absolutely absurd and meaningless. I could not find any sense in anything I had ever done. I was desperately trying to find something that I could hang onto. But whatever I could bring up, the next experiential sequence would mercilessly destroy.

For example, I came up with the idea that knowledge makes life meaningful. And the next thing that happened was that I saw myself spending thousands of hours in libraries studying and it was immediately followed by a vision of myself as an old man not being able to remember what I had for dinner! That would be the end result of my quest for knowledge and intellectual excellence. Another example was the idea that having children gives meaning to one's life. But then I saw these children facing the same predicament—growing up and dying after having lived a meaningless life. So I realized that unless you can find meaning in your own life, creating more beings whose life is as meaningless as your own, was not a solution.

That experience was what is called in the spiritual literature the "dark night of the soul." I realized that while I was experiencing this crisis, I was trapped not only philosophically and spiritually, but also mechanically, in a very concrete sense. I was experiencing tremendous pressure on my head and jaws, I felt crushed, and had difficulties breathing. Somehow I recognized that I was actually reliving my biological birth. I started feeling that I would not be able to resolve this situation and be born, if I could not succeed in finding meaning in the life that I was going into.

After three and a half incredibly difficult hours of clock time—that internally felt more like eternity—this experience suddenly opened up into light and bliss, and I instantly felt that life was great and meaningful. I did not resolve the problem of the meaning of life intellectually, but I felt it was great to be alive, to participate in existence and in consciousness. So, that was my first encounter with the *profound* effects of LSD, one which went far beyond the more aesthetic or psychodynamic experiences that I had experienced earlier.

What I realized during that experience was that there was a place within myself, in my unconscious psyche, that I was trying to run away from. I realized that many things that I was doing in my everyday life were inauthentic, because they were nothing but a way of unsuccessfully attempting to cope with this stuff. There arose a tremendous urge in me to get rid of it, to purge it out. I realized that life could somehow be simpler, more rewarding and satisfying, that I could surf through life rather than fight, grope, and stumble through it.

I discovered the source of the kind of strange linear drive, which I had felt in my life. I had never experienced anything even remotely approaching clinical depression. So it was not that I was suffering in life. I actually thought I was enjoying myself most of the time. But my life had a kind of a driven quality to it. I would read a book and think about ten others that I should read. Or going on a vacation, I would take several books with me. I would be in the mountains, skiing and enjoying the blue skies, the fresh snow, and the beautiful sunny day. I never got to read those books, but as I was skiing, I was thinking about them. They were on my mind and interfered with my ability to be fully in the present moment.

In my psychedelic sessions, I recognized that this drive was somehow related to the unfinished gestalt of my birth. I had been born anatomically, but had not completed the process emotionally. Something in me had not caught up with the fact that I was already out and free. On some level I was still in the birth canal, entangled with my mother, and trying to get out. I was projecting this feeling onto various situations in my everyday life and felt driven towards something, some solution, that was always in the future. In its extreme form, this situation can result in what some of my clients referred to as "treadmill" or "rat race" type of existence. The existentialists call it "auto-projecting," always imagining something better for oneself in the future and ceaselessly pursuing various goals.

In my pre-psychedelic days, there was never enough time for anything. Life was too short for everything I wanted to accomplish. *Vita brevis, ars longa* was my motto. My high-dose LSD experiences started bringing me into the present and gave me more capacity to appreciate what was available. I could enjoy my present resources rather than focusing on what was missing. I could look around and see what was happening, rather than always pursuing something in the future.

Could you say more about how you came to recognize the importance of the birth trauma as part of your psychological system?

It was a combination of what I was seeing in my clients and what I was experiencing myself. The general idea came fast, but the details were added over the years. This happened when I worked with people with different clinical diagnoses—from depression, claustrophobia, asthma, and migraine headaches, to psychoses, or what my wife Christina and I call "spiritual emergencies." I gradually realized that in all these conditions there was one common denominator—a significant contribution from the trauma of birth.

When people were able to relive and integrate the memory of birth, their symptoms were substantially alleviated or even disappeared. I started seeing that there was this deep perinatal pool of difficult emotions and physical feelings in the human unconscious, which is the source of various forms of psychopathology. The emotional and psychosomatic disorders of psychogenic origin do not start from scratch after we are born, during our infancy and childhood, but rather their roots can be traced to the trauma of birth and difficulties of prenatal life.

But even that was not the whole story. Later I discovered that many, if not all, of these disorders also had deeper roots in the domain of the psyche that we now call transpersonal—karmic, archetypal, and phylogenetic. This confirmed the ideas of Carl Jung, who talked in this regard about the collective unconscious in its historical and mythopoetic/archetypal aspects. I started seeing a much richer picture of psychopathology, realizing that emotional and psychosomatic symptoms were multilevel dynamic systems. I saw that their roots reached deep into the fabric of the cosmos and existence, rather than being relatively superficial products of individual postnatal biography, as they are portrayed by mainstream psychiatry.

What was the outcome for the patients you were working with who had some of these disorders you are talking about—asthma, psychosomatic disorders, and so on; did they improve?

We saw some remarkable improvements in our patients suffering from a variety of disorders, from severe depressions and neuroses to psychosomatic disorders and psychotic states. This was both surprising and impressive, considering that we specifically selected difficult cases for the LSD study—people who previously had not responded to any of the conventional treatments.

Were there particular kinds of patients that were less responsive?

We had the greatest difficulties with patients suffering from severe obsessive-compulsive disorders (OCD), who were extremely resistant to the effects of LSD. I have in one of my books a case history of a patient with a really severe obsessive-compulsive neurosis, in whom I started therapy with 100 micrograms and there was absolutely no response. I subsequently increased the dosage to 200, 500, 1000, and finally 1500 micrograms. Following the initial lack of response to ingested LSD, I also used intramuscular application, because I questioned if it was a problem of absorption in the gastrointestinal system.

After he had received 1500 micrograms intramuscularly, absolutely nothing happened. About three hours into the session, he was bored and a little hungry, so I took him to our kitchenette. His mental functioning was so intact that I let him use a large kitchen knife, cut his bread, open a can with liver pâté, and make himself a sandwich. He ate it and then, on the way back to the session room, we passed by a social room, where he saw a couple of patients playing chess. He liked to play chess, so he joined in and he was actually capable of playing a good game.

It took about thirty LSD sessions before this patient started regressing into childhood and having a more usual response to LSD. But we never really made any major progress in treating his obsessive-compulsive symptomatology. His OCD was so severe that he was in the category of patients who, in earlier years, would have been sent for lobotomy.

What about schizophrenic patients? How did they tend to respond?

Before I answer that question, I have to address the diagnostic problems with the term "schizophrenia." In Europe, the term schizophrenia is much narrower than in the United Stated. Psychiatrists in German-speaking countries, where the name schizophrenia originated, often narrow it even further and speak about *Kernschizophrenie*—core schizophrenia. Hallucinations and delusions are not a sufficient reason for this diagnosis. There have to be primary symptoms: autism, dissociation between thought and affect, extreme ambivalence, and specific disturbance of associative processes. When I came to the United States, I found that the diagnosis was often used much more loosely here.

We did not use LSD therapy in the classical kinds of schizophrenia: simplex, hebephrenica, catatonica, or paranoides. But I worked, sometimes quite successfully, with several patients who had other types of severe mental disorders that certainly fell into the category of psychosis. For example, one of these patients had a brutal alcoholic father, who had for years physically and mentally abused him, his mother, and his sister, before he himself committed suicide. When this patient had found his dead father lying on the floor in their home, he immediately went into a state of panic and ran away from home. He roamed around the countryside, feeling that his father's ghost was chasing him and fearing for his life. During this time, he slept in the parks and woods and completely neglected basic hygiene. This was not just a short-term acute psychotic reaction; it persisted for months and resisted all treatment.

Another such patient was a psychologist, who suffered from erotomanic delusions and hallucinations. She was desperately in love with her boss and believed that he shared her feelings. Although she had never had an orgasm in her actual sexual life, she now experienced ecstatic raptures of a tantric nature. She was convinced that her boss was engaging her in sex from a distance and was responsible for these wonderful experiences. This situation culminated when she hallucinated her boss's voice telling her that he had arranged for her divorce, and he was inviting her and her children to move into his apartment. Which she did, to the great surprise of her boss's wife, who understandably called the police.

How many patients have you treated with psychedelics?

I do not know off the top of my head how many patients I have treated, but I counted some time ago that I had conducted over the years more than four thousand psychedelic sessions. These were sessions, both in Prague and in the United States, in which I was present for at least five hours.

Can you tell us more about how the sessions were conducted?

The approach that we used in Prague is usually referred to as "psycholytic therapy." We used medium doses of LSD (100–250 micrograms) on numerous occasions. With this approach it was not required that the patients keep their eyes closed, so they spent a significant part of the sessions looking at the environment, looking at me, talking, and so on. This approach turned out to be extremely interesting in terms of mapping different layers of the psyche and understanding the processes that were involved.

Psycholytic therapy also offered fascinating insights into the mechanisms of perceptual changes, particularly the optical illusions during the psychedelic experience. I spent a lot of time trying to understand why my clients and other experimental subjects perceived me illusively transformed in a particular way. For example, they saw me as a panther, primeval reptile, slave-master, Egyptian pharaoh, Native American chief, supreme judge, Indian guru, Hitler, great shaman, devil, compassionate Buddha, or a magician. The optical illusions involving the environment were equally fascinating. For example, the treatment room changed into a cabin on a pristine Pacific island, the Garden of Paradise, the inside of the Maharaja Train or a Zeppelin, a torture chamber of the Inquisition, hell, a bordello, a prison cell, or death row.

We spent much time after the sessions working with free associations, trying to understand this process. This work was quite similar to what one would do with dream images in psychoanalysis. However, at some point I realized that this strategy, which reflected my Freudian past, was not ideal for psychedelic therapy (and probably even for psychotherapy in general). It became obvious to me that the psychological insights it provided were obtained at the expense of therapeutic efficacy. The primary therapeutic task was to orient the process vertically, toward the deep unconscious, not to dilute it by creating horizontal pseudosituations and the risk of problems caused by transference and projection.

I discovered that nonordinary states of consciousness can have remarkable therapeutic mechanisms. These mechanisms are far superior to the process of tediously untying the knots in the unconscious by making inferences from material emerging in discussions with the therapist. Typically, when we increased the dosage and internalized the sessions, the process rapidly reached deeper levels of the unconscious—perinatal and transpersonal. This then provided access to powerful therapeutic mechanisms and possibilities of radical personality transformation unknown to, and unimaginable for, mainstream psychiatrists and psychotherapists.

After I came to the United States and joined the Spring Grove research team in Baltimore, we systematically used this alternative strategy: high dosages, eyeshades, headphones, and hi-fi music. This is usually referred to as "psychedelic therapy." We worked with various groups of clients—chronic alcoholics, narcotic addicts, and neurotic patients. We also did a large study with patients dying of cancer, exploring whether or not mystical experiences can alleviate fear of death. And we had a program that involved LSD training sessions for professionals.

The results of this treatment modality—psychedelic therapy as compared to the psycholytic one—are generally much better and are obtained faster. But the price paid is that we do not understand why it happens. Psycholytic therapy provides better understanding, but the results are not as impressive as they can be with the psychedelic approach. The two approaches are thus complementary, one offering better and faster results, the other one offering the missing understanding of the territories involved.

How have psychedelics affected your beliefs on human nature?

I was brought up with psychoanalysis, where the picture of human nature is pretty grim. According to Freud, our deepest nature is bestial and any positive values are either reaction formations to, or sublimations of, our primitive base instincts. If we could express our true nature, we would kill others with little hesitation, steal, and indulge in various deviant forms of sexual activity. The reason why we do not do it is a result of repressive forces of human society, which we create because we are afraid of nature, and because of the influence of the superego—the introjection of parental injunctions and prohibitions.

This image of human nature that I inherited from my Freudian training rapidly dissolved for me when I started doing psychedelic work. All of the elements of the psychological underworld that Freud talked about are certainly there—the sexual impulses of problematic nature, violent aggressive impulses, greed, jealousy, and so on. But these turned out to be more like a screen that separates us from who we really are, rather than representing our true and deepest nature.

The picture of human nature that emerged from my work with psychedelics and my own psychedelic experiences was diametrically opposite to Freud's view. In fact, it was very similar to what the Hindus talk about: our true and deepest nature is not bestial, but divine. We are not what the Hindus call *namarupa* (name and form), or what we in the West call "body ego." Rather, we are *Atman-Brahman*, the creative principle of the universe—the Universal Mind or Absolute consciousness.

I also repeatedly saw people involved in responsible work with psychedelics developing in the direction that Abraham Maslow described as self-actualization or self-realization. That is, they moved from values imposed on them by their parents and society, to meta-values and meta-motivations. They discovered within themselves true senses of justice and beauty, genuine love and altruism, compassion, and so on. And they developed a deep sense of connection with the cosmos, with other people, and with nature, which resulted in more ecological awareness.

How have your experiences in this domain affected your view of death?

Coming from a materialistic medical background, I used to think of myself as a body, as a material object with Newtonian properties. I had no doubts that my consciousness was a product of neurophysiological and biochemical processes in my brain. From this perspective, it seemed obvious that when I die, this will be the irrevocable end of my consciousness and of who I am. This perspective has changed significantly during the years of my research into nonordinary states.

Many of my psychedelic experiences took me into the realm that Tibetan Buddhists refer to as *bardo*, the intermediate state after death and before reincarnation. And these experiences were very convincing. I can not say that I am absolutely sure, but I feel that it is pretty plausible that when my body dies, this will *not* mean the end of conscious activity; that my consciousness and existence will in some form continue beyond death. And I believe that this continuation is going to be similar to what I have experienced in some of my psychedelic sessions.

Probably the most interesting study we did was psychedelic therapy with terminal cancer patients. We conducted high-dose LSD sessions with over 200 cancer patients with quite remarkable results—dramatic alleviation of fear of death, spiritual opening, and improvement of their general emotional condition. LSD also often had a favorable effect on the patients' chronic pain, even in some cases where this pain had not responded to morphine or other narcotics.

In this group we had several instances when patients who had had psychedelic sessions with us experienced, at a later time as the cancer advanced, *actual* near-death experiences. For example, one of these patients had an obstruction of the ureter by a metastatic tumor and when they operated on him, he went into cardiac arrest. This was after he had had two or three psychedelic sessions. When we talked with him afterwards, he told us that he was very glad that he had had the psychedelic sessions, because he knew the territory; the near-death experience took him to the same realms that he had visited in his sessions. So he actually compared the two experiences and found them similar. These observations thus confirmed my own intimations about this matter.

Were psychedelics essential to the development of transpersonal psychology?

They were an important part of it, but they were not the only source. Transpersonal psychology had valuable input from some other areas, like Abe Maslow's study of spontaneous peak experiences. And it also reflected an awareness of the founders that academic psychology had ignored, mis-understood, and pathologized some crucial areas of human life—such as ritual, spiritual activity, and Eastern philosophy—and left out vital dimen-sions such as love and creativity. But certainly psychedelics were a power-ful catalyst for transpersonal psychology.

When I came to the United States, I was invited to conduct work-shops at the Esalen Institute in Big Sur, California. In one of my first workshops there, it was pointed out to me that my theories of conscious-ness were very similar to what Abe Maslow had been talking and writing about, only he studied spontaneous mystical experiences.

At that time I had a thick volume, a manuscript entitled *Agony and Ecstasy in Psychiatric Treatment,* summarizing my psychedelic research in Prague. This work has never been published, to this very day; I later expanded the material that it contained and distributed it into five of my future books. So I sent this manuscript to Abe Maslow, and I got an enthusiastic response from him. He invited me to come and see him.

I went to Abe's house, rang the bell, and his wife Bertha answered the door. When I saw her, I had a distinct feeling that I was not welcome. It seemed to me that she was blocking the way into the house with her body and did not want to let me in. I felt strange and I did not know what was happening; this was our first meeting and we had no history with each other. It seemed very peculiar.

Later, when we all had dinner together and had made a good personal connection, she gave me an explanation, and we all laughed about it. When Abe received my manuscript, he was recovering from a serious heart attack. When he began reading my material, he got so excited about the parallels between my work and his own observations that Bertha was con-cerned about the effect of such strong emotions on his health. So when I came to spend an entire day talking about matters of our shared interest, she was worried that Abe would get so activated by our discussion that he might have another heart attack.

Shortly after our Boston discussion, Abe's dream came true. He was given a scholarship that provided him with a house in Palo Alto and enough money to free him from academic duties. From then on, all he had to do was to think and write; it was his image of Paradise. At this point, he and Tony Sutich became aware that humanistic psychology, which they had launched in the 1950s, had a serious flaw—it did not include the spiritual dimension. So they discussed the need for a new school of psychology that would correct this omission. They initially labeled it "transhumanistic psychology."

Abe and Tony invited me to join a small discussion group that met regularly in Palo Alto, which was formulating the basic principles of this new psychology. Its other members were Jim Fadiman, Sonja Margulies, and Gaby Margulies. In these discussions, psychedelic research was an important part of the picture. I contributed to these discussions on the basis of my clinical material, and Tony, Jim, Sonja, and Gaby all knew about psychedelics from their own experiences.

I talked about an important category of psychedelic experiences. These were experiences, the existence of which I saw as a mortal challenge for the current paradigm in academic psychology and monistic material-ism of Western science. I coined for them the term "transpersonal." Abe and Tony liked the word so much that they decided to use it for the new psychology, replacing their original term "transhumanistic."

And Maslow endorsed it, even though he had never taken any psychedelics?

Oh yes, very emphatically! He loved the material and would actually have liked to have a session. We discussed it, but a psychedelic session for him was out of the question, considering his heart condition.

What precipitated your leaving Czechoslovakia for the United States?

For a number of years, we could not travel at all under the Commu-nist rule, initially not even to Russia, but in the 1960s, the situation started opening up. I was invited to present at the 1965 International Conference on LSD Psychotherapy in Long Island. I came to the United States in May 1965, stayed here for a couple of months, and was invited to give some talks. One of these talks was at Yale University. The dean of Yale University heard my lecture and offered me a one-year scholarship, which I planned to use to start a psychedelic research project at Johns Hopkins.

I returned to the United States in March 1967, ready to launch my research project at Johns Hopkins University in Baltimore. Unfortunately, about a week prior to my arrival, a paper on the effect of LSD on chro-mosomes had been published, which generated public hysteria concerning possible deleterious effects of LSD on heredity and developing fetuses. This chromosome scare later turned out to be unfounded and based on bad science, but at the time it was decided that it would not be politically wise to launch a new psychedelic research project at Johns Hopkins.

However, synchronistically, it happened that the last surviving psychedelic project was actually being conducted right there in Baltimore. So instead of starting a new project at Johns Hopkins, I joined the Spring Grove team. As I was already assigned to Johns Hopkins as a Clinical and Research Fellow, I had to make a compromise. So I taught part-time at Johns Hopkins and conducted research part-time at Spring Grove State Hospital. Ultimately, I ended up spending most of my time with the Spring Grove group, where my heart was.

It was very exciting. Not only was I free from the straitjacket of the Communist regime, but I suddenly had a small group of people who all were interested in the same things I was interested in. It was amazing to finally be able to talk openly about the most important aspects of the psychedelic experience.

There were some remarkable people in that group. Walter Pahnke, known for his Good Friday experiment which involved the administration of psilocybin to a group of theology students, joined the Spring Grove team. With extraordinary energy and enthusiasm, he initiated the project of psychedelic therapy with terminal cancer patients. Sandy Unger was the "mastermind" behind the Spring Grove project, and Charles Savage, one of the pioneers of psychedelic research, was also there. There were some talented younger therapists present too: Bill Richards, Bob Leihy, John Reid, Richard Yensen, and Franco DiLeo. I could not believe my good fortune, being able to do what I was interested in, with such congenial colleagues and friends, and getting paid for it.

You left Spring Grove and the Maryland Psychiatric Research Center to go to Esalen. Could you explain this move?

In 1972, I married the anthropologist Joan Halifax, who joined me in Baltimore. At that time, it was becoming increasingly difficult to get financial support and permission for new projects involving psychedelics. I had an enormous amount of research data, both from Prague and from Baltimore, that I had not had time to analyze and write up. And Joan had difficulties finding a reasonable job in Baltimore.

In 1973, within a month, I got twelve different offers from American publishers to write a book about psychedelics! LSD was making newspaper headlines and attracting a lot of public attention. By that time Walter Pahnke had died in a diving accident in the Atlantic and I inherited his job. I was now heading the last surviving official psychedelic research in existence, and was thus a logical source of scientific information about psychedelics. Under the circumstances, it was an exciting prospect for me to be able to take a year off, just to analyze the data and write a book. So I signed a contract with Viking Press for my first book, *Realms of the Human Unconscious.*

Around that time, I ran into Michael Murphy, the cofounder of Esalen, whom I had known since my first trip to the United States. He asked me in passing what I was doing and I told him that I had an advance from Viking Press to write a book. As it turned out, his response radically changed the direction of my life. "If you have a year to write a book, why don't you come to Esalen? Big Sur is an ideal place for such a project. We will give you a house in exchange for teaching some workshops." I gladly accepted Mike's generous offer and soon fell in love with California and decided to stay.

Why did the government end up effectively banning research with psychedelics?

The most important reason was the fact that the use of psychedelics moved from supervised clinical work to unsupervised experimentation by the counterculture, and became a mass phenomenon. The invasion of the Dionysian element into the rigid, Puritanical structure of our society, that came with the mass use of psychedelics, threatened the establishment. In addition, the people who were involved in this cultural revolution did not use what the Buddhists call "skillful means." They were provocative and clearly identifiable: they were the hippies.

The hippies violated the social codes. For example, they were strange in appearance and wore different clothes. Men grew long hair and wild beards, women did not wear bras and did not shave their armpits. Both genders advocated free sex and enjoyed nudity. They painted their cars in psychedelic colors and patterns. On top of it, the hippies were the troublemakers who protested the war in Vietnam. The unbridled use of psychedelics by the young generation was probably the most significant factor in the administrative and legal measures that ensued.

What effect did this abolition of sanctioned investigation have on the field of psychiatry?

It was a disaster! It arrested relevant progress in the psychiatric field and slowed acquisition of knowledge about the human psyche and consciousness for many decades. The government miscategorized psychedelics into the class of Schedule I drugs, meaning that they have no therapeutic value, thereby making them extremely difficult to use or even to study. In removing them from the hands of professionals, the government has taken away the most promising research tools and the most powerful therapeutic approach that psychiatry has ever had.

Do you think the culture these days is more ready for such work with psychedelics?

There have been important developments that are certainly favorable for the eventual reintroduction of psychedelic therapy. For example, there now exist powerful non-pharmacological methods of psychotherapy, which can trigger the same spectrum of experiences as administration of psychedelics: primal therapy, rebirthing, holotropic breathwork and other methods of working with breath. There are also marathon sessions, Paul Bindrim's aqua-energetics, and on occasion even gestalt therapy. In addition, many therapists now also feel comfortable working psychotherapeutically with individuals undergoing "spiritual emergencies."

There is increasing awareness that routine pharmaceutical therapy seeking to suppress symptoms is not a solution and is actually associated with problematic side effects. And there are professionals who are comfortable with experiential therapies that involve intense emotional and physical experiences. Such experiences are seen, not as a nuisance, but as a great opportunity. For them, bringing in psychedelics would be a logical step to enhance and deepen what they are already doing.

Finally, in the last several decades, there has been an increasing erosion of the most fundamental tenets of the old paradigm in science. The philosophical implications of quantum physics, the holonomic theory of David Bohm, the holographic model of Karl Pribram, Rupert Sheldrake's theory of morphogenetic fields, Ilya Prigogine's concept of dissipative structures, and chaos theory, are the most salient examples. As a result, today's professionals are better equipped to deal with theoretical implications of transpersonal phenomena than their colleagues in the 1950s.

In view of these facts, it is astonishing that academic circles still refuse to accept the theoretical implications of the findings of modern consciousness research. These implications are staggering, and some of them are well known even to the general public, such as the observations of out-of-body experiences in near-death situations. One has to admire how little the physicists needed in the early decades of the twentieth century to accept the phenomenal conceptual shift from Newtonian physics to Einstein's theories of relativity and then to quantum physics. By comparison, psychiatrists have managed to ignore for decades a true avalanche of paradigm-breaking evidence of similar conceptual relevance.

There are other factors that might influence the attitude toward psychedelics. People who are now coming into positions of power were on the campuses in the 1960s and they do not have the same kind of fear that the old generation had of these substances. Many of them had personal experiences with them. I think that should not be underestimated either.

How should society regulate psychedelics?

In the early 1970s, when I was still working at the Maryland Psychiatric Research Center, people from the National Institute of Mental Health asked us the same question. We were at the time the last and only team conducting official government-sponsored research of psychedelics. They were very concerned about unsupervised use of psychedelics by the young generation and turned to us as experts, asking for advice. They did not like our answer, and certainly did not follow our advice.

What we suggested was to create a network of centers, where people who wanted to experiment with psychedelics could go and have supervised sessions with pharmaceutically pure substances. The data generated by this work could then be used to promote our knowledge about psychedelics and nonordinary states of consciousness. This would have remedied the paradoxical situation that existed at that time—and still exists—in the United States. While hundreds of thousands of people are experimenting with psychedelics, exploring deep recesses of their psyches, those who know the least about these substances and experiences are law-abiding professionals. Yet these are the people who are expected to offer effective help to those folks who get into trouble as a result of experimenting with psychedelics! Paradoxically, government-sanctioned use of psychedelics in such centers might also take away part of the motivation of young people, who like to do everything that is forbidden.

Part Three

Culture and Consciousness

Culture and Consciousness

For several hours after drinking the brew, I found myself, although awake, in a world literally beyond my wildest dreams. . . . Transported into a trance where the supernatural seemed natural, I realized that anthropologists, including myself, had profoundly underestimated the importance of the drug in affecting native ideology.

—Michael Harner[1]

As psychedelics and altered states imploded into Western consciousness, anthropologists naturally turned attention to their role in other cultures. And what they found was startling. Fully ninety percent of the world's cultures have one or more institutionalized altered states of consciousness, and in traditional societies these are almost without exception sacred states. As the anthropologist Erika Bourguignon put it, this is "a striking finding and suggests we are, indeed, dealing with a matter of major importance."[2] Psychedelics are one method used to induce these sacred states, and have played a role in shaping cultures, especially tribal cultures, in areas as diverse as ritual, art, spirituality, and myth. Moreover, their long history of use extends back over thousands of years.

Anthropologists quickly learned that psychedelics are used conscientiously in these cultures. They are traditionally employed ritually for specific sacred and healing purposes. Their use is almost invariably regarded as beneficial to the individual and community.

Such an approach contrasts starkly with their popular use in the West. Especially in the turbulent 1960s, though many benefited, there were also casualties, misuse, and abuse. However, from a cross-cultural perspective this is hardly surprising; there was little understanding of their use, minimal social support, and no established ritual or sacred context to draw upon. Far from being valued by the wider community, psychedelics were quickly banned.

This raises an intriguing question: What exactly determines a drug's acceptability in a culture? Surely the overwhelming determining factor should be the extent of morbidity and mortality it produces. But a moment's reflection suggests that this plays merely a minor role. Witness, for example, the wholesale but perfectly legal massacre produced by smoking tobacco, which accounts for nearly half a million deaths in the United States each year[3] and over four million worldwide.[4] Contrast this with the far smaller, but still tragic, approximately seventeen thousand U.S. deaths from all illegal *and* pharmaceutical drugs combined.[5] Yet the U.S. government spends billions to imprison marijuana growers and until recently spent billions to subsidize tobacco growers.

With regard to a drug's cultural acceptability, several factors other than toxicity seem much more important. The first of these is how long a drug has been in use in the culture. When initially introduced to England, tobacco use was viewed as disgusting and punishable, while Russian smokers were flogged and had their nostrils slit. However, the longer a drug remains in a culture the more likely it is to gain acceptance.

A second factor is the lag phase between use and the onset of complications. Strychnine is said to produce an impressive high, but since death may follow within minutes it has never attained popularity.

A third factor is economic: How deeply is the drug imbedded in the economic system, and how many people profit from it?

Then there is the distribution of drug use across social classes. When a drug is used primarily by people outside the mainstream, it is likely to be stigmatized and illegalized. On the other hand, as the saying goes, "a drug is not a drug when members of the ruling class use it."

A final factor seems to concern the congruence between the experiences produced by the drug and the values of the mainstream culture. Psychedelics can clearly produce experiences outside, and often antagonistic to, the conventional Western world-view. As such they seemed threatening and were soon ruled to be illegitimate.

Clearly the cross-cultural study of psychedelics has much to teach us about consciousness and cultures, including our own.

NOTES

1. M. Harner, "The sound of rushing water," in *Hallucinogens and Shamanism,* ed. M. Harner, 16–17. (New York: Oxford University Press, 1973).

2. E. Bourguignon, ed. *Religion, Altered States of Consciousness, and Social Change,* (Columbus: Ohio State University, 1973), 11.

3. Drug War Facts web page, www.drugwarfacts.org/causes.htm#tobacco (accessed February 13, 2004).

4. World Health Organization web page, www.who.int/tobacco/health_impact/en (accessed February 13, 2004).

5. Reconsider.org web page, www.reconsider.org/issues/public_health/ estimated_deaths_.htm (accessed February 13, 2004).

8

Peter T. Furst

Ancient Altered States

Born May 23, 1922 • Peter T. Furst is Professor Emeritus of Anthropology at the State University of New York at Albany, a member of the research staff of the University Museum, and on the Graduate Faculty of Anthropology at the University of Pennsylvania. He is a noted authority on contemporary Mexican Indian religion, symbolism and pre-Columbian and North American art, and the ethnology and cultural history of psychedelic plants. His books include *Hallucinogens and Culture*, *Flesh of the Gods: The Ritual Use of Hallucinogens*, and *North American Indian Art* (with Jill L. Furst).

MY INTEREST IN HALLUCINOGENS began in the late 1950s. At the time I was a journalist living in California and writing about science, natural history, and anthropology for a magazine called *Fortnight*. I had a friend in the Hollywood police department who was ranting about how peyote drives people to sex crimes and so forth. So I thought, "Wait a minute. I want to know something more about this."

I planned to write a major article for *Fortnight* about freedom of religion related to peyote and the Native American Church. But before I got it into print, the magazine folded. I didn't think about hallucinogens again until about 1965, when I started working with the Huichol Indians as an anthropologist.

I worked with the Huichol artist Ramón Medina, who was training to be a shaman. Barbara Myerhoff came down to Mexico in 1966, in search of a topic for her doctoral field research, and I introduced her to Ramón. One day Ramón remarked, "You'll never understand the Huichols until you've eaten peyote." So he fed us peyote, and it was awful tasting. It's absolutely the worst. Also, I was a child of my own culture, and here's Ramón with unwashed hands and a dirty penknife, and some very dirty

151

peyote. He's cutting pieces and feeding them to us, and I could just *see* the amoebas dancing.

I will never forget my reaction. We were in Ramón's hut, and all of a sudden I exclaimed, "God damn it!" So Barbara asked, "What's the matter?" I replied, "Well, here you are having this wonderful experience, and I feel absolutely nothing." She asked, "What experience am I having?" And I said, "Well, you're floating on this beautiful luminous blue-green sea." Which was in fact *not* her experience at all; she actually had a rather scary one. She was chased by a cactus person that wanted to embrace her and pierce her with spines.

You had your own vision of her, which wasn't her experience at all?

Right. Ramón later invited us to come on a peyote pilgrimage with him. We did that in December of 1966, and afterwards Barbara wrote her doctoral dissertation and a book about it.

I haven't had all that many psychedelic experiences myself. An Indian man down in Chiapas invited me to partake in a mushroom session. We've never actually determined whether mushroom use in Chiapas was indigenous, or was introduced by Mexican hippies who discovered that the mushrooms grow wild in the Palenque area. For a while we thought that it was probably indigenous, but now I'm no longer sure. Although there is no question that the Maya knew about mushrooms, because the dictionaries make that very clear.

There are two early dictionaries that give Maya names for various kinds of mushrooms, one of which is called the "mushroom of the underworld." The Spanish Franciscan friar, Bernardino de Sahagún gives a good description of the use of mushrooms by the Aztecs. But for the Maya we have the circumstantial evidence of the mushroom stones that go back to the first millennium BC, which may not necessarily have been Maya; they might be late Olmec or Izapa. And we have the dictionaries put together by Franciscans and Dominican priests, which give names for the mushrooms; the "mushroom that drives one crazy" is one of these, for example. I'm sure the Maya knew about this stuff.

Did you do your doctoral thesis on hallucinogens?

No. I did my thesis on West Mexican shaft tombs and their figurines, and related them to shamanism. I became increasingly interested in shamanism cross-culturally and through history, and researched shamanism in the Americas, South America, and Asia. In all these places, psychoactive mushrooms were available.

The main mushroom in use in Europe was not a *Psilocybe*, but rather the fly agaric, *Amanita muscaria*. Fly agaric use was suppressed by the Church and condemned. Ironically, it has survived as the quintessential Christmas decoration—you know, the white-stemmed mushrooms with the red caps. When I grew up around these mushrooms, we were always told that they were deadly. They clearly are not, although they can cause unpleasant gastrointestinal distress if you eat them fresh. But I know people who have used them, especially in the Northwest. I don't know why we can't find any really indisputable evidence for the use of mushrooms generally by American Indians. But R. Gordon Wasson came across a Chippewa medicine woman in Michigan who knew about it.

North American Indians didn't know much about peyote either, right? Peyote came from Mexico, didn't it?

Well, no. Interestingly enough, some of the earliest known archeological remains of peyote are from Texas. The Witte Museum in San Antonio has a collection of material that was excavated from painted caves in the Trans-Pecos and the Big Bend areas. Peyote is not native to that region but to the lower Rio Grande, which is quite a distance away. The earliest date that we used to have for peyote in this area was AD 800.

It has always been assumed that what the ancient desert culture people were principally using was the seeds of *Sophora secundiflora*. This is a small flowering tree, and the seeds are dangerous. They contain cytisine, which when consumed could stop your heart. The shamans knew how much to administer—but one little bit too much and that's it.

So the Witte Museum gave me two dried peyote buttons that had been excavated from one of these caves. I sent these to the UCLA radiocarbon dating laboratory. And, my God, they tested-out as being from about 5000 BC! So, in 5000 BC they were already using peyote that had been traded up to that area from either the lower Rio Grande or from northern Mexico. The amazing thing about these ancient peyote buttons is that they were still active, although not terribly potent.

As you look at the spread of peyote use, what do you think has been really happening with this phenomenon?

The exact kind of ecstatic visionary experience is to some degree driven by culture. What you see is not simply the effects of the alkaloids interacting with chemical structures in the brain—it is also culturally determined.

Did you have any contact with Carlos Castaneda?

I met Carlos in 1962, when we were both graduate students at the University of California at Los Angeles (UCLA). My professor at UCLA was the German Johannes Wilbert, who studied tobacco and shamanism in South America. Johannes did something for us that was absolutely wonderful. There's a nice German tradition called *doktorvater*, with the professor acting in his role as a substitute father. He started a Thursday night informal seminar at his house for about a dozen of us, at which we would come back from the field and share our experiences.

One day there was this short guy—very friendly, very funny—who told us about having met don Juan Matus. He said right off the bat that this was not the man's real name. He had concocted the name out of don Giovanni, the famous lover, and Mateus, a cheap Portuguese wine favored by impecunious graduate students. He said that he met this old Yaqui Indian on a bus-stop bench in Tucson. Which is perfectly okay, because there's a Yaqui community in Tucson. That much of his story, I'm convinced was true. And don Juan said, "Come with me to Sonora." Well, Carlos had been given $500 by the UCLA Laboratory of Ethnic Arts to buy a dozen or so Yaqui masks. That's how that relationship started, with this character who was an old herbalist. All the rest, of course, was invention by a fertile imagination.

I have long been convinced that Carlos wrote his first book as an act of revenge against a professor who had given him a hard time, and he was going to show him up for the gullible fool that he thought he was. If you look at the first book, he says at the end, "I will never write about this again, I'm too scared." I think he was absolutely on the level with that. But then the money started rolling in.

The first book, *The Teachings of Don Juan*, he gave to the University of California Press. You don't give a book to an academic press with any expectation of royalties or fame! There were several professors who endorsed it as a new way of looking at the world, and the book came out in 1968. Then all of a sudden it caught on, and Ballantine Books moved in and bought the contract. When I read the original manuscript I had some misgivings, which I mentioned to Barbara Myerhoff. She replied, "Oh no, he's on the level. Maybe there's some graduate-student hyperbole there, but I think this is all true."

Right? A few years later she realized it *wasn't*, mostly through reading Richard De Mille's book, *Castaneda's Journey: The Power and the Allegory*, which exposed the fraud.

De Mille said that Castaneda lifted some of his tales from Myerhoff's story of Ramón Medina, right?

Yes. That really shattered her. She felt that was real betrayal, because she had told him those things in confidence.

As far as you know, Castaneda never went to the Huichol country himself, right?

Right. Still, I've never had any bad feelings about Carlos. I wish he had not pretended that his books were factual. They would have been just as interesting as allegory, as Richard De Mille suggested.

In November of 1975, I went to the American Anthropological Association meetings in San Francisco with my wife Jill. We came down for breakfast, and Carlos Castaneda, who I hadn't seen since 1971, was sitting there. So I said, "Hey, I'll introduce you to Carlos Castaneda." Jill met him and later she told me, "You guys were so gullible. I never believed one word of Carlos's stuff."

What is your opinion of the long-running debate about the role of psychedelics in religion? At one extreme there are people who agree with the religious scholar Mircea Eliade, who said that the use of psychedelics represents a decadent form of religious practice. At the other extreme are people who agree with the ethnomycologist R. Gordon Wasson, that psychedelics were the origin of all religion.

Well, I think that Wasson went too far. But I talked to Eliade about six months before he died. There was a conference on consciousness in Switzerland, and Eliade was supposed to go. But the organizers called me and said, "Eliade can't come. He's too ill, but he's asked us to invite you in his place," which was quite an honor. So I called him and we talked for a long time. I told him that I disagreed with his take on hallucinogens, and he said, "Well, you have to remember that my book was written in the early 1950s. *Shamanism: Archaic Techniques of Ecstasy* came out in France in 1951. What did we know in the early 1950s about these things?" For example, he did not know the antiquity of hallucinogens in America. He also believed that Siberia and the Arctic were the places where shamanism originated, right? But that's no longer tenable.

It isn't?

No. It certainly is the area in which shamanism was best studied. The first reports on shamanism came out in the 1600s and 1700s from German travelers. But the Arctic wasn't even settled until about four thousand years ago. So to say the Arctic was the place of origin of shamanism can't be right. It's certainly one of the purest expressions of shamanism, but shamanism has to be much older than that, if you assume, as I do, that shamanism is a kind of Ur-religion. I think it's Paleolithic in its origins.

What did the Neanderthals know about hallucinogenic plants? Well, for example, in Iraq there's a Neanderthal site, which dates to about eighty or one hundred thousand years ago. When they excavated this site, they identified eight plants—seven of which are still used in the same area for medicinal purposes, including *Ephedra*. That means that one hundred thousand years ago these people had a knowledge of healing plants, of medicinal plants. Well, if they had that, then why not also a knowledge of hallucinogenic plants?

Some Scythian graves have been found with Cannabis.

But those are much later. The Russians excavated one of the Scythian mounds in Central Asia, and found tripods holding bronze kettles with marijuana seeds in them. In the fifth century BC, Herodotus wrote about the rituals of the Scythians. He described the tripod, the kettle hanging down, the seeds, all placed over a fire. Then they put a tent over the whole thing and they breathed in the smoke. And he talked about the "howling Scythians." Actually, he said they were weeping, because these were funerary rites. And then came the Russian excavation that showed that Herodotus was reporting history and not myth.

So your view is that hallucinogens were involved in the origin of some religious traditions but not necessarily all.

No, I think that's also going too far. The use of the so-called "hallucinogens" is a *function* of religion, not its origin.

What about the mushroom images from Tassili in Algeria?

The Tassili rock paintings? Those are quite late, no earlier than Neolithic. We know practically nothing about that culture, except that they had wonderful rock art and they may have used mushrooms.

There is also the question of mushroom use by the early Christians in Europe, reported on by Giorgio Samorini. He found a considerable number of mushroom images in Christian iconography and published some dramatic photographs. Amazing stuff! His images are very convincing.

Could you talk a little bit about frogs and toads, and how they were used?

Regarding frogs, there is the work of Robert Carneiro, who is at the American Museum of Natural History. He wrote a paper on hunting magic among a South American people called the Amahuaca. Members of this tribe will set fire to a branch and then burn holes in their skin. Then they rub tree frog poison into it, and they become unconscious and froth at the mouth. It can be deadly. Then they have certain experiences they interpret as visions of birds, where they can understand the language of the birds. Or they have a vision of where a bunch of pigs are assembling, so that they can go out and hunt them. That poison is so potent that the toxin of one of these little frogs could kill ten grown men. It's the most potent natural toxin known.

Changing the subject from frogs to toads, Andrew Weil proposed a theory that the toxic portion of toad secretions, such as those obtained from Bufo alvarius, *might be deactivated with heat. So if you just lick the toad you could get poisoned, but if you smoke the secretions, the toxic portion is destroyed and only the psychoactive part of it is delivered.*

That could be. But Michael McBride, a clinical pharmacist friend of mine in Texas, has been doing pioneering research for years on toad poison. Among other things, he has been looking into what happens when toad poison is combined with a fermenting mixture. He found that yeast is able to degrade the bufodienolides—one of the three main toxic compounds of toad poison—while the "visionary" bufotenine is left unchanged. There are also other enzymes that degrade the bufodienolides. This is important research, as it helps explain how toad poison might have been effectively used by indigenous peoples without killing them.

It certainly shines some light on an account from the early 1600s by an English priest named Thomas Gage. He reported that the Quiché Maya of highland Guatemala threw toads into fermenting maize beer to "strengthen" it. Some people have interpreted this as "superstition" or just pure symbolism. In reality, there appears to have been a scientific basis for the approach they were taking, based on observation and experience.

Perhaps this destruction of toxins, might be true with Bufo marinus, *too. Because* Bufo marinus *has some pretty poisonous chemicals in it, along with the potentially psychoactive ones.*

Sure. Michael D. Coe found *Bufo marinus* skeletons at an Olmec site in Veracruz. And he says they couldn't possibly have been used for food, as there's very little meat on them.

There's so much in this field we don't know, and there's so much that we're probably never going to know. It's pretty frustrating, and the drug laws make investigation even harder. I can see why there could be a good argument against legalization of addictive drugs. On the other hand I think there's also a very good argument for pulling the rug out from under the world market for drugs, by legalizing them. Make the focus a public health problem, and not a legal problem.

What areas do you think our society should pursue, in terms of research and application related to psychedelics?

Perhaps the time has come for something new. We had all the hysteria of the late 1960s. Remember that story about those kids who took LSD and stared at the sun and became blind, which then turned out to be completely fabricated? I think we're way past that, and we can return to scientific studies. We really need to look at positive applications for these drugs. Alleviation of nausea and wasting sickness are a couple that *Cannabis* can target. Unfortunately, most states aren't yet like California, Arizona, and those few others that have made medical marijuana legal.

We should be studying traditional cultures and their shamanic knowledge of these plants. Not just going in and isolating the one "active" drug, but looking at the whole thing. It's very complex chemistry. Dick Schultes once called peyote a veritable factory of alkaloids. There are over fifty that have been identified in peyote, and they all do different things. An integrated approach to the botany, chemistry, and ethnomedicinal use of shamanic plants would be very useful for research projects. That's what I've always been interested in myself.

9

Michael Harner

Tribal Wisdom: The Shamanic Path

Born April 27, 1929 • Michael Harner is widely acknowledged as the world's foremost authority on shamanism and has had an enormous influence on both the academic and lay worlds.

Within academia, he conducted extensive fieldwork in the Upper Amazon, western North America, the Canadian Arctic, and Samiland (Lapland). He did pioneering studies of the Jívaro Indians of the Amazon (now known as the Shuar), and wide ranging studies of shamanism.

He also played a major part in alerting academics to the central role of psychedelics in shamanic practices and many tribal cultures. Harner's description of his own initiatory ayahuasca experience in the Amazon jungle, which is described in his book *The Way of the Shaman,* has become a classic example of the power of these substances. It provides a superb account of their importance to some shamanic traditions, their ability to introduce new world-views and effect personal transformation, and their capacity to render researchers more sensitive to, and comprehending of, the cultures and practices in which they are used.

After this experience, Harner went on to undertake extensive shamanic training, first with Shuar teachers, and then throughout many areas of the world. His combination of anthropological training, academic expertise, studies of shamanism in multiple cultures, and personal shamanic training, has produced a rare, perhaps unique, breadth and depth of expertise and influence.

In 1987, he left academia to devote himself to full-time work with shamanism, and created the Foundation for Shamanic Studies. The foundation funds research and publications, offers worldwide trainings in shamanic practices, has an international membership, and—in an intriguing cultural reversal—has reintroduced shamanic practices to parts of the world where the tradition was lost or suppressed.

His many publications include the books: *The Way of the Shaman, Hallucinogens and Shamanism, The Jívaro,* and a coauthored novel, *Cannibal.* What Yogananda did for Hinduism and D. T. Suzuki did for Zen, Michael Harner has done for shamanism, namely bring the tradition and its richness to Western awareness.

I CAME TO THE UNIVERSITY OF CALIFORNIA at Berkeley in 1950, expecting to become an archaeologist. But then in the course of my archeological fieldwork, I found that the Indians living nearby were like encyclopedias that nobody was opening, and this alerted me to the incredible amount of knowledge that was available just by asking the tribal elders.

In 1956–1957, I did my doctoral dissertation research in eastern Ecuador among the Jívaro people, who are now generally called the Shuar. I returned to the Amazon in 1960–1961 to study the culture of the Conibo in eastern Peru, and I returned to the Shuar in 1964 and 1973. Around 1966, I went to Columbia and Yale Universities as a visiting professor, and then accepted a professorship at the Graduate Faculty of the New School for Social Research in New York. I stayed there from 1970 on, sometimes also teaching at Berkeley. During my later years at the New School, I increasingly took academic leave to focus on shamanic work and teaching, and then in 1987, I pulled out of academia entirely in order to devote myself to shamanism.

How did you initially hear about the use of psychoactive plants?

I was aware of peyote and had read of ayahuasca use, but I had no comprehension of their importance. Then in 1956–1957 among the Jívaro, I suddenly found myself in a society of shamans. About one out of every four adult males and a much smaller proportion of females were shamans. In the course of my fieldwork, I interviewed them, and they said that I really should go on a vision quest at a sacred waterfall and take this drink of theirs. I realized that this was important, and I was just about to do it when the rainy season came and logs started dropping over the waterfall. So it was too dangerous—because if we bathed in the waterfall, we could get fatally clobbered. Some years later, I did do it with them, but not until after being with the Conibo of the Peruvian Amazon in 1960–1961.

I first took ayahuasca at that time, with the Conibo. My fieldwork was in its later stages at that point, and I was attempting to get information on their spiritual system. The Conibo said there's only one way to learn about it—you've got to take the drink. So I took the drink.

I really didn't have much in the way of expectations. They had said you could see frightening things. They said it was known sometimes as the "little death;" that it could induce an experience like dying, and that some people in rare cases actually did die. But in the villages where I lived, the vast majority of the shamans were using it almost every night, so it was not that big a deal. My book, *The Way of the Shaman*, has a detailed description of that first experience of mine.

When you came down from it, what was different in terms of your own sense of yourself and what you were doing there?

At first, it wasn't so much the sense of myself that was different. But I was completely in awe of the fact that a whole other reality had opened up. This was a reality that could not be fantasy, because the experiences that I had were also experiences that the Conibo who took ayahuasca were having independently, down to concrete details, without us ever having talked about them with me beforehand. A shaman said afterwards that I really could become a master shaman—that I had gotten so much from my first experience that this was what I should do. Since it was a rare opportunity, I decided to avail myself of it, and that's when I actually got involved in shamanic training.

Ayahuasca was taken in every session; they didn't do much shamanism without it. At one time historically, the Conibo had the *muraya*—shamans who worked only with tobacco—and they were very respected. But by the time I was in the Amazon, there were no muraya around. However, I did use tobacco water with the Jívaro, which was a shaman's drink. You soak green tobacco leaves in cold water and drink the water or inhale it through the nose.

Did the tobacco drink induce visionary experience?

It heightens your perceptions, at least with that particular kind of uncured tobacco. It's very powerful. You're taking it to feed your spirit helpers, who love tobacco. It is also used to increase alertness, so that if there's a sorcerer who's working against you, your spirit helpers will be alert and protect you. The Jívaro were very much involved in feuds and wars, in contrast to the Conibo.

Would the Jívaro use ayahuasca to determine whether or not to go on a raid or start a war? Would they use it to make a collective decision about their culture?

Well, first of all, we'd better all get in the habit, and I should lead the way, of calling them Shuar, because they want to be called Shuar.

No the Shuar did not and do not use ayahuasca to make collective decisions. I know that's been *reported* for the Jívaroan Achuar, but it is not true there either. The Jívaro proper—the Untsuri Shuar (also called Muraya Shuar, or Hill Shuar), the people I worked with—felt strongly that normally only one person at a time should take ayahuasca, otherwise the contact with the spirits would be diluted or altered. However, sometimes two shamans would take it together, such as for healing work.

The Achuar is a different tribe?

Yes. They are a closely related Jívaroan tribe, with a mutually intelligible dialect, but some important aspects of their culture are different. For example, unlike the Shuar, they did not take and shrink heads. But anyway, getting back to your earlier question, *natemä*, which is the Shuar name for ayahuasca, might be taken for divinatory purposes by a shaman prior to a war raid. However, he would take it just to get some idea of whether they should do the raid, whether there were bad or good omens—in other words, whether it was propitious. It was also taken to divine if someone, through sorcery, was responsible for an illness or death. In the latter case, such a divination could result in an assassination raid.

What about sorcery? Among some peoples sorcery seems to be associated with ayahuasca use.

Yes, that is true. Over my decades of work in shamanism I've come to certain conclusions that helped me understand the Shuar, including their preoccupation with sorcery, or bewitching. In other words, "sorcery" commonly implies hostile or amoral action, and it is typically contrasted with healing.

First, let me say a few words about what shamans have discovered worldwide about the shamanic cosmology of nonordinary reality: there are three Worlds: the Upper, Middle, and Lower. The Upper and Lower, above and below us, are completely in nonordinary reality, and beyond pain and suffering. In contrast, the Middle World, in which we live, has both its ordinary and nonordinary aspects. It is also the World in which pain and suffering can be found, occurring in both realities. Sorcerers specialize in doing their work in the Middle World. The Shuar are very much involved with Middle World spirits. There are Middle World spirits of all types, just as there are humans and species of all types here in the ordinary reality Middle World. Middle World spirits have not transcended Middle World consciousness. So the Shuar shamans can have at their disposal spirits who have a variety of personalities and behaviors, who have not emerged from the preoccupations of ordinary daily life. These can be spirits of any beings: animals, insects, or humans.

Working with Middle World spirits is both difficult and dangerous, and this is the world in which the Shuar shamans are enmeshed. They do not work in the Upper World, unlike a lot of other shamanic people. They also only go a little distance toward the Lower World—that is, only into the lakes and the rivers. A culture that is stuck with Middle World spirits is a culture that is going to have sorcery.

Sorcery is typically hostile action. In my ethnography on the Jívaro, I called it bewitching. There are terms in Shuar culture for someone who does this. One is *wawek*. A *wawek* is a shaman who's gone bad. They are regarded as bad shamans, even if they are in one's own family and are directing their efforts at dealing with common enemies, of whom they have many.

I can contrast that with the Conibo. They also have shamanism, but don't have this kind of aggressive behavior, and they include much travel to the Upper and Lower Worlds in their shamanic journeys.

I take the reality of spirits very seriously. In fact, their reality provides a parsimonious explanation for otherwise inexplicable phenomena. This parsimonious explanation was unfortunately thrown out of Western science in the so-called Age of Enlightenment. I think shamanism will eventually lead to a reevaluation of this antispirit belief, which I think is an Achilles' heel and missing link in science. So I work a lot, and very successfully, with the spirits.

How do you define a spirit?

A spirit could be considered to be an animate essence that has intelligence and different degrees of power. It is seen most easily in complete darkness and much less frequently in bright light, and in an altered state of consciousness better than in an ordinary state. In fact, there's some question whether you can see it in an ordinary state of consciousness at all.

You've taken ayahuasca with both the Conibo and the Shuar. They sound like rather different contexts: different kinds of mental sets and perhaps different settings. Were your subjective experiences also different?

Yes, they were. I picked up on the local spirits and the activities in the area. What I would encounter would be not only cosmic knowledge, but knowledge of specific local spirits, the local peoples' spirits, and specific matters involving patients. So the local spirits do impinge on the experiences.

Could you say more about the "cosmic knowledge?"

My views of the cosmos derive from more than ayahuasca experiences, which were my lead-in to a broader view. But subsequent experiences of altered states of consciousness and shamanic states of consciousness independent of ayahuasca also had an effect.

When I came back from my first ayahuasca experiences with the Conibo in 1961, I started going through the anthropological literature with great excitement and expectations. Because I was convinced, like R. Gordon Wasson and others at that time, that all religions had their origin in plant-induced experiences. We all went through this stage.

Some of us are still in it.

Yes. But when you experience other methods of access besides the plants, then you discover that it's bigger than plants—that there's a whole other reality, and that there are different entrances into it. *That's* the really exciting thing, because you can no longer be a reductionist saying "the plants are doing it." This is what excites me. I see general patterns, cosmological patterns, regardless of whether ayahuasca or sonic driving is being used. So I take the idea of another reality very seriously. I take very seriously the idea that death is not death, and life is not life. [laughs] But they're useful constructs.

Would you say that your thinking about the world evolved after you came back from your fieldwork with the Conibo and the Jívaro?

Yes. I published *The Jívaro* ethnography in 1972, and then my book *Hallucinogens and Shamanism,* based upon a symposium Claudio Naranjo and I organized at the American Anthropological Association meeting in 1965. The early 1960s were the critical period in our excitement about this field—wondering where we were going and what we were discovering. With regard to the evolution of my ideas, at first I thought it was all about the plants. I even got into the Haiti thing in those years and figured out there was a plant infusion being used to make zombies.

As an anthropologist I was interested in the role of these plants in human life and traditional knowledge. Although I tried some of the new chemicals that were becoming available at that time, they were generally not what I was interested in. I was, and still am, an anthropologist. I want to understand how things got to be the way they are and what the native peoples really know. I've never viewed natives as laboratories for our experiments in social science theory or psychological theory. I view them as teachers. The problem is that most Westerners are not ready for their teachings. I don't have anything against Sasha Shulgin's concoctions and so on, but they just don't interest me. I have greater interest in time-tested things and their historical consequences for humanity.

Eventually, I came to many dead ends. For example, I was sure that *pituri, Duboisia hopwoodii,* used by the Australian aborigines, was going to turn out to have *Datura*-like effects, but it apparently did not. The Inuit shamans seemed like another dead end because I couldn't find any psychotropic plant use among them, and they were certainly having strong spiritual experiences. The evidence was staring me in the face for a long time, but I didn't see it; that in perhaps 90 percent of the world's shamanic cultures they use a monotonous percussive sound to enter altered states of consciousness, rather than significant psychedelics.

Finally I got around to trying drumming. I had a bias against it being able to *do* anything, but lo and behold, after various experiments, it worked. Later I spent some time with Northwest Coast Indians who used drums in a very effective way for reaching the shamanic state of consciousness. I now have great respect for monotonous percussive sound—particularly at 4–7 hertz, in the theta range of EEG waves—for producing similar experiences and allowing one to get to the same altered states, if one has the proper training. Obviously there's always a difference between a specific drug and some other technique. But those differences are not changes in the underlying cosmology or changes in the basic conclusions one arrives at.

So my path involves monotonous percussive sound or sonic driving. And that's what has made it so easy for me to teach shamanism through the years, because it's a legal, safe, effective, and ancient method. It teaches people that there's more than one door to nonordinary reality, which is something that shamans in so many parts of the world already knew. Of course some silent meditators can get to similar places. You don't have to have monotonous percussion sound; it just makes it a lot easier.

Would you say that such sound allows one to reach realities similar to those produced by visionary plants or drugs?

Yes, I do feel very strongly that way. But the path is usually more subtle and takes longer. On the other hand, access is constantly available and permits doing shamanic healing.

In an article you wrote on the use of Datura-*type plants in European witchcraft, you suggested that their effects are quite different from, for example, ayahuasca and the tryptamines, or peyote and the phenethylamines.*

It's virtually impossible to function under a strong dose of one of these tropane alkaloids. I had used *Brugmansia-Datura*-type solanaceous plants among the Shuar—and also had actually tried out the "witches" flying ointment back in the early 1960s in the United States. My conclusion, and the hypothesis I presented in that article, was that it was not possible to do shamanism using this very strong drug, which commonly made one unconscious for as long as thirty-six hours.

In my opinion, European shamanism had to give up the drum because of its noise, leading to persecution by the Church. An exception was in the remote north, in the Arctic, where its use was continued among the Sami—the Lapps—until the missionaries finally arrived there. In the more southerly European areas where the drum was given up, they shifted especially to mixtures involving the solanaceous plants, plants of the nightshade family. But these incapacitated you if you used enough, so you couldn't perform acts of healing and divination, having very little control over your experiences in nonordinary reality.

In that sense, it wouldn't really be very useful for shamanism.

This is why I think they distinguished the sabbat from the esbat, as I indicated in my book, *Hallucinogens and Shamanism*. The sabbat was probably the journey where all the nonordinary things happened to the "witches" in an altered state potentially produced by these plants with the spirits, and the esbat the formal meeting of these shamans together in ordinary reality. It's just a theory, but it would explain why there is this peculiar dichotomy in European witchcraft, which was really a form of shamanism. This dichotomy wasn't there among the Sami in northernmost Europe in the beginning of the twentieth century, because they were still using the drum.

Are you saying that the Central Europeans used drumming also, and they had to give it up?

I don't have hard evidence to back up this theory, but I cannot conceive of them *not* having the drum. The drum was still being used in shamanism into the twentieth century in northernmost Scandinavia, the area where religious persecution occurred the latest in Europe. Teresa de Avilar was able to use the drum in her spiritual work in Spain, but she was a nun "in the service of Christ."

There's also Mediterranean art showing the drum.

Yes. I think what happened is that they couldn't use drums if they wanted to avoid being discovered by the Inquisition, they had to have a silent way. The plant ointments were quiet and less discoverable. I've found the same thing in Inuit villages. They're not about to do shamanic drumming within hearing of other people, because they'll be singled out and reported to the Christian authorities. So the drum is really a liability in a situation of persecution.

Did you find any evidence of alternative plant use in Europe? Trypta-mine-containing plants? Psilocybin-containing mushrooms?

I pursued that, of course. There's no hard evidence I know of, but presumably berserkers were using the *Amanita muscaria* mushroom to get into that state. There's some indirect supportive evidence proposed by R. Gordon Wasson.

Have you tried the Amanita *mushrooms?*

No, they are not in my experience. Among the Samoyed peoples—one of the most Western of Siberian groups, not that far from the Sami of Scandinavia—shamans and nonshamans both sometimes ate or burned dried *Amanita muscaria* to help change consciousness for spiritual purposes. It's not something I've published yet, but as far as I know, that's the most westward evidence of psychotropic mushroom use in a native context in Eurasia. I think it's probable that this kind of knowledge was known slightly farther to the south and west in Scandinavia in the old days, à la the berserkers. The berserkers were violent Norse warriors who were likely possessed by the power of the mushroom, much as nonshaman Siberians still can be when they wish to have extraordinary physical strength and endurance.

Did you eventually "graduate," to use a Western term, as a shaman? Did your teachers tell you that you were ready to go out and practice?

You never graduate as a shaman. It just goes on and on. Your teachers almost never tell you you're ready.

Just like psychoanalysis.

Ordinary teachers never know if you're ready. There are two types of teachers. One is the ordinary teacher, which is what I think you were referring to—somebody like myself or shaman teachers I worked with among indigenous peoples. Then there are the spirit teachers, who are the real teachers. The spirit teachers may tell you, and do tell you, what you can do, but all the ordinary living human teachers are just expediters. The ultimate authorities are the spirits you work with, and they tell you what to do and what you can't do. That's one of the reasons that I feel it's usually a mistake for anybody to characterize themselves as a shaman, because the power can be taken away at any time. Anyone who claims to be a shaman starts getting focused on his or her ego. He or she, however, is almost nothing, for one is only a shaman when the spirits want that person to be a shaman.

Were you given any visions or insights by these plant spirits about the culture you come from? It's such a world-dominating culture. Are the spirits commenting on this?

Our culture is considered to be deformed and out of contact with these truths. I think that compassionate, healing spirits have a mission to try to communicate their existence to us so that they can get on with their work of trying to reduce suffering and pain in our reality. But they are not all-powerful. They can't do it without the help of intermediaries, and shamans are especially strong intermediaries. And so, precisely because the spirits need help in this, they will teach you surprising things to encourage you to help them. But they are in one reality and we're in another reality, and the only way they can penetrate this reality, except in very rare circumstances, is with help from our side. We have our power; they have their power. When we go into alliance with them, that's when healing miracles and miracles of knowledge can come through.

So the main thrust that I had in the Amazon using plants continues in my present work using sonic driving. The main thrust was that they were attempting to alert me to the reality of the spirits, to get me involved, and to teach and involve others. But they never said explicitly why this was. Implicitly, however, it was to reduce spiritual ignorance and suffering in ordinary reality.

Can you can meet the same spirits, whether you access these worlds via plants or via drumming?

You can meet some of the same spirits, but not all the same spirits, because the spirits of specific plants can possess you to varying degrees. Much depends on what the spirits feel you are ready for and need to access at a particular time. Some of the spirits that I worked with as allies in the Amazon I still often work with, but there are now others in addition. Some are less dominant than they once were, and others are stronger.

In addition to the compassionate spirits, are there malevolent spirits?

Yes. Here in the Middle World the spirits have the whole range of personalities that also occur in ordinary reality. What is "malevolent" is an interesting thing. Other species may view us as malevolent, such as when we kill and enslave them. But we don't view ourselves as malevolent, and we don't see our whole species as malevolent. So a lot of the so-called "evil spirits" are often basically just trying to make a living and exist in their own way just as we are. More often than not, they don't even know they're dead. They're just doing the same old thing, but they're doing it in a

Middle World of nonordinary reality. And this can include simple things like insect spirits who intrude into people.

What conclusions have you arrived at about different kinds of spirits? You mentioned the Middle World vis-a-vis the Upper and Lower Worlds. And there are spirits of animals, spirits of plants, spirits of ancestors, other deceased humans. Are there others that are neither human nor animal? Are there extra-terrestrial spirits?

I'll start with ancestors, as they are very important. Compassionate spirits—whatever species we're talking about—are especially found in the Upper and Lower Worlds, and these spirits have compassion for suffering beings in general. But ancestors tend to focus on compassion for their descendants. That's one of the reasons that many shamans use ancestral spirits so much for help.

You wouldn't say that extraterrestrials could be Upper World spirits?

No. From our point of view all the galaxies in the astronomers' universe are still Middle World. Extraterrestrials, as much as we've tried to look for them, seem like an uninspiring search. If there are extraterrestrials, which I assume there are, that's fine. To me, that's not a spiritual matter. They're just people making a living somewhere on another rock. [laughs]

The Upper World extends beyond the material world. Consider the Tuvan shamans in Central Asia. When they go past the stars, they get to the nine heavens, and then there's the white heaven above. The Upper World is beyond ordinary reality, beyond the astronomer's universe. And the center of the universe for any shaman is right where the shaman is located in ordinary reality. You are the center of the universe.

Are there other spirits that one encounters, neither animal nor plant nor human? Or spirits of a particular place?

Yes. You can encounter the spirits of the elements, for example. They are very powerful, but they don't have compassion. You can also have spirits of place, but it's typically a constellation of the spirits of that place, including local ancestor spirits.

Are you saying that the three worlds are located inside? That they are internal constructs?

No, I am not. The shaman is an empirical pragmatist. The worlds are where ever the shaman sees them. The idea that all this is happening inside us is, in contrast, a theory.

How would you compare your shamanic cosmology to that of the Perennial Philosophy?

What shamans discover is consistent with much of the Perennial Philosophy. I think there's an unfortunate tendency among some scholars and writers to consider shamanism as primitive. But the hypothesis of a kind of evolutionary hierarchy in which the caste-based societies of the Indian subcontinent house the highest and most developed spirituality is somewhat naive. Once the spirits get their hands on you, it doesn't matter what your original intention was—whether you were going to follow the Buddhist path, Christianity, or whatever. Once you give the spirits an opportunity to teach you, they're going to give you what you need, not what you planned according to your culture's program.

Do you feel the spirits are always around everybody, every being?

Yes, the Middle World spirits are, but usually not the Upper and Lower World spirits. And this is part of the problem. There's a lot of spiritually caused illness in the world, because people are not aware of what's around them. Take "possession," for example. In my opinion, it's fine to do ordinary psychotherapies and chemical therapies and so on with people who are deemed to be psychotic or schizophrenic. That's great. But Western treatment typically ignores the possibility there may be spiritual forces involved in the illness. In the contemporary world we've rejected the possession model and substituted something which is more acceptable to Age of Enlightenment science. We're bogged down in eighteenth century science.

Have you seen cases of psychosis that were cured by shamanism?

I am of the opinion that I have. However, it's very difficult to isolate the operative healing variables in any individual case, and also I'm not qualified to evaluate clinically what constitutes a case of psychotic behavior. Our Foundation for Shamanic Studies is a kind of university of shamanism. We train people who are already psychotherapists, physicians, and psychiatrists, and they can take home what they learn and experiment with cases of clinically defined psychosis. Certainly I've seen people exhibiting extreme behaviors, including alcoholics and drug addicts, who were then radically changed through depossession work.

The Spiritist church in Brazil, which has at least thirteen million members, embodies African, South American Indian, and some European elements in its depossession work. The president of the Spiritist church some years ago told me that a friendly Brazilian government turned over a mental institution to them for a year as an experiment. According to him, at the end of the year there were no more patients in the institution. Now, that's probably an exaggerated account. But it reminds us that one of our missions is to bring depossession work into mainstream Western life as a serious practice, in conjunction with other therapeutic practices. To make it work, however, you can't deal with people who are on mood-changing drugs. They have to be consciously present for the work to succeed. Meanwhile, one of the tragedies in our culture is the medical establishment's rejection of the possibility that there may be spiritual factors at work in these cases.

The work is really done by the spirits?

Not alone. The shaman has to work with the spirits. You have to have both forces in operation. Depossession is one of the most exciting healing approaches that I know of. We introduce only our most advanced students to it, after they've done at least three, and usually many more, years of work. Then they get the depossession training.

An interesting thing about possession illness is that it's relatively unknown in the New World native cultures. There is a little bit on the Northwest Coast, and some glimmers of it among the Inuit. It seems to be much more an illness associated with the Old World. There is some mystery here—why it's such an Old World thing, and lately imported into the New World.

Maybe it has something to do with the influence of the Church, denying the reality of the traditional spirits. If you deny the reality of the spirits, it makes you more vulnerable to unconscious possession. Whereas if you're working with the spirits directly, you would be protecting yourself more.

One typically gets possession illness when there has been significant soul loss through traumas, and loss of one's spiritual powers. If there are no shamans around, little can be done, but if there are shamans around they can remedy soul loss. So I think you're on the right track. When people are pretty empty spiritually, that's when there's room for involuntary possession.

On a personal level, how has the work with plants and shamanic drumming changed your own world-view about life, death, and spirituality?

Radically. I no longer view ordinary reality as the only reality. There's a whole other reality, and that reality is the bigger one. This one is just a transitory experience; you're only here for a certain number of years, but the other one is infinite. Whether you come back again, that's another question. Personally, I am not interested in reincarnating, because once you've been out "there," it's ineffable ecstasy and union. I feel this material world is basically just a short pit stop. But we should do the best we can to help here, because, compared to the Upper and Lower Worlds, this is a reality of suffering and pain. This is a Darwinian reality.

In fact, I consider our definition of life to be a very biocentric view. We are biological entities, so we define life in our own terms. But to me the whole universe is living, and it doesn't have to be only in biological form. Biological forms, by their very nature, go through the process of natural selection and evolve. Natural selection involves competition, and to survive competition requires that you have fear. Of course, you are also rewarded with the pleasure of the sexual act in order to create the next generation. We're talking now about DNA wanting to persevere. So the Middle World that we live in is a world where, in order to survive, one must experience fear.

When somebody has a great shamanic journey, that person is sometimes reluctant to return from the ecstatic experience, far away from the fear and pain of the Middle World. So we have very definite safeguards to ensure that one comes back. It's well known that some shamans can leave permanently, when they want to, but the trick is to come back here and do the healing work. We aren't given ecstatic knowledge just so that we'll look forward to our deaths. We are given this knowledge, and the spiritual empowerment that goes with it, so we can help to reduce suffering, pain, and spiritual ignorance here in the Middle World.

Death is no big deal. I'd like to stay around as long as possible to see how this life comes out, and to stay with my beloved wife, Sandra. But I certainly don't fear death the way I once did.

I'm still very much an imperfect human being, and it's never been my intention nor capability to be a perfect one. It's not an intention of shamanism to teach people to lead inspiring model daily lives and to be gurus. Shamans are supposed to reduce suffering and pain through the hard work of healing others. That's their job. They also help the dying and the dead, because shamans also heal the dead stuck in the Middle World, if they want help.

Shamanism is very emotionally rewarding, in both acquiring shamanic knowledge and helping other people. My students often say what a privilege it is to do this work. And what is the work? The work is helping others, but shamanic practitioners end up feeling better about themselves! What looks like a sacrifice to the outside world is really the high point of the person's life. It changes your perspective. And of course you take less seriously things that should indeed be taken less seriously.

At the same time, a shaman is typically enmeshed in daily life, has a wife or a husband, has children, is a hunter, farmer, banker, computer operator, or whatever. Part of your daily routine is spent in ordinary reality, and that's fine. It's all the better that you be grounded in that, so you have sort of a microvacation. Then when you are called upon to do really serious spiritual work, you'll be recharged and go back to it with full force.

The idea in shamanism is not to try to be a gentle exemplar for everybody else all the time, and not to be in a constant mystical state. That's fine, but that's a different tradition. So you'll often find shamans engaged in joking and mildly outrageous behavior when they're off duty, much like you might find emergency-room physicians and nurses having an "inappropriate" sense of humor about things. Nonshamans often can't understand this. Then when you go back to work, boom! You're back in the trenches.

Do altered states implicitly convey something about ethics? Do they teach people to live more ethical lives?

Experiencing an altered state that occurs in the Middle World would not necessarily do that. However, outside the Middle World, the shamanic state of consciousness gets you in touch with the teachings of the compassionate spirits. These are concerned about reducing pain and suffering, and do indeed make it more difficult for you to be unethical. It's not that you can't be unethical, but you're going to have a harder time being unethical.

Similarly, people who begin to study with us may not at first have any interest in ecology. But after a few journeys they start having a different view, one they never expected, about the interconnectedness of all species and the planet that is their home. Once you start realizing we're *not* superior to the rest of the cosmos, but that we're just part of it, this creates a more compassionate and ethical orientation. And if you know that material reality isn't the whole ball of wax, you can drop your focus about getting everything you can in this reality before you die. A fellow wrote a book he actually called *Die Rich*. What an amazing concept, huh? I think he made a lot of money doing it, but I don't know if he's still alive. [laughs]

Someone else wrote a book about dying empty—giving everything away before you die.

That's more like it, yes.

The spirits may help you do what you do, but you're still choosing to do it, right?

I think it's a two-way thing. The spirits have an effect on you, and you're never utterly disentangled from them. There is a kind of osmotic effect, so that the spiritual connections permeate you. Right now, while I'm talking to you, I'm seeing several of them. Not because I'm calling them in, but because I'm touching on a subject that they feel strongly about.

But the real effect is when you're on duty and not in your ordinary life. Your ordinary life is often quite imperfect. I think that's the way it's supposed to be, because if you were too satisfied with your ordinary life you wouldn't have the attraction to this other reality.

Most people who really take this path seriously have suffered significantly. Perhaps not in the dramatic, traumatic way it's portrayed in some of the Siberian literature, but they have suffered. They're hoping there's more to life than this.

Once you start interacting with these spirits, they guide you in certain ways that are no longer entirely your free choice. You may go on a journey wanting something, and then they give you what you need, not what you want. So, there is that feedback.

But what about those who take a path of sorcery; they're making that choice, right?

Persons who go down the sorcery path have often been unknowingly possessed by suffering Middle World spirits who have hostile orientations. To that degree, "free choice" can be a questionable term. The compassionate healing spirits will stay with you as long as you don't go down the sorcery road, but if you do, they'll leave you. We're like rechargeable batteries, and we get spiritually recharged constantly as long as we're working in alliance with compassionate healing spirits that want to reduce suffering and pain here. When, let's say out of anger, we make a big mistake and decide to "get even" with somebody, then the healing spirits disengage. They will not support you in such actions. You still have that residual power—the battery was charged—and you can do damage for quite a while. But ultimately it's going to fail you because the power source will be gone. And whatever you put out there comes back to you multiplied. That's when it's disastrous for you, for your protective power has left. There are sorcerers who can keep going for awhile, who are drawing on spirits other than the compassionate ones, but it's a big mistake to go down that path.

One advantage of shamanic education is that you learn you can get angry at somebody, but still protect him/her spiritually, and thereby protect yourself. But people who aren't trained shamanically usually won't have the discipline of knowing that they should control their spiritual powers when they get really angry.

Have you ever tried the combination of plant medicine and drumming at the same time?

With peyote, of course. But peyote is so mild that it's easily done. However, with a strong dose of ayahuasca you don't even want to hear a dog barking or a child crying. It's too overwhelming. With ayahuasca you want to hear the songs, which are great, and they can connect you very strongly to your spiritual allies. But they involve no drumming.

Carlos Castaneda renewed interest in shamanism and had a tremendous influence on contemporary psychedelic culture. What do you think of Castaneda?

He performed an important role. He showed the Western world that non-Western peoples could have a fascinating and radical perspective on reality, even if they were barefoot. And he also helped provide some sort of framework for people in the psychedelic movement who were having a hard time figuring out how to organize their experiences.

As a matter of fact, Carlos himself had quite a difficult time organizing his own early experiences. That's how we first met. After I came back from the Conibo to a position at the University of California at Berkeley in 1962, I gave a talk one evening on "Drugs and Reality in the Upper Amazon." Carlos was a graduate student, and he read about that talk, so he looked me up at the 1963 meeting of the American Anthropological Association. He said he was curious about how I organized these experiences conceptually, because as yet he had no framework. So I shared with him the Upper Amazon perception of reality through ayahuasca and other substances.

Then when I heard him start talking, I was blown away by his accounts, because they were so beautiful. In fact, I encouraged him to write them up. So within a few weeks he came back to Berkeley with an account of his first peyote experience, which later became a chapter in his book. It was great, and I encouraged him to write more, and he brought some more a few weeks later. At *that* time, I think he was pretty much on the level about what had happened to him.

I encouraged Carlos to write a book-length manuscript, which he then did. He eventually published it with the University of California Press, because the New York commercial publishing establishment wasn't ready for it, and couldn't cope with it. In fact, the first review in the *New York Times* of Carlos' book, *The Teachings of Don Juan*, was written by a specialist on the don Juan of Europe, of the Renaissance! He wrote a short, very critical, uncomprehending review of it. The *Times* had no idea of what was happening. Much later, after Carlos was popular, the *New York Times* assigned more appropriate reviewers.

One of Carlos' most important contributions was introducing the terms "ordinary/nonordinary" reality, which remain immensely useful. The American anthropologist Robert Lowie had earlier used "ordinary and extraordinary," but nothing quite works like "ordinary/nonordinary." Unfortunately, in later books Carlos didn't really distinguish adequately between those anymore. The first two books were closer to shamanism and to what I consider to have been experiences with a psychedelic base. Later, Carlos shifted more into his own world. His later books have very little to do with shamanism and a lot to do with Carlos' own world, such as his construct of Toltec shamanism—nobody knows who the Toltecs *really* were. It's simply an archaeological concept.

Many today believe that most of what Castaneda wrote was a sham. Do you think that don Juan, his mentor shaman, was a real person?

I think don Juan was real. However, I think some aspects of him described by Carlos were composites, and other aspects, described in the later books, were "dreamed" by Carlos. Early on, Carlos invited me to go visit don Juan. Unfortunately, I didn't have time to travel with him down to Mexico, and I've kicked myself ever since. But don Juan and I were in contact through Carlos. Carlos wanted to get that book published. When he mentioned this, don Juan said that he didn't really know if it was important, but if Carlos really wanted it, he'd help. So he had three power masks made. One was for Carlos' literary agent, one was for Carlos, and one was for me. I can tell you that these masks are the *real* thing. They are, in fact, very dangerous masks.

These are actual physical masks? Why are they dangerous?

Yes. I can show you mine if you want to see it. I just ask you not to handle it, okay? They are dangerous because they have immense spiritual power that's of the Middle World.

Carlos never got out of the Middle World. You'll never find any reference to the Lower World or the Upper World in his books, nor do you find any reference to healing. He was in the world of the sorcerer. Not surprisingly, the people that are attracted to his disciples' workshops often are not people who are oriented toward compassion and healing, but rather to power alone.

They're trying to amass power?

Yes. However, power alone is not shamanism. But I loved Carlos. He was a great raconteur, and he spoke the way he wrote, but with humor. You could sit for hours listening to him. You would have been enthralled. But Carlos was really not interested in shamanism, per se.

Have psychedelics been a part of your life in more recent years?

Not in recent years. I haven't felt that they are important anymore. I felt that they were important at one time—useful as an entree. But these days I don't want to get too deeply in there, except when I'm working. And then I usually like to get out after half an hour or so.

What do you say to students who want to take psychedelics?

It's fine if they want to do it; that's their business. But I don't want my students to get the idea that they *have* to do that. I want them to get the bigger picture—that there's another reality and that it's accessible by various means.

What legacy would you like to leave to future generations?

Well, if I were to die tomorrow, I'd feel that I'd done more than I had ever hoped. I feel very lucky that way. I never envisioned this path, and I never envisioned so many students wanting to seek it. I am satisfied with what has already been accomplished, because now there are so many people who are well-trained and prepared to work with and learn from the spirits shamanically, so that I'm no longer essential. The movement has its own momentum. So, I'm now very relaxed. What is my legacy? Well, my students as much as anything, because they will carry on, and some will go farther than I have ever gone.

10

Laura Archera Huxley

More Recipes for Living and Loving

Born November 2, 1911 • Laura Archera Huxley was born in Turin, Italy. Displaying remarkable talent playing the violin as a child, she studied with several masters in Berlin, Paris, and Rome, where she earned her Professor of Music degree. As a teenager she moved to the United States, making her debut in Carnegie Hall. After further studies at the Curtis Institute of Music in Philadelphia, she put her music career aside to pursue other means of creativity and development. Over the next several decades, she produced documentary films, was a film editor at RKO, played in a major symphony orchestra, and was engaged as a psychological counselor, lecturer, and seminar leader in the human potential movement.

In 1956 she married the English writer and philosopher Aldous Huxley, with whom she explored the potentials of psychedelics. In 1963, at his request she administered LSD during the final hours of his dying process. Powerfully influenced by her consciousness expansion work and psychedelic visions, she went on to launch organizations and conferences focused on improving the condition of children. In 1977 she founded Children: Our Ultimate Investment, a nonprofit organization dedicated to the nurturing of human potential. "The predicament of the human situation," she says, "begins not only in infancy, not only before birth, but also in the physical, psychological, and spiritual preparation of the parents before conception." She is the author of several books, including: *This Timeless Moment, You Are Not the Target,* and *Between Heaven and Earth.*

Huxley has received widespread recognition and numerous honors for her humanistic achievements, including an Honorary doctorate of Human Services from Sierra University, Honoree of the United Nations, Fellow of the International Academy of Medical Preventics, and Honoree of the World Health Foundation for Development and Peace, from which she received the Peace Prize in 1990.

I FIRST BECAME AWARE OF PSYCHEDELICS while I was on a plane returning to Italy. During that flight, I read Aldous' book *The Doors of Perception*. I had met Aldous and heard him speak about psychedelics, but I didn't really realize what they were. However, I felt there was some connection with the mind state described in *The Doors of Perception* and the work I was doing as a counselor, because I noticed that some people would go into a similar state of mind during therapy.

In 1957, I asked Aldous if I could have a psychedelic session. He said, "Yes, you can have mescaline, but so you know what it is like, you should come and give it to me first." I thought that was courageous, because I knew nothing about it, but I responded, "Yes, I'll give it to you. What do we do?" He replied, "You have to be free for the whole day." So I went there for the day, and he had a beautiful voyage.

Days later, I was accompanied to his house and this time he gave me mescaline. Initially, I became a little nauseated, which is expected with mescaline, and which only lasts a short time. Then he smiled and said, "You are on your way."

The previous week I had visited an orphanage in Tijuana where there were eighty-six infants being cared for by six nuns. The children were in little cribs and these valiant nuns were running from one child to another, changing their diapers and giving them bottles. My mescaline experience became much stronger while reexperiencing the plight of the nuns and children, and the event and I were almost fused as one. So that was my first experience, which changed in character later on in the day, lightening up with some laughter. I described this experience in detail in my book *This Timeless Moment*.

These days you work with young people, educating them about how to dis-
cern whether or not to have a child. Do you feel that this early psychedelic
experience shaped your work in the world?

That experience was very much the first impulse. When you have such a powerful impulse, you end up finding the things that feed the impulse. So that initial experience was indeed very important for me.

Why did you visit the orphanage in the first place?

I was living with my friend, Ginny, who was interested in children. We were asked to go see if we could do something for these children, so we went. Ginny later adopted two children, and my adopted grandchild is the daughter of one of the children.

In what ways do you feel that your experience with psychedelics has affected your perception of the world around you?

Psychedelics allow you to be much more vulnerable and open. You become more aware of your daily theatricals. You are much more careful not to hurt other people. Psychedelics make you aware that everything is alive.

You remarked that the psychedelic experience makes one more sensitive to the feelings of others. How is this connected to your interest in serving people in the world?

Let's think of service as a circle where giving and receiving are balanced. The ideal kind of service is a roundabout thing. In service, one may think, "I give." Well, I give, okay. But I *receive* as well.

I don't like how the word "sacrifice" is used. People will say, "Oh, how I sacrifice for my child." But you don't *sacrifice* for your child; you just do whatever you have to do. The word in Latin means: to make sacred. So the meaning of the word "sacrifice" is quite different from how one typically uses it. In the Catholic viewpoint, for example, there is *always* sacrifice. Jesus Christ sacrificed, and you sacrifice, and I sacrifice. If one thinks of the real meaning of the word, to make sacred, it's much better.

In what ways have your psychedelic experiences affected your beliefs about religion and mysticism?

I feel very lucky in this respect. I was brought up Catholic, and we went to church, but it was not a very big deal. When I was fourteen, I decided the course of my life. Among other things, I thought, "What is this? They tell us that if we sin for one hundred years we go to hell for eternity. It doesn't make sense. I'm not a good mathematician, but I can see the difference between eternity and one hundred years." So I just let it go, and I never suffered as many Catholics do when they leave the church. Later, through my psychedelic experiences, I saw that religion is not necessarily spirituality.

With applied spirituality, you aim to cause no harm. Psychedelics made this viewpoint so clear for me, and I probably had the realizations sooner than I would have if I hadn't used them. But it's a natural, obvious thing, in the end. Although I don't know that we are all naturalists at heart.

In the 1950s and the early 1960s, you and Aldous were among the first pioneers exploring the psychedelic experience, and you were both enthusiastic about the potentials they held. However, as we can now see, their acceptance by our culture has been very difficult. Why has our culture had so much difficulty with the psychedelic experience?

One way to look at it is very simple. There was a sensationalized case of a suicide, which made for powerful television sound bites. But one hundred people sitting quietly and having good will and good feelings isn't exciting for television.

And then there is the usual thing with human beings—simply that we have difficulty with change and with accepting novelty. Change causes a feeling of insecurity. The acceptance of a new concept usually takes at least one generation. Perhaps we are better prepared to work with psychedelics these days, because so many people have had the experiences. I hope so.

Aldous described the mystical experience as "gratuitous grace," and remarked that "it's up to the recipient of the gift to cooperate with grace." Could you say a little bit about that?

Aldous speaks a good deal about being a recipient of gratuitous grace in *Island*. That book is his legacy. *Island* is what he wanted to say as he was going out. The kids in the book, when they are around fourteen, fifteen, or sixteen years old, are introduced to gratuitous grace. But first they have to make a difficult and dangerous ascent up a mountain, where they are roped together. It is dangerous not only for themselves, but also for their companions. So, a crucial aspect relates to caring for another person—the other life is just as important as one's own. While the entire book of *Island* is suffused with psychedelic experience, it's actually only mentioned specifically on one occasion.

If one receives the grace, one can just take it, and that's the end of it. But it is the *cooperation* with grace that brings it alive. The responsibility of cooperating always comes back to each of us. Some people have had one psychedelic experience, and it has changed their lives. Others might have a few hundred experiences, and yet no basic change occurs.

In my own life, I have not taken psychedelics often—I think altogether, probably eight times. I did LSD a few times with Aldous, and then I did it again after he died. I did synthetic mescaline and psilocybin. I took ayahuasca tea twice, and I did MDMA once.

Do you feel that psychedelics have potential for psychotherapy?

Psychedelics are extraordinary tools when used with psychotherapy, because in one day you can let go of so much, and have insight into so much. Sometimes more than in a year of traditional psychotherapy. Yes, I certainly think they should be used in psychotherapy. But I don't know who should be entrusted with the toolbox—priests or psychiatrists? That is the difficulty.

Whoever uses psychedelics should treat them with the greatest respect. When Aldous and I used them, we prepared the ambience and ourselves the day before. The day of the session was kept as a holy day, and there were beautiful fruits and flowers around. The result was that we had no negative experiences. I realize now how lucky those of us were who approached LSD before it had either the demoniacal or the paradisiacal vibrations it has now—when it had no echoes of gurus and heroes, doctors or delinquents.

Toward the end of his life, Aldous began to hear about bad experiences. Careful protocols like the one that we followed when we used psychedelics were sadly not incorporated by all people who took the voyage. One thing that can really help reduce negative experiences is to have a sitter present. The sitter has to be ready to have no secrets, because the person will see completely what is going on. The sitter also has to be ready to do nothing, which is difficult. It's like achieving silence in meditation. So the sitter must just be completely there, completely respectful and loving, but do very little, unless there is another kind of prior agreement. For example, if the person gives you a list of items that he or she wants help working on, then you generally remind the person that you were asked to do this. In fact, with that first session that Aldous had me give to him, he said that he wanted to inquire about a special time in his life that he could not remember. I was ready to use methods that can help to take people to repressed or forgotten memories, but then I saw that it was unimportant, and I shut up. He was in such an extraordinary state that I had no right to intrude.

In one of those early sessions that you described, you mentioned that Aldous talked about the difference between knowledge and understanding, with understanding being based on direct experience.

I think that this probably applies to what we were saying before about religion. One has knowledge of religion, or one has an understanding of spirituality. Aldous thought that knowledge was very important, but that without understanding, knowledge falls short of helping. He also said that understanding alone, without knowledge, is not productive enough. It's the combination of the two that works.

He said a similar thing about love. Knowledge without love may be dangerous, but love without knowledge is not as effective as it could be.

Did Aldous express to you what he thought would happen with psychedelics? Was he optimistic that they would be accepted by society? Or did he express concern that society would reject them and force them underground?

For a while he didn't have any such concern, but eventually he became worried. He suggested that one example of how to approach the use of these substances is provided by the shaman. The shaman has a tremendous responsibility, not just to give an herb, but to guide a soul.

What was your sense of how Aldous viewed Timothy Leary?

Well, he said that Tim was an Irish shaman. But clearly Tim's approach was another concern that Aldous had near the end of his life. Once when they were on a drive together, I heard Aldous say, "Please Tim, keep it quiet." And two days later there were headlines about Tim and psychedelics in the papers. [laughs] That was just Tim. I mean, what can you do?

Who do you think should have access to psychedelic drugs, given an ideal society? And what about young people?

The question of who should have access is perhaps the most difficult of all. But then saying who should *provide* psychedelic experiences is difficult too. My granddaughter had one experience and then wrote me quite an enlightened letter, saying, "*Now* I know who I am. Don't ever let me forget." It was the most beautiful event, but it's not always like that for everyone.

Sometimes it isn't so good. At the risk of being judgemental, I think these raves—with so much noise and all kinds of drugs, including alcohol—can be really damaging. They give all kinds of illusionary power and can be physically dangerous. I would not want to have that kind of situation.

Psychedelics make you aware that everything is alive, sacred, and connected. I presume and hope that everybody will ultimately come to that conclusion; it cannot possibly be the privilege of the few. But it is everyone's right to first be given the basic necessities of life: nourishment, safety, and respect. After this, the psychedelic experience can become available.

Has your experience with psychedelics affected your understanding of death?

Yes, very much. Although I can only speak about death without having experienced it, so I don't really know. [laughs]

I don't know how I'm going to act when the body goes away. But I have the feeling that not all of me will die when my body dissolves. Psychedelics have given me a better sense that there is something beyond. However, I actually feel that I "die" several times a year—this feeling has been happening to me all of my life. So I don't know if my view of death comes entirely from psychedelic experiences.

Are you comfortable talking about Aldous's death experience, the decision to give him the LSD, and what that was like for you?

Well, the reason that it was not as difficult as it might have been is because we were prepared: the moment he asked me to give him an injection I knew. He spoke about his death once in a while, but as he was approaching it, he didn't speak much about it. But when the time came, then it was very clear. I knew what he wanted me to do.

I thought it was so beautiful how you guided him toward the light in those moments. How did you know to guide him toward that place?

I don't know. I had never read the *Tibetan Book of the Dead*—it's a big book. But Aldous had guided his first wife as she died according to this book. There is also a beautiful description in *Island* of how a husband guides his wife's death, with the same principles described. Aldous had said that psychotherapy is actually similar to death. You have to let go of the past and move on. So I didn't have any doubts about what he wanted.

Had you discussed with him previously what he would like you to facilitate for him at the time he was dying?

No, he didn't say, "You do so and so." No.

But he wrote "100 micrograms" down on a piece of paper?

That's right. We hadn't specifically discussed it previously. But I had the vials and everything there, because he had spoken about that generally. He had been working with a psychiatrist in Chicago who used psychedelics with cancer patients. Aldous had taken a painkiller, for the last week or so of his life, but no LSD. Although he hadn't previously said, "When I die give me LSD," he had mentioned to me earlier that he thought LSD might help in the transition. He was referring at the time mostly to people in physical pain, to detach them from the pain. But that was not his own case. When he was actually dying, he was totally clear, and wrote his own prescription: "100 micrograms."

Did he talk at all after the LSD?

No, I just squeezed his hand, and he answered once, and then at the end he did not answer any more. It was so smooth a passage, you can't imagine. It was just a gentle diminuendo.

Would you be willing to read this quote? This was Aldous's favorite passage, with which you end your book.

Well, yes. This is from Aldous' grandfather, Thomas H. Huxley. He wrote a letter to Charles Kingsley, and I quote:

Science seems to me to teach, in the highest and strongest manner, the great truth which is embodied in the Christian concept of the entire surrender to the will of God. Sit down before fact like a little child, and be prepared to give up every preconceived notion, follow humbly wherever and to what ever abysses Nature leads or you shall learn nothing. I have only begun to learn content and peace of mind since I have resolved at all risk to do this.

This is from the man that created the word "agnostic."

Agnostic. Really? Did he have a conversion experience later in life?

No, but agnostic doesn't mean that you don't believe in God. It just means that you don't know. It's a confession of ignorance.

What are you most passionate about now in your life?

What I'm most passionate about now is to see that children are born wanted and prepared for, and that they come into a world that respects them and welcomes them. The idea is to prepare young people so that they don't have babies when they are babies themselves. They are children, and they want to be loved, and they think the baby is going to love them. Well, the baby *is* going to love them, but it also has to be loved and prepared for and taken care of. Teen pregnancy has been linked to poverty, limited education, child neglect (sometimes abuse), health problems, drug abuse, and violent crime. Sadly, America leads the world in teenage pregnancies.

I have a program called Teens & Toddlers. A few times a week, a teenager takes care of kids two or three years old. Two- or three-year-old children are not so easy. Teens & Toddlers has demonstrated an effective, preventative approach that can be replicated in schools anywhere. Although the program began in America, my foundation, called Children: Our Ultimate Investment, has expanded the program to the United Kingdom with outstanding success.

The project includes two key elements. First, there is regular one-to-one contact between the young adolescent and a "toddler," whom the adolescent befriends and establishes a relationship with. And second, there is classroom time spent focusing on child development issues, parenting skills, sexuality, and relationships.

I have another program that I have been pursuing for many years, called Project Caressing. The most significative form of communication an infant has with the world is through the skin. For the nine months of gestation, he feels no boundaries between his body and that of his mother. The shock of birth is partly due to that separation. Suddenly he is alone in an incomprehensible, possibly inimical universe, and he longs for and needs one thing more than any other—skin contact.

For Project Caressing, we envisage in every city block a serene, sound-proof, pastel-colored room, furnished only with comfortable rocking arm-chairs and pillows. In this room adult participators would hold a baby, knowing that their warmth and affection will magically infuse that baby's entire life with responsive tenderness. No words will interfere with the soft melting of loneliness into silent loving communication: only soothing humming in the caressing room, or golden silence. For in the infant's world, it is contact with a living body with a beating heart that counts. Busy mothers and fathers will be able to leave the infant in the caressing room, knowing that only affection and tranquility will be given, instead of the catastrophic noises, lights, radiations, and vibrations of TV, so often used as a built-in, never quiet, never caring, never touching baby sitter. And the older people, who are increasingly separated from their grand-children, will feel the joy of giving—not money or work or things—but giving themselves and their love for the sheer pleasure of it. They will hold a baby, and by the magic of touching, *they* will be touched.

Is there a legacy that you want to leave to these children, in terms of your own wisdom?

Well, there is a prayer that resonates with me. I have no ownership of this prayer. I did not write it, I just wrote it down. It is the *Prayer of the Unconceived.* It can be published anywhere without permission as long as it is quoted in its entirety:

> Men and women who are on Earth
> You are our creators.
> We, the unconceived, beseech you:
> Let us have living bread
> The builder of our new body.
> Let us have pure water
> The vitalizer of our blood.
> Let us have clean air
> So that every breath is a caress.
> Let us feel the petals of jasmine and roses
> Which are as tender as our skin.

Men and women who are on Earth
You are our creators.
We, the unconceived, beseech you:
Do not give us a world of rage and fear
For our minds will be rage and fear.
Do not give us violence and pollution
For our bodies will be disease and abomination.
Let us be where ever we are
Rather than bringing us
Into a tormented self-destroying humanity.

Men and women who are on Earth
You are our creators.
We, the unconceived, beseech you:
If you are ready to love and be loved,
Invite us to this Earth
Of the Thousand Wonders.
And we will be born
To love and to be loved.

Part Four

Religious Implications

Psyche, Soul, and Spirit

Religious Implications

Psyche, Soul, and Spirit

> There is a continuum of cosmic consciousness against which our individuality builds but accidental forces and into which our several minds plunge as into a mother sea.
>
> —William James[1]

Psychedelics certainly startled and shook the Western world. But one of the greatest surprises was that psychedelics produced religious experiences. A significant number of people, including staunch atheists and Marxists, claimed to have found *kensho* in a capsule, *moksha* in a mushroom, or *satori* in a psychedelic. In fact, these claims proved so consistent over so many years that some researchers have renamed psychedelics "entheogens," substances that facilitate awareness of God within.

Religious scholars immediately split. For many of them, psychedelic epiphanies were considered pseudo-spiritual at best and delusional at worst. How could mere micrograms of a curious chemical possibly replicate the heights of human experience traditionally hard won over decades?

On the other side of the isle stood researchers like Ram Dass, Rabbi Zalman Schachter-Shalomi, and Huston Smith, who argued for the possibility of experiential equivalence between contemplative and chemical mysticism. They drew on research such as the famous Harvard "Good Friday Study" and on theories such as the "principle of causal indifference."[2] This principle suggests that if states are experientially identical, then the fact that they have different causes may be irrelevant.

The debate has raged for decades. At the present time, both research and theory suggest an answer to this question. That answer is a highly qualified "yes." Yes, it seems that psychedelics can induce genuine spiritual and mystical experiences, but only on *some* occasions in *some* people under *some* circumstances.[3]

Whatever the conclusion, the debate and the psychedelic explosion which set it off, turned attention to the intriguing relationship between drugs and religion. It soon became apparent that the religious use of drugs to induce sacred states of consciousness has been widespread across numerous cultures. Historical examples include the *kykeon* of the Greek Eleusinian mysteries, the Australian aborigines' *pituri*, Hinduism's *soma*, the wine of Dionysis Eleutherios (Dionysis the liberator), and the Zoroastrians' *hoama*.[4] Contemporary examples also abound, such as the use of marijuana by Rastafarians and some Indian yogis, Native American peyote, and the South American shamans' ayahuasca.[5] No matter what the current debate in the West, it seems clear that for centuries other cultures have agreed that psychedelics are capable of producing valuable religious experiences.

Unsuspecting Westerners who experimented with these drugs were not immune to their religious and spiritual impact, and this impact took three forms. The first was a spiritual initiation. Many people had their first significant religious-spiritual experience on psychedelics. Among the contributors to this book, James Fadiman and Ram Dass are striking examples of people whose lives were dramatically reoriented in this way.

Those who were already committed to spiritual concerns, such as Rabbi Zalman Schachter-Shalomi and Huston Smith, found a deepened interest in, and understanding of, various aspects of religion. Spirituality, mysticism, and Eastern philosophies proved particularly intriguing for many people, and the influx of Hinduism and Buddhism into the West was one result.

A third effect was to encourage people to begin a spiritual practice in order to deepen and stabilize the experiences and openings they had glimpsed. For it rapidly became apparent that, while psychedelics might sometimes grace the user with a glimpse of the transcendent, it often lasted no longer than the drug's effect did. As Huston Smith concluded, "Drugs appear to induce religious experiences; it is less evident that they can produce religious lives."[6] The challenge is to transform peak experiences into plateau experiences, epiphanies into personality, altered states into altered traits, transient states into enduring stages, or as Huston Smith so eloquently put it, to transform "flashes of illumination into abiding light." This challenge played a large role in the popularization of practices such as contemplation, meditation and yoga.

In short, psychedelics had a major impact on the understanding and practice of religion in the Western world, and Ram Dass, Rabbi Zalman

Schachter-Shalomi, and Huston Smith were at the forefront of investigating the religious significance of these substances.

NOTES

1. W. James, *William James on Psychical Research.* (New York: Viking, 1960), 324.

2. W. Stace, *Mysticism and Philosophy.* (Los Angeles, CA: J. Tarcher, 1964/1987), 29.

3. R. Walsh, "Entheogens: True or False?" *International Journal of Transpersonal Studies* 22 (2003): 1–6.

4. H. Smith, "Do drugs have religious import?" *Journal of Philosophy* 61 (1964): 517–30.

5. H. Smith, *Cleansing the Doors of Perception: The Religious Significance of Entheogenic Plants and Chemicals.* (New York: Tarcher/Penguin, 2000).

6. M. Harner, ed., *Hallucinogens and Shamanism.* (New York: Oxford University Press, 1973). R. Walsh (2005), *The Spirit of Shamanism,* 2nd ed. St. Paul, MN: Llewellyn Publications (in press).

11

Zalman Schachter-Shalomi

Transcending Religious Boundaries

Born August 28, 1924 • Rabbi Zalman Schachter-Shalomi was born in Poland and raised in Vienna, Austria, from which he fled following the Nazi takeover of power. Emigrating to the United States in 1941, he was ordained as a rabbi in 1947 and received his doctorate from the Hebrew Union College in 1968. Rabbi Schachter-Shalomi has held the World Wisdom Seat at The Naropa Institute and is Professor Emeritus at Temple University. He has been recognized as a major scholar of Hassidism and Kabbalah, and was a founder of the Jewish Renewal movement. Rabbi Schachter-Shalomi's approach to Judaism has been described as a novel synthesis of the Chabad/Lubavitch Hassidic tradition with contemporary spirituality. In his numerous articles and sermons, he has examined the significance of the psychedelic experience and the literature of transpersonal psychology and religious mysticism. Over the past decade, he has pioneered the practice of "spiritual eldering," working with fellow seniors on coming to terms with personal aging and training them to be spiritual mentors for young adults. His books include: *Paradigm Shift, Wrapped in a Holy Flame: Teachings and Tales of the Hasidic Masters, First Steps to a New Jewish Spirit: Reb Zalman's Guide to Recapturing the Intimacy and Ecstasy in Your Relationship, Torah and Dharma* (with Tetsugen Glassman Roshi) and *From Age-ing to Sage-ing: A Profound New Vision of Growing* (with Ronald Miller).

I'VE BEEN A RABBI SINCE 1947. My sacred studies were at the Lubavitch Yeshiva, a seminary for Hasidim. In many yeshivas, you mostly do intellectual study of the *Talmud* and legal codes, but Lubavitch also emphasized meditation and prayer. This, more than the other things, was very important to me.

What drew you to this particular perspective?

The best I can put it is the way my daughter expressed it later on. She asked, "Abba! When you're asleep you can wake up, right? But when you're awake, can you wake up even more?" The drive to "wake up even more" was something that I can remember ever since I was young. I was very curious about things below the surface. I was always wondering, "Why are these people doing such and such religious activities? What is it that they get out of these practices?"

I was raised in Vienna, and in the winter of 1938, after the Kristall-nacht, they deported my father, who then snuck back into Austria illegally. So we had to get out before they could harm him. We crossed the border into Belgium illegally. That was an awesome thing, going between the mines of the Siegfried and Maginot Lines, getting across safely, and then coming to Antwerp.

It was in Antwerp that I met the people who really opened me up spiritually. They were diamond cutters, and I learned how to cut diamonds with them. While they worked, they also studied. One guy sat there with a microphone, and the others had earphones on because there's a lot of noise with diamond cutting. So this one person would read, and the others would keep on working. If they wanted to talk they'd hit a switch, stop the machines, discuss what they had to discuss, and then go on. Often they would sing some of those beautiful Hasidic melodies at the top of their voices. They initiated me into contemplative Hasidism.

Later on we had to flee Belgium during the Blitz, and we were interned in France. When we got out, we went to Marseilles, and I met the person who became the Lubavitcher rebbe, who recently passed away. The way in which he talked about the evolution of consciousness made a fantastic impression on me. I met his father-in-law later on, who was his rebbe, and he became sort of my root spiritual master—Rabbi Joseph Isaac Schneersohn, with whom I had many private encounters for guidance. It was he who sent Rabbi Schlomo Carlebach and me out to visit university campuses to spiritually inspire students.

This was at the end of the 1940s. At about that time I began reading a lot of psychology, and eventually in 1954, I came across Aldous Huxley's book *The Doors of Perception*. Everything that he described fascinated me and was so close to the Hasidic tradition: the various levels of consciousness, the worlds to which one can go, and what "soul" is like. I was consumed by this seeker's curiosity, I very much wanted to have some direct experiential knowledge, and at the time I was studying Hinduism and Catholicism.

Later I heard that Abe Hoffer and Humphry Osmond were conducting psychedelic research at a mental hospital in Saskatchewan. I asked them whether I could have an experience, and they said, "Yes, if you come here." I wasn't particularly interested in going to a crazy house to get "opened up." I thought, "This is like doing major surgery on a dunghill. I don't need to pick up all that psychic stuff." So I had a conversation with Gerald Heard and he agreed. He said, "Don't go there. I have some friends at Harvard," and he told me about Timothy Leary and Richard Alpert.

Just prior to meeting Tim, I had been in New York to see the Lubavitcher rebbe. I went outside for a moment to talk to a friend, while everybody else was singing and saying the *l'chayim*—"to life." Someone called me in from outside and said, "Zalman, the rebbe asked, 'Where is Zalman?' He said teasingly, 'Maybe he's gone for a retreat, maybe he's gone for a meditation.'"

So I came in and the rebbe said, "Drink l'chayim—a big *cappo grande*. Drink two of them." I was given about eight ounces of schnapps the first hit, which I drank and said "l'chayim" to him. But he didn't answer, so I drank the second one. I figured he would answer for the second one, but his mind seemed to be wandering. The he focused on me again and asked, "Why don't you drink?" So someone hit me—after the two vodkas—with some rye. I said, "l'chayim," and drank down the rye. And he said, "That was for the retreat. Now for the meditation." There was no more schnapps, so someone gave me wine for a chaser. When I had it down the rebbe said, "L'chayim. Have a good retreat and a good meditation," and he began singing. By then, the alcohol had hit my brain and I started to jump and dance. So, two weeks later, when Tim Leary took me on my first psychedelic voyage, the last image that came to me before I started to tumble was the rebbe saying, "Have a good retreat and a good meditation."

So you were finally able to have the psychedelic session you had been looking for, with Timothy Leary as your guide?

Yes, it was Tim who guided me the first time. I asked him, "What should I pay attention to?" and he responded, "Never mind. There's only one thing you need to do: trust your travel companion and float downstream. Okay?" So that's what we did and a remarkable night happened.

It was done at an ashram, so you can understand how different it was from doing it at a mental institution. The setting was extraordinary: the chapel of the ashram. To have this psychological set and in that setting was amazing!

Before that time, I had read some remarks made by Theodor Reik, who talked about how we all have totem life inside us. He described a Jewish totem being a sheep. Leary was certainly a cat, a tiger—the way he moved around. At one point during the experience I looked at him, and I saw him as a tiger and myself as a sheep, and I said, "If you're hungry you can eat me." You know, it didn't matter. The whole business of paranoia wasn't there. It was a very wonderful journey. I subsequently had some other trips where there were descents into hell, but that first one was just wonderful.

How did your psychedelic experiences, both the positive and the difficult ones, shape your perspective toward spirituality and Judaism?

The wonderful thing about psychedelics was the "mind move" that occurred—the recognition of the fluidity of consciousness. My reality maps were no longer absolute. I used to have absolute reality maps based on traditional creeds, and felt that if I just thought of things in a particular way, everything would be clear. With psychedelics, I could see how all cosmologies are heuristic and it depends on what you want to do. I could get into various viewpoints; if I wanted to see the universe from a Christian perspective, I got it. All I needed to do was give a little mental wiggle and I saw it that way. That was a very important discovery for me.

Another thing I learned was how important it is to do one's contemplative homework afterwards. Leary said to me that time, "Imagine how potent this is and what it might do for people. And imagine how, if this is misused, it's not so good." Ram Dass would say in those years, something along the lines of: "For grass you should have the equivalent of a driver's license. And for LSD you should have the equivalent of a pilot's license." He emphasized the preparation and the responsibilities that go with it.

It's been said, "If you want to do grass, you have to have three days: a day for preparation, a day for doing it, and a day for digesting it. If you want to do LSD, you have to have a week: three days of preparation before it, and three days for doing your homework afterwards." Everything happens so fast in the psychedelic experience and so many worlds are being traveled through. If somehow there is no womb made for the seeds that are received at that time . . . well, these *need* to be nurtured so that they can grow. One has to do a lot of contemplative homework after a psychedelic experience.

The report that I wrote about psychedelics, "The Conscious Ascent of the Soul," was first given to a group of rabbis who were doing something unusual. We met, not as rabbis, not as Orthodox, Conservative, or

Reform, but as a group of people who were interested in theology across the spectrum. We would read our papers to each other that we didn't dare give elsewhere.

After I had that experience with Tim, I read them that report. One person asked, "Well, if this was such an important experience, did it make you into a saint overnight?" I said, "No." But then I asked him, "Tell me, what would you call the paradigm of the great revelation?" He replied, "Mount Sinai." So I said, "That's good. And forty days afterward they worshipped the Golden Calf."

So the experience only opens you up to greater vision. When you have the vision, you have a burden to carry that vision out. In other words, it makes demands on you. But you can also ignore the demands, shut the doors again, and then the places that have become transparent become opaque. To keep the transparency, homework is crucial, but it can be quite difficult to do such work on one's own. It's beneficial to have someone with you who will help you harvest the experience.

The big difference between psychedelics and meditation is that in meditation you can steer. When you get close to the abyss, you can steer away, rather than tumble through it. But with psychedelics you can't help but go down Niagara Falls. When you get to the blind spots in your soul, the places where the neuroses are centered, of course you want to avoid them. That's the time when you want to go pee; you want to make love. In fact, you want to do *anything* but stay with the things at the core of your anxieties. People talk about the fixation—your flaw around which everything circles. It takes different forms, but it's always the same issue. For a moment the door opens up and you see it. If you have someone with whom you can talk this over, it really helps. I didn't have someone, so I had to take time out later and think about it. I regret that I didn't keep a journal at that time.

Did you discuss your LSD experience with the Lubavitcher rebbe?

Yes, I told him about it. In fact, I hoped that he and I would do it together. Forget it! The nice thing was that he never pooh-poohed it, but he kept saying, "Just remember, it's only an experience, okay?"

I remember a cartoon with the caption: "Just the same old cosmic truths." After a while the experiences were less momentous, and there seemed to be a need to wait between sessions. In those years I felt that it was important to have a psychedelic experience at least twice a year, once before Yom Kippur and once before Passover, to revisit that place and check out what was happening there.

Is the use of psychedelics inconsistent with the Hasidic tradition?

It depends on who you ask. Some experiences in Lubavitch are catalyzed by vodka, and vodka people don't like the other approach. I remember once coming to a Hasidic *farbrengen,* a traditional gathering where they were having vodka, and I had brought my pipe along with some good grass. You want to have your high, you have your high; I want to have my high, I have my high. By and large this wasn't done in the open, but the hidden scene was a different story.

I understand that there are some seminaries where groups of people have looked at sacred texts while high on grass. Leary and Alpert did this with psychedelics, looking at the *Tao Te Ching* and the *Tibetan Book of the Dead.* They said, "Lets go through all these texts under the influence of those drugs, and see what they look like. Then we'll rewrite them—recast them out of that experience."

I was eager to try this with the *Book of Job* or the *Book of Ecclesiastes,* because the *Book of Ecclesiastes* is the most Buddhist book in the Hebrew Bible. For everything, turn, turn, turn; there is a season, et cetera; nothing is permanent. It could be a remarkable study. But that all got undercut because psychedelics became used more for recreation, than for mining the soul. People would drop acid and then go to see The Beatles' movie, *Yellow Submarine.* I think *Yellow Submarine* is acid enough!

Do you feel that recreational use made the spiritual approach unacceptable?

Well, there were excesses in those days, and some psychedelic advocates even talked about putting LSD into the water supply. That kind of attitude created paranoia and a backlash.

At the University of Manitoba, where I was working at that time, I said something about having tried psychedelics. Right away there was an inquiry, and the dean called me onto the carpet. My daughter was teased by the kids in school who asked, "Does your dad give you LSD in your orange juice?" By that time prudence said, "Go underground, don't talk too much about it."

Also, when psychedelics became illegal, the paranoia of that illegality created further problems. If substances are not available in a kosher way, the people who use them are lawbreakers, and this creates problems. In other words, the substances get contaminated with the bad attitude.

Back in their heyday, somebody interviewed me and asked, "What do you think about LSD and psychedelics?" I replied, "When God saw that people didn't turn to Him, but turned instead to their medicine cabinet, He made himself available in the medicine cabinet. So what did Satan do?

Satan became the pusher." You get a sense that in manufacturing these now illegal substances, the newly created underworld charged them with a lot of negative energy. The shadow costs hit us in the face.

The great social experiment of psychedelics in the 1960s ultimately unraveled, and in many respects the dark side took over. Nowadays, could psychedelics be integrated in a wholesome way?

Attitudes have indeed changed. I can look back at the times when people tuned in, dropped out, and blew their minds. But then came the time when those people with the blown minds dropped back in again. They became the people who worked on Wall Street and made their mint, or went to work with Microsoft on the computer revolution, and brought a new mind-set to the whole business. Nowadays, these folks are coming into their elder years, and I have the sense that they will want to look at the spiritual use of psychedelics at this point in their lives in a much more serious way.

I remember when I first met the great psychologist Abraham Maslow. I was flying back from the Lubavitch dressed in my Hasidic outfit, and this guy sitting next to me was reading a psychology text. I looked over his shoulder and saw that it was good stuff he was reading. In those days the stewardesses would check with you to see what your destination was. So she came down the aisle and asked: "And your name?" to which he replied, "Maslow." "And where are you going?" "To Regina." He was going to see Humphry Osmond. So I turned and asked, "Are you Professor Abraham Maslow from Boston?" "Yes," he replied. So we started a conversation about humanistic psychology. I mentioned the peak experience available via psychedelics, and he said to me, "It's like the cable car up Mont Blanc; it's not quite fair."

But later, after his heart attack, he took the cable car, because he could no longer climb the mountain himself. It was part of what made him move from humanistic to transpersonal psychology, which was a remarkable turning point for him.

I bring this anecdote up because I feel that Maslow figured, "I don't have much time left to live and I want to see what's going on beyond the physical." And what Maslow tried to do is something that's going to happen for the boomers now coming into their elder time. I think they will approach spirituality with a lot more responsibility. I feel that homes for the elderly should be able to create programs in which people could better prepare to let go of their outworn views and cosmology and embrace a Gaian understanding.

Part of my eldering work has been to help people move from just merely aging to sageing. In order to become a sage—it's not just years that do it—you have to do inner work. So my deep sense is that if we could get people to do that opening up and to look at their life—to have a life review and contextualize their failures, and see how their failures have been the root of their successes in life, and harvest their life experience—out of that, such wonderful things could happen. A corps of elders who have been seasoned through this kind of process could then go to Bosnia, to the Middle East, and so forth. Instead of sending young people, who still have their lives ahead of them, a person who has lived a long life would be able to say, "All right, if they're going to kill me they kill me." It's an easier way out than disability and diminishment.

How were your subsequent psychedelic experiences?

At one point I went to Millbrook for an experience. By that time Leary was there and the enthusiasm was fantastic. They had a roof over their heads, there was money available, and it was all very exciting. That session was well planned, and I worked on some key questions for my dissertation during the experience.

There were unplanned moments, too. It was around the time that Marilyn Monroe had committed suicide, and she came into my experience, with her despair. For the first time in my life I understood why people would want to take downers. I felt so stretched and overwhelmed from being up for such a long time and doing such strong work, that I wanted to be *less* conscious. I wanted to go to sleep; I wanted to escape into a dim, mushy feeling.

Yet I can see how psychedelics could be useful to work through depression. You could go into that deep place, and look at the depression. But one would need a lot of support doing that—someone to hold one's hand.

For an entirely different take on how to use psychedelics, let me talk about the Mexican psychiatrist Salvador Roquet. Here was a person who took people to hell and back. I called him the most compassionate cruel man in the world. The cruelty was that he made you meet your shadow, meet your death, meet your abyss, all that kind of stuff. Sometimes on acid, sometimes on ketamine. Later on he did it in what he called convivials, without drugs, but these were still very powerful experiences.

I did a convivial with Roquet in Mexico once. In one exercise you looked into a coffin. There was a mirror on the bottom of the coffin, and you saw your own face in there. Then you had to imagine you had only two hours left to live, and you had to write someone a letter. I wish we had documentation of the protocols used during these sessions, because I think they were very useful in helping people go to their dark places, and I really would like to see such approaches on the record.

At one time I was going to do an article on capital punishment. I proposed that instead of killing a criminal, he should be made to take LSD and look at pictures that the police had taken of his crime. The criminal would then see what his victim looked like, and on the acid, identify with the victim. Because that kind of identity shift happens in that mind state. I think that this would be both the best rehabilitation and the most humane way of dealing with such criminals.

What did you learn from your own encounters with the dark places?

The dark places in those experiences taught me that there was no escape from them. There are times when you die every death in the world. I died every death, I suffered every sickness. It all came through, and there was no way out but to bear it. While in that place, bearing it, I understood what Good Friday was all about in Christianity. I had the sense of the atonement, the at-one-ment that occurs at the time you experience death. This time I'm lucky—I'm me. But I could also be one of the Tutsis in Rwanda, since we are really deeply one being.

Once I took morning glory seeds. Oy! That stuff did bad things to my stomach. But I had a vision of myself in a cave with other people, and everybody was sitting in warm water. Some people were asleep, some people were having nightmares, and some people were happy and looking around the cave. I took a dip under the water, and I saw that beneath the water we were all one being. Then I tried to alert them: "Hey! Take a dip and see what is really going on! Stop having your nightmares!" But they got angry at me for attempting to break them out of their individual experiences, and I lost it myself. Nevertheless, I got to see the whole cycle of "one and many" in that experience.

We are brain cells of the global brain. An organismic understanding of the universe emerged for me out of my psychedelic experiences, and allowed an awareness of Gaia. We are each vital organs of the planet. The optimal contribution we can make is to be the most noble self that we can be.

How would you go about regulating psychedelics, or handling the whole drug controversy in general?

The whole drug policy is crazy. It's like the Cold War! The more money you throw at it, the more money the other side throws at it, and the more evil is generated. The fear of legalization is absurd—it comes from a lack of understanding.

Young people need initiations rather than wild experimentation. Having participated in peyote rituals, I see what a remarkable thing sacramental initiation can be when it is socialized. Solo meditation, as good as it is, isn't enough. We need to have social meditation, because in spiritual intimacy, powerful bonds are created, and this is a glue that allows us to collaborate.

These days, society has pretty tenuous bonds. Since the Renaissance, the focus has been increasingly on the individual, and we don't have extended families now. How brittle society has become.

What would you say to young people who are interested in trying psychedelics?

I would not want to begin with dire warnings, but with gentle experiences. Under the right circumstances, I would like to see *bhang* made available, so that people could have a mild marijuana inebriation with which to hear the great myths of the world retold, to bring back such dreams. Because all of us have run out of myths. The United States, Israel, the United Nations, all of them have run out of myths, and we need people who will dream new myths. To invite young people, under the right circumstances, to dream the myths of their idealism for their lifetime would be wonderful. That's what the raves are doing in some crazy way. It's not even crazy, but it could be done much better.

If you had to die now, what would you most regret having done or not done?

I've been over that territory so many times that I feel everything was right. It doesn't mean that I did right each time, but that I learned from each situation. Part of eldering is that you try to repair issues and relationships. I don't feel I have anybody in my jail of contempt anymore, or any unforgiven stuff. Years ago I might have accused myself for relationship issues: I'm in my fourth marriage, so there was a lot of stuff around that. But I see now who my spouses were, and we are not in the spousal relationship, but in a coparenting relationship in which we still honor each other. So I don't feel that I have a lot that I regret.

These days I'm working on my inventory, as it were, trying to complete things so that if I go, everything is handled. In the other room I have a folder with the Hebrew word *halila* written on top of it, which means "God forbid." The folder contains my cemetery deed, wills, and copies of financial things—who gets what. All that is organized, so I don't feel so bad about going.

How would you imagine using psychedelics in the training of rabbis?

My sense is that a psychedelic experience could be very helpful in deep counseling. It could help with understanding and working through many issues, such as developing appropriate motivation, reducing the inflation that can come from being a rabbi, and seeing things from multiple perspectives.

Psychedelics could add a post-triumphant point of view. Rabbis have been trained for generations with the notion of Judaism *über alles*, believing that all other religions are not as good or as important. Likewise, priests have been trained that Roman Catholicism is the cat's meow. Psychedelic experiences often generate a sympathetic view of other religions, so I think that such experiences could be important for ecumenicism. They could also foster an appreciation of feminism, and of something for which I coined the word "ecokosher." For instance, if I drank out of a styrofoam cup it would be more kosher than if I drank out of a glass that had some pork inside, but it would be less ecokosher. Nowadays, kosher has to be hooked to ecology.

Up until about the 1980s, not one of the official seminaries—except the Lubavitcher Yeshiva where I studied—taught Jewish mysticism. They all focused on exoteric Judaism, and didn't go any higher. I can't imagine a better way of introducing people to the worlds of Jewish mysticism than via the psychedelic path.

For instance, in one remarkable Zohar text, the prophet Elijah opens the discourse. But instead of talking *about* God, he talks *to* God. If you want to listen to the conversation, you can listen. He says, "Thou art One, and not just a number. Thou art the origin of origins, the cause of causes. No thought can grasp Thee at all." Now, when you get into a text of this sort with a fluid mental approach, you begin to understand. But if you hit it with a hard fundamentalist mind, you don't get it. I think to understand the depth of a religion, one needs to have firsthand experience. It can be done with meditation, it can be done with sensory deprivation, it can be done a number of ways. But I think the psychedelic path is sometimes the easiest way, and it doesn't require the long time that other approaches usually require.

12

Ram Dass

Walking the Path: Psychedelics and Beyond

Born April 6, 1931 • Ram Dass has been one of the most influential spiritual teachers of our time. Born Richard Alpert, he became a professor of psychology at Stanford University, and then at Harvard, where he met Timothy Leary and was introduced to psychedelics.

The results were monumental for Alpert and for our culture. He redirected his personal and professional life to study these drugs and, when offered the choice to abandon this work or face expulsion from Harvard, he continued his research. The result was the infamous firing by Harvard of both Alpert and Leary.

Alpert's life took yet another dramatic turn when during a trip to India, he met his spiritual teacher, and thereafter devoted himself to spiritual practice, teaching, and service. As one of the first Westerners to dive deeply into Eastern religion, he led the way for subsequent generations of seekers. The name "Richard Alpert" was given up, traded for "Ram Dass," which signified his shift toward leading a spiritual life.

Instead of describing religious practices in the musty terms of outdated theological systems, Ram Dass spoke directly from his own experience in a manner that Westerners could understand. He described processes such as training attention, transforming emotions, refining awareness, and of living ethically in order to reduce craving. Here was someone who could marry his scientific and psychological training to his spiritual insights, and thereby communicate them afresh.

By presenting examples from his own life and using contemporary language and concepts, he became what Carl Jung called a "gnostic intermediary," and thereby overcame the ritualization of religion that pervades Western traditions. Ritualization occurs when people no longer understand or practice truly transformative disciplines, settling instead for the mere repetition of old rituals. To combat ritualization, gnostic intermediaries engage in authentic practices, experience a tradition's timeless truths for themselves, and translate their insights to inspire others. Ram Dass, one of the great gnostic intermediaries of our time, has served as a bridge between ancient and modern worlds, between East and West, and between spirituality and psychology.

Gandhi's statement, which Ram Dass is fond of quoting, applies equally to him: "my life is my message." Ram Dass' messages are many, but can be summarized under three categories: practice, karma yoga, and service.

- Practice: Ram Dass has written and lectured widely, but above all he has practiced and applied what he has learned on his spiritual path, and he encourages others to do likewise.

- Karma yoga: Everything in our lives can become "grist for the mill," as one of his books is titled. By dedicating one's activities in the world to a higher goal, while simultaneously relinquishing attachment to a specific outcome, karma yoga transforms all activities into means for awakening. As Martin Buber put it, "any natural act, if hallowed, leads to God." By his own admission, Ram Dass is first and foremost a karma yogi.

- Service: After years of intensive inner work, Ram Dass found himself increasingly drawn to service. In doing so he was following an ancient cycle of first withdrawing to heal and transform one's inner world, and then returning to share that healing and transformation with others. He has done this by teaching, counseling the dying and distressed, assisting numerous causes, writing books such as *How Can I Help?* and creating service organizations such as the Hanuman Foundation and the Seva Foundation.

In 1997, Ram Dass suffered a severe stroke. Initially completely paralyzed on one side and unable to speak, he has since made a difficult but steady recovery. Not surprisingly, he has used the stroke, like everything else in his life, as grist for the mill, and in doing so has offered us yet another gift.

Ram Dass' classic book *Be Here Now*, together with *The Only Dance There Is*, and *Journey of Awakening*, introduced many people to spiritual practice; *Miracle of Love: Stories about Neem Karoli Baba* offers accounts of his guru; *Still Here: Embracing Aging, Changing and Dying* brings a spiritual perspective to aging; and *One Liners: A Mini-Manual for Spiritual Life* collects some of his pithiest aphorisms.

❧

MY INTRODUCTION TO PSYCHEDELICS was via Tim Leary, whom I met as a colleague at Harvard. He was headed to Mexico one summer, and I had decided to fly my plane there, so he suggested we meet in Mexico City. When I got off the plane, he told me about the psilocybin-containing mushrooms that he had taken, and said, "I learned more about psychology from those mushrooms than from graduate school." That certainly piqued my interest!

After our vacation, I got a job as a visiting professor at the University of California at Berkeley for a semester, while Tim went back to Harvard to research these mushrooms. By the time I returned from Berkeley, the details for the prisoner recidivism project and the Marsh Chapel Good Friday experiment were being worked out.

I was very eager to try the mushrooms, so in March of 1961, we took some psilocybin pills at his big fancy house in Newton. Tim and I took the psilocybin pills together with Allen Ginsberg, who was there too.

I left Tim and Allen in the kitchen and went into the living room where it was dark. Eventually, I noticed that there was someone in the corner of the room, and tried to see who it was. And I realized that it was me! Me, in my various roles—pilot, academic—all my roles were out there somewhere. I was living those roles, so it was quite difficult to see them "over there." I thought, "This drug is going to make me not know who I am. If those are my roles over there, what's going to be left?" Then I thought, "Well, at least I have my body." That was my first mistake, because I looked down at the couch and I saw the full couch with no body there! That scared me. Being a philosophical materialist at the time, I really considered my body to be solid. With a sort of Jewish humor, I wondered, "But who is minding the store?"

I ended up going inward to a place in myself where I had never been before. It was a feeling/tone that conveyed the message of being "home." It was a safe home, an ecstatic home. And I racked my brain to see what

I could recall from my psychology texts that pointed to this—this place in me, this perspective.

Eventually I came out of that experience, and realized that we'd had a snow storm. Tim's house was on a hill, and I rolled down the snowy hill, ecstatic. I had truly been affected by those psilocybin pills. Tim's house was only about three blocks from my parent's house, where I grew up. So I walked to their house in the snow. When I came to their walk and saw that it was not shoveled, well, I felt that as the young buck in the family, I should shovel the walk for my dear old parents. So I shoveled the walk. Unfortunately, it was about four in the morning. My father and mother appeared at their window with a look on their faces that said: "What's wrong with you, you damn little fool?"

Now, ever since I was a baby, I always looked to my parents' attitudes to determine my behavior. Later in life, I looked to their surrogates for this: professors and heads of departments. But in my inner self, in this "home" inside, it felt very good to shovel their walk. And so I danced a jig down below, and I waved, and I shoveled snow. That was the first time I had ever bucked authority.

And you've been doing it ever since.

But that was the key one, during that psilocybin trip.

Very shortly after this, Aldous Huxley gave us a copy of the *Tibetan Book of the Dead*. I was fascinated. I had taken a psychedelic on Saturday night, and he gave us the book on Tuesday. I started to read the book and it was as if it were filled with descriptions of my Saturday night trip. Here was a book designed to be read to dying monks, so for me to identify with it so strongly was a shocker.

The *Tibetan Book of the Dead* gave me a feeling that Eastern psychology described the internal workings of this feeling of "home" that I had experienced. So this turned me toward studying the East, because Western psychology didn't seem to provide an answer. I didn't know anything about Eastern spirituality; I just thought that it would be able to provide an explanation of what had happened to me on my psilocybin trip. Eventually Allen Ginsberg, Tim Leary, and Ralph Metzner all went to India, and I thought I should go too. I figured that since the East seemed to have these sophisticated maps of the mind, then maybe I'd find myself a "map reader" in India. We couldn't read the maps because of our cultural limitations and blinders.

But in the meantime, I became fascinated by what "the moment" included. It was like multilayered baklava. Like planes upon planes, and some of them were nuts, and some of them were honey. For example, there was an ecstatic state, where colors and music became so incredibly vivid that it seemed as though Mozart must have had access to, and listened in on, these realms.

Aldous Huxley once gave a speech where he said that we are fond of precious jewels because they remind us of the pebbles from these higher planes. Well, until I took that psilocybin I hadn't seen any of these planes.

So psychedelics gave you a much wider view of consciousness and its possibilities?

Yes. They actually introduced me to my consciousness, something that my studies of psychology had not done. And I liked it very much. It was a vehicle I could now use to travel to these other planes.

What do you think shifted in your values as a result of your psychedelic sessions?

It's hard to separate the influence of the experiences from the influence of Tim Leary. Tim was upset by authority, so I became upset about authority, although that in itself didn't really have anything to do with the drugs.

But your life shifted very dramatically. You were an academic, playing the academic game as a professor, and then . . . ?

Then I wasn't on that track any more. I looked at my colleagues in Harvard and I felt sorry for them—because they didn't know that "home," and they were valiantly opposing us. The professors in the building we shared held a meeting to chastise us. But we knew we were right. We had experienced expanded awareness of our consciousness, and we couldn't just ignore it.

The press came to this meeting, along with students and faculty. The professors said we weren't doing good science. Of course, this attitude was because they were behaviorists and we were introspectionists. But in fact, *they* were missing the boat on good science. Tim explained what we were doing, pointing out that we *were* doing good science.

I stood up and stated that I would like to "change categories." I told them that I was going to leave my scientific role and was going to become a datum, which they could study. Because I didn't want to have anything to do with academics at that point; these experiences were that profound. When a boy from Boston laughs at Harvard, *that* is a shift in values!

Can you say some more about the project? You mentioned the effects of psychedelics on prisoners? You showed a dramatic reduction in recidivism among those prisoners who took part in the experiment, right?

No, we *wanted* to show a dramatic reduction in recidivism. Indeed the prisoners were *happier* after the experience. Of course, very few prisoners get the okay to be drugged in prison, and have the drugs provided for them! Tim wanted to show that giving these prisoners psychedelics would give them a new perspective and allow them to stand aside from their game. Prison is a school for losers; they had all lost at their game. But the experiment was not particularly successful and there was no dramatic reduction in recidivism. Tim thought this was because the prisoners had inadequate support, such as halfway houses, after they were released. Well, perhaps he was right, but some of these prisoners were triple murderers. I didn't like the prison project, as you can tell.

But the Good Friday Project, that was a perfect study. It was run through the Divinity School at Harvard. The subjects were twenty divinity students from Andover Newton Theological School, and the experiment was run in the basement of the Chapel of Boston University. Half of them experienced a Good Friday service under the influence of psilocybin, and the other half got niacin, which we used as an active placebo. The students would go into the room, and one would say, "Oh that rose is so beautiful." Another would say, "Well I guess I didn't get the drug, because all I have is itchy skin."

Walter Pahnke, who ran the study, was an MD who was taking his PhD in divinity, and he interviewed the subjects. These interviews were then given to theologians throughout the country, who were asked: "Did the subjects have a genuine mystical religious experience?" Nine of those who took the psilocybin were determined to have had genuine religious experiences; but with the control group that took niacin, the number was something below four. *Time* magazine got wind of this, and wrote it up as "Religion in a pill!" People like Walter Houston Clark and other religious scholars confirmed that the mystical experience had indeed happened. So this was a much better study, with better results, than the prison study.

You have mentioned a couple of times the sense of tasting "home." What do you understand that home to be?

It's the *Atman* in Hinduism. The Quakers call it "the small still voice." It's a plane of consciousness in which we are privy to the universe subjectively. Normally, if I look at a tree, the tree and I are two separate objects. But when I commune with that "home," I know the tree from the inside. That's something! It's a perspective that includes everything as one large meta awareness. You go in through your own awareness, to *the* awareness.

Until psychedelics came along, I'd had negative experiences with religion. I was a member of a conservative temple in Judaism which never told me about mystical experiences, and never taught anything about the Kabbala. So I ended up being a social Jew. My father did that too; we had a political and social religion. My view of psychology was also very limited. In behavioral psychology, we psychologists were imitating physicists. We treated humans as objects and paid no attention to their inner world.

Your first psychedelic experience happened with Tim Leary. So in spite of all the problems he created, he actually had a beneficial influence on your life.

He was my first guru.

But you subsequently moved on to a spiritual guru, when you went to India. What stopped Tim from making the transition to a spiritual perspective himself?

I think he was too attached to his intellect. Tim's poetry does show a concern with spiritual matters, but, primarily, he couldn't get away from his intellect.

Why were you more amenable to the spiritual?

You know it's a funny thing. Tim traveled to India for his honeymoon and went by the temple that I ended up in five years later. Hari Das, my teacher, got on the bus and sat down next to Tim, and he wrote on a chalk board in perfect English. Tim was flabbergasted. Hari Das walked into the temple, and Tim went to follow him. But just then the bus driver blew the horn letting the customers know that it was time to return, and Tim went back to the bus. Tim could have been studying with my guru, five years earlier! But he ended up taking a very intellectual approach. I, on the other hand, gravitated to a guru who was not intellectual, but rather more *bhakti* or devotional. So I was, and have been, more in tune with my heart, while Tim was more in tune with his head.

So you went to India and your life changed once again, when you met your guru. I understand there was quite a story behind that meeting.

My meeting with Maharajji is a great story. I was taking a walking tour of Buddhist temples with a young Westerner who got a letter from the government telling him that he had to leave India, so he immediately decided he had to go see his Hindu guru. In contrast, I was turned off by Hinduism because, in its popular Indian focus, there is so much garish "calendar art," and superficial squawking "loudspeaker sermons," and cheap statues of gods everywhere. I couldn't stomach it; I had to stay with Buddhism.

But my friend decided to go up to the Himalayas to see his guru, and he asked me to borrow a Land Rover for him from another friend. So we found ourselves in this Land Rover in the middle of the Indian plains. And I was uptight. This guy wouldn't let me drive, and I didn't want the responsibility for what might happen to the Land Rover. And mostly, I didn't want to see a guru.

That evening, he suggested that we stop for the night, as we still had fifty miles to go. So we stopped at a house and I got into bed. During the night I needed to pee, so I got up and went to the outhouse. When I was outside that night, I saw the most magnificent stars—they were like Van Gogh stars. The sight was profoundly moving, and it made me think of my mother, who had died six months earlier. Then I rushed to the toilet and back to bed, and I didn't tell anybody about this episode.

The next day, we drove the last fifty miles and parked by a little temple. My friend began to cry and said, "I'm going to my guru who is up on the hill." So he left me alone there with all these Indians. Well, I was paranoid and I didn't want to leave the car. I was guarding the car, but they were all saying, "The guru is up there, he is up there." At first I didn't react, but finally, I went to take a look at the guru.

The guru was surrounded by Indians, and the fellow I came with was stretched out on his belly, with his hands on the guru's feet. I immediately thought, "I'm not going to do that!" and I pushed my hands in my pockets. The guru said something, and one of the Indian people translated for me. "Maharajji wants to know if you came in a big car?" I said, "Yes." Then Maharajji said something else, and the translator asked, "Maharajji wants to know, will you give it to him, so that the fellow lying on his belly can have it?" Now, since I was the one responsible for the car, I started getting really uptight. All the Indians were laughing at me, which made me even more uptight. Then the guru wanted me to come closer and sit next to him. When I did he asked, "You were out in the stars last night?" I said, "Yeah," thinking anybody could have been out in the stars. Then he said, "You were thinking of your mother." He was reading my mind!

I sat there looking at the ground, wondering how he had got that. Then I thought about all the different things that I was ashamed of and had been hiding. I mentally recited these shameful memories, and then I looked up and met his eyes. They held unconditional love. Before that moment, I had spent a lot of time covering up stuff, feeling that nobody could love me if they knew this stuff. But he loved me, and he knew all that stuff. I was like a filleted fish. I spent two days crying. Someone would ask, "Why are you crying?" and I would respond, "I don't know." So that was my first meeting with Maharajji.

But the story that you are probably referring to happened later. At this meeting, he asked me if I had any "vitamins for the mind." I had brought some LSD in my bag, and I assumed that he must have meant the LSD, right? So I brought it out. There were three or four tablets, and each was a dose for someone my weight. He took one, and I pulled my hand back, but then he took another and another. Well, I was concerned because I knew how strong these were. But then I thought, "He knows everything." I thought that he took the tablets, but nothing happened. I watched him like a hawk, but he didn't get happier or sadder. Nothing happened. It was like when someone takes the bus to Chicago; but he was already *in* Chicago, so he didn't need to take the bus.

When I went back to the United States, I told people about this incident. But you know, I didn't actually see him stick the doses in his mouth, so it was possible that he didn't. I really racked my brain over this.

Then two years later, in 1971, I went back to India. When I saw Maharajji again, he questioned me, "Did you give me some medicine?" "Yes," I replied. He asked, "Did I take them?" I said, "Yes." He asked, "Do you have more?" So I gave him four more, and he took them. And nothing happened. Nothing at all.

Some of the sadhus—the yoga practitioners—use small doses of arsenic for their practice, and one of them had a year's supply of arsenic. Maharajji asked to see it, and he took it all. Quite concerned, the sadhu exclaimed, "But that was my whole year's supply!" These and other experiences caused me to feel that Maharajji's consciousness is in all planes, so these drugs and poisons don't affect him; it's like taking water for him.

Wasn't there a wonderful comment he made at the end of the second LSD session, where he said that these drugs could give you a temporary taste of the Divine, but not a permanent experience?

Yes. He said, "If you take this drug, you can meet or have darshan with Christ, but you only stay about an hour. So wouldn't it be better to *be* Christ instead?" He told me about sadhus who had used plants that produced this sort of effect. But he said that where he came from, they used hatha yoga instead, and when they were very accomplished in hatha yoga, then they could create the same state of mind without psychoactive plants.

What do you see as the relationship between the use of psychedelics and spiritual practice?

As I gained experience in the use of psychedelics, I realized that I was accessing spiritual planes of consciousness. These chemicals can get you in the door, but you don't stay on these planes like you do when you become adept at meditation. However, the psychedelics give you faith in these new, spiritual perspectives—faith which is necessary for later spiritual growth.

In the Buddhist system, faith is one of the five "spiritual powers," along with wisdom and awareness, effort and concentration. So you're suggesting that even though psychedelics may not develop these other capacities and powers, they can give an enduring faith of a certain kind.

Psychedelics can't give you a permanent spiritual immersion. But they can give faith about the existence of these other planes, and you need faith as a foundation for spiritual practices. Psychedelics gave me the faith that allowed me to get to Maharajji. So psychedelics can open doors, and if later you want to revisit these spiritual planes, having had such experiences will make it easier.

But on the other hand, if the psychedelic experience is too mind-blowing, it can detract from your ability to recognize the spirit in this moment. Because this moment doesn't necessarily have the pizzazz of the psychedelic moment.

So you're saying that psychedelics can offer extraordinary gifts, but can also lead to some spiritual traps, right?

The spiritual trap that psychedelics offer is too much pizzazz. Yet for me, psychedelics did indeed provide the faith that I needed. Later I managed to experience ecstatic states without drugs, because I knew that these states existed. Some of these states are beyond life and death. Even though Maharajji died in 1973, he is with me all the time.

How have these chemicals affected your understanding of death and dying?

I think I've found my soul, which doesn't die. My ego dies at the end of each incarnation, but my soul doesn't. My soul goes through repeated incarnations. This information comes from the view of the universe that Maharajji shared with me, spiritual books, and my intuition.

When I teach at the Zen hospice, I ask the volunteers, "Who is your patient? Is your patient this body, this personality, or this soul?" After hearing their response, I'll say, "If the patient is a soul, you had better continue to support the soul after death, because this is a long transition. Even if the body has stopped breathing, the soul is still around." I can say that because of what I have learned from psychedelics and from Maharajji. And I can say it with conviction.

You've written a book titled Still Here: Embracing Aging, Changing, and Dying. *How have psychedelics informed your views on these topics?*

The end of an incarnation is like the end of a chapter in a book you are reading. You don't grit your teeth over it. I think psychedelics allowed me to move into the "witness place."

With regard to my stroke, I became a witness of the stroke. And this position didn't cause nearly as much pain or suffering as I might otherwise have.

If it weren't for psychedelics, I would be like the rest of the culture, and I wouldn't be interested in dying. But psychedelics made me conscious of dying. And now, when I'm old, I think such consciousness has a great place in aging.

Psychedelics helped my ability to "see our souls." After I took psychedelics, if I was in a library, for example, I'd pass the murder mysteries—which I used to guzzle—and go straight to the big, thick, dusty, spiritual tomes. I just honed in. I couldn't figure what was the matter with me, because I had become so captivated.

I'd get energy because I was going to be in a room where a baby was born, or in a room where people had died. Those were the places where one sees behind the billboard at the edge of town into the hidden mystery in life. That's what psychedelics turned me on to.

It seems as though psychedelics opened you up to the bottomless mystery of consciousness, and your life has been about exploring that ever since.

Being an explorer is a role that I like. Tim Leary and I were explorers. When I went to India, I was exploring. I've been exploring my mind and I'm exploring inner exploration. As an older gentleman, I spend hours and hours just sitting. And I'm constantly coming back to identify with my awareness, and letting the river of thoughts go by. Yum, yum, yum.

I'm exploring states or planes of consciousness. Planes of conscious-ness are like places—like Boulder or Los Angeles. In India, I saw that people identify their souls with spiritual planes or states of consciousness. But when I landed in New York, there wasn't a culture there that identi-fied with their souls. A culture where people identify with their souls can take death as a given of life, but our culture can't do that.

You mention cultural attitudes. What insights have psychedelics given you into the nature of society, and how have such insights affected you personally?

I was surprised at how the culture at Harvard reacted to psychedelics. Here was a tool that would allow the culture to grow, but they didn't want such tools. We were a pseudopod of a culture, and they wanted to cut us up.

Our current evolutionary stage is one of communication focused out-ward: radio, television, etc. But in the next evolutionary stage, we will have to meet *inside*, like we did through experiences with LSD. Such meetings lead us to identify ourselves as the One.

When psychology was uppermost in my thoughts, my individuality was uppermost in my thoughts. Now that I have moved my consciousness past that, I feel that I am merely a cog in a wheel. I'm doing my gig, I'm living my life for God. These would have been pretty "far out" things for me to say, back before my exposure to psychedelics. So that's what psy-chedelics did for me: I learned that reality is much greater than I thought it was.

Each of us is a cog in the wheel in that plane of consciousness where we realize the One. When there, I am free of my fear. I'm free of having to make decisions about my life, because *that* Consciousness makes deci-sions for my life.

The second time I was in India, I was searching for my guru Mahara-jji, and I couldn't find him. At that time, Western seekers visiting India were all going to Bodhgaya to meditate. So I went there to meditate, but about the third week, I again felt the pull to find my guru. Meditating with me was a girl who wanted to meet my guru, and she had a friend who had brought a school bus over from England. So we decided to take the bus to search for my guru. Of course, the other meditators got wind of this. Well, most of them didn't want the whole thing—the guru expe-rience, as it were—but they heard about "the bus," and so thirty-four of us decided to leave. We left on the bus sometime after twelve noon and headed directly toward a five star hotel in Delhi. We had been meditating, and you know how you get, right? We wanted ice cream sodas and soft beds!

On the way, we went through Allahabad, which has a spot where two rivers converge. It is considered spiritually valuable to bathe in that water, so hundreds of thousands of seekers come to bathe at that point in the river. It's a very colorful scene.

There was some lively discussion about whether we should take the path to the spiritual power spot, or the path to those ice cream sodas. But we finally decided on the power spot, and we saw a Hanuman temple and decided to park there. Two men started walking in the direction of the bus, and one of them was Maharajji! So we jumped off the bus, and touched his feet, and he said "follow us."

They had this little rickshaw, and we drove behind them in our big bus. They pulled up to a building, and Maharajji and the other man, who turned out to be an economics professor, stopped and got out of their rickshaw. The professor's wife came down the steps and said, "It's good that you came. Maharajji told me at six this morning that I needed to get up and make preparations, as we were going to have thirty-five for supper." Now, I hadn't decided to leave on this bus trip until noon. That made me suspicious of my "deciding" to take the trip. Who was really deciding?

Changing the topic, I'd like to talk a bit about medical marijuana. My stroke has given me all sorts of opportunities. Before my stroke I'd say "Maharajji, I want a parking space by the bank," and a car would pull out, and there was my parking space. That was a little bit of grace. Now, since I had the stroke, I get handicapped parking spaces. So that's a different sort of grace. I also get medical marijuana now, and it's great to be able to smoke it without the paranoia of doing something illegal. Medical marijuana alleviates my muscular spasticity, and makes my pain irrelevant.

The medical marijuana I have is very strong. When I am on the road giving lectures, the pain gets very intense, so I usually take the marijuana before speaking. So that marijuana affects more than just me: one joint and a thousand people got stoned!

I don't know if it's really the marijuana. Maybe it's because of Maharajji's presence in me. Or maybe the audience is primed for such an experience by coming to a spiritual talk in the first place. I'm not sure what it is.

When I speak, about half my audiences have used psychedelics, and their consciousness is *ready* to travel. Nowadays I'm finding more and more sympathetic people in our culture.

Is there a particular age when the use of psychedelics seems most appropriate?

I think a person has to first be grounded on this plane—socially, economically, sexually. When I have guided psychedelic sessions, I have noticed that there are usually two places where a bad session can occur: going out and coming back. Coming back, it can be horrible to see the life you've created. A well-grounded 60-year-old can withstand that experience, but a 20-year-old might not be grounded enough. It's not that I distrust adolescents, but they have other work to do at that age, which may be more pressing than studying consciousness.

What do you think the role of psychedelics was in the 1960s?

Psychedelics were the bedrock of that time. People took psychedelics, first went inward, and then turned outward to make changes based on what they had learned. They were involved in social movements such as antiwar and the civil rights, and their ideas fed into these movements. I can't think of any social movement of that time that didn't have this influence.

There were many technologically sophisticated folks who worked with psychedelics. My friends from silicon valley all used acid, and they took what they learned from psychedelics into technology. The creation of personal computers and the Internet was inspired in part by psychedelics.

Why do you think our culture is so fearful of psychedelics?

I think it has to do with change. Psychedelics undermine both individual and cultural illusions, and can bring you closer to truth. But society doesn't want that to occur, because our society isn't founded on truth or truth-based values.

In what ways have psychedelics impacted our culture?

In art, in science, in rock 'n' roll, the Beat poets. In every one of those areas, psychedelics had an impact. Then there are more serious areas, like civil rights, the Vietnam War, the sexual revolution, and the ecological movement, too. I've heard of many people who have had psychedelic experiences in which they realized the horrifying damage we are doing to our planet.

You yourself have had an enormous impact on our culture as both a social activist and a spiritual teacher. You've also introduced Eastern perspectives and raised ecological concerns. It's remarkable that so many of these contributions can be traced in part to your psychedelic experiences. Thank you for your contributions, and for sharing your insights with us.

Thank you.

13

Huston Smith

Do Drugs Have Religious Import?
A Forty Year Follow-Up

Born May 31, 1919 • Huston Smith is one of the most influential scholars of religion of our time. Born of missionary parents in China, he took
his doctorate in religious studies and philosophy. He then went on to a
distinguished academic career as professor of philosophy at the Massachusetts Institute of Technology, as the Thomas J. Watson Professor of
Religion and distinguished adjunct professor of philosophy at Syracuse
University, and most recently was visiting professor of religious studies at
the University of California at Berkeley. He is the recipient of twelve honorary degrees.

Smith did something all too rare for a professor of religion: he not
only studied and analyzed religious traditions intellectually, he also practiced them. And he practiced them very seriously. To his Christian and
Chinese heritage he added in-depth practice in several major religions,
and spent considerable time in retreats, contemplation, and yoga.

While it might seem incomprehensible to anyone who understands
the power of such practices, the unfortunate reality is that the academic
world of religious studies is largely populated by people whose knowledge
of the religions they research and teach is purely intellectual. The result is
that all too often the greater meanings, or what philosophers call "higher
grades of significance," go unrecognized. As philosopher Immanuel Kant
long ago pointed out, intellectual understanding without relevant experience to underpin and fill it out results in "empty concepts." Consequently,
Smith has long been an inspiration to the growing number of religious
scholars who appreciate the contemplative and mystical depths that spiritual *practice* unveils.

Huston Smith's thirst for direct experience led him to test for himself
the startling claims for the possible spiritual value of psychedelics. With

their help, he finally tasted some of the higher transcendent experiences and insights that he had devoted his life to studying. Though he took the substances only a few times, they had a profound effect on him, and through him on our culture.

In 1963, Smith published a landmark article titled "Do Drugs Have Religious Import?" in the *Journal of Philosophy*. This article proved to be one of the most influential of all publications on psychedelics, and is the most reprinted article in the journal's history. In this article he took issue with the prevailing view that drugs produced pseudospiritual experiences with little religious value. Smith's conclusion? Drugs can *sometimes* produce authentic religious experiences in *some* people, but it is by no means certain that they necessarily produce religious lives. His conclusion remains compelling to this day.

This and other important papers on psychedelics were published in the book *Cleansing the Doors of Perception: The Religious Significance of Entheogenic Plants and Chemicals*. He also coedited (with Reuben Snake) *One Nation under God: The Triumph of the Native American Church*, describing the Native American Church's battle to defend their religious right to use peyote as a sacrament.

Had he made only these contributions on the topic of entheogens, Huston Smith would still have left his mark on history. But he has been prodigiously creative in many other areas covering a spectrum of religious topics, philosophical reflections, and social issues. His book *The World's Religions* is the most widely-read religious text book, while *Forgotten Truth: The Primordial Tradition*, lays out core assumptions of the Perennial Philosophy. His award-winning *Why Religion Matters: The Fate of the Human Spirit in an Age of Disbelief* asserts the contemporary importance of religion and defends against one of the most pervasive yet subtle threats of our time: the spell of scientism, which is the mistaken belief that science alone provides valid knowledge. Other books by Smith include *Beyond the Postmodern Mind*, which stresses contemporary issues in philosophy, education, and society; *Islam: A Concise Introduction*; *Buddhism: A Concise Introduction*; an anthology, *The World's Wisdom: Sacred Texts of the World's Religions*; and a collection of interviews titled *The Way Things Are: Conversations with Huston Smith on the Spiritual Life*.

He has also been a major media presence. He produced three award-winning documentary films, and in 1996 was the subject of a five-part television series by Bill Moyers: *The Wisdom of Faith with Huston Smith*. In light of all this creative activity, it is not surprising that he has been one of the most influential scholars of our time. The following interview can be seen as a follow up to his article "Do Drugs Have Religious Import?"

I REGARD THE WORLD'S GREAT RELIGIONS as the winnowed wisdom of the human race—with a lot of dross, of course. One thing that first attracted me to studying them was the tremendous exuberance of the vision that they hold out for human life. In my own spiritual *sadhana* practice, I always begin the day—along with meditation and a little yoga—by reading a couple of pages of sacred scripture.

At the moment, I'm working my way through the New Testament. In doing so, I came upon a phrase in *Peter*—a little letter towards the end; the phrase in which he refers to "those things on which angels themselves long to gaze." Wow! I mean that will do it for the day. Talk about exuberance! And this is what they are aspiring for—a vision that even the angels would give their eye teeth to have. So that is the dominant mood of these traditions.

The mood is not one of denial—in the psychological sense of denial—of the difficulties and evils of life. I recently came across a definition of denial. It's like thinking that you can see the world better by closing one eye. One of the virtues of the wisdom aspect of the world's great religions—what I call the wisdom traditions—is their realistic awareness of the difficulties, atrocities, and problems along the way. This combination of exuberance and realism is what drew me to the wisdom traditions, and it is the dominant note that I hear sounded in them.

Starting with that broad framing of the wisdom traditions, let's begin to address the question of what relationship the psychedelics or entheogens—and the experiences that they can help to bring about—have had with the wisdom traditions? What role did they play in your life, and what role could they be playing in other people's lives?

All right. It sounds like you've asked everything you need to ask in the three parts of that one question. I spoke of the exuberance in these traditions. But they also refer repeatedly to occasions when the validity of this exuberance breaks through on people in unmistakable, undeniable, and life-transforming ways. And it not only breaks through for the people involved directly, but also sometimes for their successors. A primary example would be Gautama the Buddha under the *bo-gaha* (wisdom tree). After six long years of preparation, according to the classic account, one night the heavens finally opened and in came his history-transforming illumination. Then one can go on from that. Jesus came out of the river Jordan at his baptism, and the heavens opened. Then on Mount Tabor there was the transfiguration, when three of his disciples saw his face shining and his raiment transformed. When Saint John was on the Isle of Patmos, again, the same thing happened to him. For Jakob Boehme, the remarkable seventeenth century German mystic and cobbler, it was when he was looking in a pewter dish. In all these cases there's not just *news* of a different world, but the *experience* of a different world—one is *in* that world.

Now I fully believed the master accounts in these traditions; I took them on faith. So when I heard that there were techniques for achieving transcendence, well—I was whoring after the Absolute. Nothing could hold me back. And so I broke in my legs through meditation—ten years faithfully. I went to Japan and entered a Zen monastery. But I discovered that experientially I was pretty flatfooted. I gave it everything I had. And I think that my wife Kendra, who put up with this obsession of mine, would validate that I gave it everything I had. But I didn't get much off the ground. A little bit, but not very much.

Then Aldous Huxley's *The Doors of Perception* came along. I already knew Huxley, having sought him out after reading his book *The Perennial Philosophy*. He was something of a guru for me at that stage, and when he produced *The Doors of Perception*, I was more than interested.

I was at the Massachusetts Institute of Technology at the time, and I played a part in bringing Huxley there for a semester. He arrived at MIT as a distinguished visiting professor of humanities in exactly the same week that Timothy Leary arrived at Harvard.

Leary had taken his vacation that year in Cuernavaca, Mexico, where he first consumed those seven sacred mushroom that so strongly influenced his life. Leary had an incredible reputation as an early genius, and he had a dream assignment—three years at the Center for Personality Research at Harvard University with no strings attached. He could turn his creativity in any direction he wanted.

Well, what was burning a hole in his head was the question of what to make of that mushroom experience. He knew, of course, of Huxley's little book, and so it wasn't long before they got together. And since I was volunteering to be Huxley's social secretary, I too eventually met up with Leary.

On New Year's Day, 1961—quite a way to begin a decade—Kendra and I arrived in Leary's living room. After coffee and pleasantries he produced a vial, shook out some tablets from it, and told us that one tablet was a mild dose, two was a medium dose, three was a heavy dose. I believe these were psilocybin, on that occasion. "Be my guest," he said. I took two, while Kendra, more venturesome, took three. After about an hour, I was into the experience that for the previous fifteen or twenty years I had been trying to get by other means.

Now, I had no doubt from the start that it was an authentic experience. First of all because it experientially validated my world-view that was already in place. In philosophical parlance, this was the Great Chain of Being which envisions all reality as proceeding from the infinite at its apex, and that infinity contains within it every virtue. The apex of the Great Chain has been described in various ways. The Hindus call it *sat, chit, ananda*—infinite being, infinite awareness, infinite bliss. Plato calls it "the good, the true, the beautiful." At the apex, everything is smelted down into its virtuous mode, which is—according to the Great Chain of Being—the only true mode; because the dross enters as one falls away from this sacred source.

I had no doubt that my experience was valid, because it was retracing exactly what I was convinced was the nature of reality. However, I had not previously experienced the upper echelon personally, and it brought an element of surprise. That's a confession, because the texts should have prepared me for this surprise, but obviously I sort of passed over that bit. This surprise was the element of fear—or more precisely, awe. Awe, I came to see so clearly, is the distinctive religious emotion because it combines two emotions that otherwise tend to be opposite: fear and fascination.

In awe, you want to move toward the fascination, because this is not only unknown territory but territory that one could not have imagined actually exists. What could be more fascinating than that? So that draws you to it. But on the other hand it's new territory, and are the natives friendly? Is the atmosphere viable? You don't know, and so that causes you to hold back. The result is this unique blend of fear and fascination, and I experienced both. The intensity built as I mounted the links of the Great Chain of Being, until I got to the penultimate level—next to the infinite, the Absolute. And there I paused to take a second look at this question, "Do I want to make that final step, or do I not?"

Tim was sort of in the background, observing during the day, but at that moment he was in another part of the building. Kendra was also in a different room, alone. Just as I was debating: "Do I want to take that final step or not?" Tim walked in, pleasantly relaxed, and asked, "How are things going?" I blurted out, "Tim, you better watch out and be aware of what you're playing with here, because if I decide to take this final step, you might end up with a corpse on your couch. The emotional intensity is increasing so exponentially that if I take that step, I feel it might be like plugging a toaster into a power line. And then you would have my dead body on your hands."

"Don't worry," I continued. "I have a loving family and I don't find life intolerable, so I'm not going to take that step. But I want to register this point. I'm well aware that I am under the influence, but that doesn't in any way undercut what I'm saying. At this moment, it feels very clear to me that if I *do* take this step, it will shatter my physical frame."

Well, in retrospect, I think I was wrong about that. I'm not aware of reports of any deaths occurring to normally healthy people through these substances. So I think I was mistaken there. But nevertheless, my sentiment rang true to what I was experiencing.

To consider the effect that these substances have had on my life leads to the baffling question of behavior change in general. How do you measure behavior change? And what causes it? If any psychologist, anybody, got a firm grip on those questions . . . why, to say their reputation would be made is an understatement! So when I consider my life, I have no idea what it would have been like without these substances. What's the basis for comparison? There is a saying, "Isn't life strange?" To which someone replied, "Compared with what?" And it's a little bit like that, when I'm asked what effects these substances have had on my life. I have no basis for comparison.

But several things are very clear. One of these is that I am immensely grateful that I had that experience, and several others which followed. I must have had a half-dozen—including the Good Friday experiment[1]— that were very powerful. After which, the utility seemed to go down quickly and the bummers increased; I had some very negative experiences. So I came to the same conclusion as the Alan Watts' admonition: "When you get the message, hang up the phone." It seemed to me that I'd gotten the message.

In my case I can't think of any value to these bad trips, except that the spirit bloweth where it listeth—one can get the human spirit under one's thumb, but it's like a ball of mercury. One can set up all kinds of precautions—set, setting, and substance—and yet one cannot predict the result.

The classic case for me was when Stan Grof was conducting his perfectly legal research at Spring Grove, Maryland. He was flying in people whose accounts he wanted to accumulate. I was flown in, and maybe I was kind of set up for a fall. I'm not comfortable with this, but I got a little whispering, "Boy, we've really got a big fish here," because I had spent so much time studying the world's mystics and so on. "This is going to be a real blowout!" Well, maybe that in itself was a negative inducement.

And there was another problem: I wanted Kendra to be with me. However, she could not arrive on time; she arrived in midstream, so I felt that we were out of synch. I don't think she took the substance at all in that case. So maybe it was that I was in and she was out. Whatever the reason, it was just eleven hours of cacophony and Indonesian monkey dances and so on. [laughs] It was bad news. But I don't think I learned anything except maybe these little trivia that I've reported.

So I find myself to this day in an intellectually curious situation. I have fallen into the pattern of saying that these experiences comprise one aspect of the three most important experiences of my life. The first one is my marriage and my children. The second, my first trip around the world, where my eyes were opened to this world's phantasmagoria. And then the third aspect is the entheogenic experience, which introduced me to another order of reality—what Carlos Castaneda referred to in the title of one of his books as *A Separate Reality*. This reality was not *just* separate—although that's very important, as distinct and different—but incredibly more mysterious, more awesome, and more wonderful than "normal" reality. So I'm in this very curious situation, where entheogenic voyages constitute one aspect of the three most important experiences of my life, and yet I have no desire or inclination to repeat the experience.

That's puzzling! I don't think I've gotten to the bottom of it, but I have some reason for not continuing the experiential side of this path. One reason may be that the element of awe includes fear, and so that fear may contribute to my reluctance. A second reason is that I feel like I know where that place is, and I know that it *is* there. Now the work is to transform the components of my life so that they more approximate that state. Now I have an agenda and that's my job, rather than going on a kind of spiritual R and R of revisiting that land.

I want to qualify that last pejorative, flippant statement of "spiritual R and R," because I think that these experiences can exert a kind of spiritual gravitational pull on my life. In themselves, they can move one's life toward a spiritual existence.

I was forty-two when I came to this, and there were about three years that I was involved with it. Three very exciting years at Harvard when there was this nucleus, at first visible, and then increasingly underground as the plot began to thicken. But the nucleus of about twenty people or so would gather once a month pretty regularly to discuss these matters and hang out together. There's a great wish to be with those who know what you're talking about. I had about a half-dozen experiences distributed over three years, so it wasn't very often. Every six months or something like that, in my case. Of course, for others it was very different.

Do you have any theories about groups like the Native American Church that do use an entheogen on a regular basis? Can such use fit into a regular practice for some people, or for some groups?

The experiences occasioned by entheogens on the one hand, and those that occur *au naturel* or spontaneously on the other, are very similar. I've done a little research into this connection. I took knowledgeable people as my subjects, and drew one pile of reports from classic accounts in the mystical traditions. But these reports were not so well known that everybody would recognize them. A second sample of reports was generated from psychedelically occasioned experiences. I shuffled the two piles, and then asked these knowledgeable people to sort them back into their original piles. They couldn't do it. It was almost 50 percent, but they were wrong 1 percent of the time more than they were right. So this to me says that, phenomenologically, these two kinds of experiences are indistinguishable. Being that close, it would be surprising if there were *not* some kind of institutional connection between entheogens and religion.

In fact, we're very sure that this has happened in history. Mexican Indians' use of the mescaline-containing peyote cactus goes back several centuries—five, nine, no one really knows—into the twilight zone of Mesoamerica. And then there is the *soma* of the *RgVeda*, the most ancient of Indian scriptures, dating back some thirty-five hundred years ago. *Soma* was an entheogenic plant used from the second millennium BC, the identity of which has been lost. And of course there were the sacred Eleusinian mystery rites in Greece that survived for a thousand years until the fourth century, where the secret *kykeon* potion produced visionary consciousness. In all three cases the substances were integrated into a full-bodied religious practice.

We know that this integration happened, but you were asking, "Why?" Well, I think it seems natural, given the affinity between the experiences, however they are invoked, that they would become integrated into religious practices. It probably wasn't calculatedly thought out. Perhaps it came over people incrementally until they eventually moved these things into place, and a solid institution with such a center was established.

So something about the institutional practice might make entheogenic experiences have more enduring value?

I think that's true. That, combined with a sacred setting. Again, we have to realize that these experiences are not for everyone. While we don't know in the case of *kykeon* or *soma*, we do know in the case of the peyote use by the Native American Church, that even in tribes where the Church is very vigorous, some people choose to join and some do not.

You've mentioned kykeon *and* soma. *In some of your writings you noted that the Eleusinian mysteries were shrouded in secrecy, and that the identity of* soma *was at first protected and then consciously forgotten. Could you explain that a little bit more, and maybe speculate as to why there was so much secrecy?*

Well, I'll try. You're asking about issues that are not well understood, so we're in the area of hypotheses. R. Gordon Wasson has made the clearest hypothesis in his book on *soma*.

He posits that something like a psychedelic down-swirl occurred, and recreational use entered. In other words, the sacred element was lost, and profane use got out of hand. According to Wasson's hypothesis, rather than have it go that route, the Brahmins decided to shut it down. I'm only reporting Wasson's theory here, as I don't have an independent theory. But his theory is as good as any I know.

Considering this most important plant/god, as well as the especially awesome tone of the ninth book of the *RgVeda*, where the hymns are entirely dedicated to *soma*, we're to believe that the identity of the *soma* plant would be just forgotten? That's incredible! How could that have happened? It cries out for a hypothesis, and Wasson's is plausible. In fact, it's the only hypothesis that has been ventured. All the other Vedic scholars throw up their hands and say this is one of the mysteries of history. But Wasson, at least, moves in with a hypothesis.

In the case of Eleusis, I don't know whether there were overt measures against it after Christianity became the established religion of the Roman Empire. I can believe that there may have been. But I have not really looked into the history of the shutdown of that awesome phenomenon. One thousand years and some of our greatest and most influential minds, like Plato and Pythagoras probably, had their philosophy shaped by that experience. And yet something *that* important was kept an absolute secret for one thousand years? Oh, that's confidentiality for you!

*Reflecting on more recent entheogen use, why wasn't the psychedelic move-
ment of the 1960s fully successful at bringing about rapid, beneficial changes?*
I think everybody realizes that the decade, the generation, was not
successful or we would have a more "flower-child" America today than we
do. Kendra and I always have some book that we are reading aloud. Our
present one is Peter Coyote's *Sleeping Where I Fall*, which is a tremendously vivid account of the 1960s and its ideals. And of course he admits,
as everybody does, that they were not fully realized.

But this is a murky area, because they *did* change America in those ten
years, and in certain ways enduringly. Civil rights, for example, was a
change for the good. But nevertheless the ideal of the "greening of America"—one can hardly claim that that has come about.

There are several reasons why many ideals weren't achieved. One
reason was . . . well, the technical word is *antinomian*. *Nomos* has to do
with law. So antinomian is going "against the law," with the connotation
that you can rise above the law—the law here meaning ethics, the basic
principles of ethics. And so, you are above the law, outside the law. And I
think *that* sentiment, neglecting the importance of ethical commitments
as a foundation for a spiritual life, was very much part of the picture.

Another reason that many ideals were not achieved is more subtle. All
the religious traditions have a wisdom-based esoteric dimension. The
common way of saying it is, "Cast not your pearls before swine." Or the
Taoists say, "Know ten things; tell nine." Some things should not be just
flaunted to the public. To go back to the pearls before swine, for example,
there's a double reason. First of all, if you cast them before swine it won't
do the pearls any good; they'll likely get trampled. And it won't do the
swine any good, because they'll get sick. So in the same way, there are
truths that if they fall on uncomprehending ears can only be distorted and
misunderstood, and I think that element was overlooked. Well, the brash-
est case was this notion of spiking the water system with LSD that Tim
Leary had at one point—I don't know how seriously—as a way to change
society's consciousness. So that's a second reason.

A third reason that many ideals were not achieved may have been due
to context, or the lack thereof. By ignoring the religious context for these
substances, one failed to create genuinely holy experiences.

In addition, the movement at that time lacked a social philosophy or
a blueprint for relating itself to society. Let's contrast this to an example
from early Christianity. On the esoteric side, for the first several centuries,

there would be a moment in the mass where some official would cry out, "The doors! The doors!" That was the point where the catechumen—who were sort of learning on the kindergarten or first-grade level—had to leave, while the Eucharist was actually unveiled and participated in. So there was a clear recognition that unless you really *understand* what's going on, this could seem like cannibalism—when you say, "This is my blood, this is my body," and things like that. In other words, this could be misunderstood. So the ritual provided a structure that prevented such a misunderstanding.

This is backtracking a little bit, but you said that one of the three most important experiences in your life was the entheogenic experience. Could you say a little bit more about why that was? What happened during some of those experiences that brought you to that conclusion?

Well, the most obvious is that I experienced—"ontologically" would be the philosophical word for it—what before that time I had only believed. So, it was like fleshing out an intellectual, cerebral understanding, with the conviction of actually experiencing that reality itself. One could think of the difference between reading a marriage manual, then suddenly you're into the real thing. So that would be the most obvious.

Then there was also an opening of the heart. This was an opening to all other beings, human and otherwise. When one is in that state, doing anything mean or mean-spirited, much less something bad, to somebody would just be out of the question.

And there is carry over. After the Good Friday experiment, people asked, "Well, are you a different person?" And I always say, "Well, I can't really say, in the long run, because I don't know what kind of person I would have been without it." But after that occasion, for six weeks or maybe longer, I was in a different mood as I went into the institute. I was not always in love and charity with my colleagues, but I was more so, and *palpably* more so. In addition, the sense of my pain and my pathos, and the sense of the pain that other people were going through, as well as the joys and so on, was far more in my awareness. If you think you're drawing closer to God, and not in fact drawing closer to your neighbor, you're just fooling yourself.

Let me move back to the virtues that are common to different wisdom traditions. There are two mechanisms by which such traditions work to inculcate these values. One has to do with precept or doctrine, and the other with practice. The first acts as a road map—one with as much crystalline clarity and detailed accuracy as possible. One must keep that road map of life's pilgrimage in place. And that includes the virtues that one should seek to cultivate as part of it.

The second mechanism is practice through setting an example. That is, not keeping it solely a head trip. There's the adage, "What you are speaks so loudly to me that I can't hear what you're saying." The most powerful way of teaching virtue is through the influence and impact of one's own attainment. But of course you have to have a huge sense of humor when you talk about spiritual attainment!

One of the reasons that I remain concerned about the issue of entheogens is that I feel I was privileged, even blessed, by them. I was accorded not just the philosophy or the theory of the way things are, but also an *experience* which validates this theory. I was incomparably fortunate to have that validation. And it makes me very sad and distressed that these days people cannot have the same validation without risking a knock at the door. I think there's something rotten in the state of Denmark where this situation prevails. Now, everybody realizes that it's a can of worms. But that doesn't mean that we shouldn't open the can and go to work sorting them out.

Having lived through the 1960s, witnessing the hopes of the psychedelic movement dashed due to the cultural reaction, what is your sense of today's culture? Here we are four decades later. Have conditions changed sufficiently that renewed efforts to incorporate psychedelics within society may be successful?

Well, I'm not a social theorist. I am concerned, but I don't spend time keeping up on the latest developments. And I'm not very good at taking a pulse of our social ethos. Are we any more open now than we were then?

I have entertained the possibility of an experimental situation in which an established religious group—let's just say a church, if it had interest in this direction—could include an entheogen in its monthly or weekly services. I would opt for monthly in the communion cup or something like this. And then bring in the best sociologists to study what happens in the church. Does conviction in the spiritual life consolidate? What about the Bodhisattva vow and humanitarian spin-offs? Are they more concerned with human beings, more compassionate? By works as well as sentiment? I would like to see that happen, and it's one sort of wedge into the issue. Let's try to be creative and constructive, rather than just bemoaning the deplorable state of affairs. I guess that's my one concrete wish.

If a young person, maybe one of your own children or grandchildren, at one point expressed an interest in having an entheogenic experience, at what

*point in his or her life do you think that would be most appropriate? And what
kind of circumstances would you want to see surrounding that session?*

Well, I'm very clear on the second question, although I don't think I
have much of an idea on the first question. I don't think they should be
beneath the "age of discretion," as the phrase goes, which would be . . .
what? Late teens, college age, or something. I wouldn't want it below that.
Now, I'm not a developmental psychologist, but I assume that at a stage
younger than the late teens, one is forming one's ego boundaries, sort of creating a mold into which to pour one's life. And I would have the same fear
of giving it to someone who already had problems with ego boundaries—
namely that they may have problems of spacing out and not reintegrating.

As to the circumstance, I think it should be with the people to whom
one wishes to commit one's life. What I mean is that these people will be
around for the long haul—these are the people that one wants to be most
deeply related to in the course of the years ahead.

*In describing your first experience in 1961, you said that you had had a
disciplined meditation practice for at least a decade and had studied the religious literature extensively. What effect do you think that had on your first
experience? And how much similar preparation would you suggest that someone else should complete before having a first experience?*

Oh, I think it very much shaped it. Again, one has to be modest in
terms of making declarations about these substances and their effects. But
in my case, I think the substances simply poured experience into the
molds of my existing world-view. But I know people for whom it just
exploded their view of reality and gave them a totally different world-view
to live in. I know three or four people who were logical positivists—materialists to the core, totally convinced—until the experience. Now they've
completely lost interest in teaching the philosophy of science. All they
want to do is teach mysticism. So, there are some surprises along the way.

*How many mystics can the world use? How many mystics does the world
need? [joking]*

How many does the world need? [laughs] Well, we could quibble
about the word, but in the way that I define the word, that's like asking,
"How many saints could the world use?" More.

*You said that when you took psychedelics early on it was a validation of
your belief system. What, though, if you took individuals who had different
belief systems? Would psychedelics validate each of those belief systems?*

Well, if I heard you correctly you didn't repeat back my qualification.
Because I said that in *my case* they did. But then I went on to describe

these logical positivists and the like, where the experience just spun their whole world-view around and left them with a new and different world-view. They couldn't have been more surprised at what happened. So, underneath those two examples is my point concerning the importance of reticence and caution about overgeneralizations and declarations with regard to the effects of these substances.

Has the psychedelic experience given you any understanding or insight into death and dying?

It has confirmed what I already believed; namely that dropping the body—as the Indians say—is not the end of our journey. I recently wrote an introduction to a new edition of the *Tibetan Book of the Dead* which, as you know, deals with the *bardos*—the stages of the after-death experience. Rereading that book reaffirms what I have experienced in this life, and the psychedelic experience acts as a confirmation to this understanding of death.

Does that include transmigration of the soul?

One of my students once asked Ram Dass, "What about reincarnation?" And in his usual inimitable, eloquent, precise way, he said, "It's there when I need it." I think that's perfect. I can't think of a more logical, more constructive—when fully understood—view that makes sense about our moral behavior. Do I actually believe it in its literalism? I do believe that our work is never completed unless we're the one in ten thousand billion people for whom this is our last incarnation. Short of that, we all have work to do after this body drops. But whether it's done on other *bardos*, or coming back into another body—the wisdom traditions themselves disagree on that. And I, too, am not really invested in that issue.

Considering the many wisdom traditions, what might it mean to live in a "wisdom society?" Or, what might we do to ameliorate some of the devastating aspects of our current society?

I think that second question is a little bit more manageable, but, again, I'm not a social theorist. I have sometimes said to my social scientist friends and colleagues that God and the Infinite I find manageable, but history is too messy—it's too complex and chaotic.

Of course, the virtues should flourish and we should cultivate those. To blueprint, one can trot out the platitudes of equality. But now how do you parse that? And then there's egalitarianism. Do we do away with all differentiation? It's easier to see the devastating flaws, like the rich getting richer and the poor getting poorer. Now that's terrible! I mean that's flatly immoral. And racial discrimination is flatly immoral, as is violence. I get a little more solidity from pointing out what is wrong, because that just jumps out at me. So, one can target it that way.

I've mentioned the virtues a couple of times, and the West tends to target the virtues, especially humility, charity, and veracity. But Asia gets to the same place by targeting the three poisons of greed, hatred, and delusion. These are what stand between us and the virtues. With a Western background, we always think it's good to accentuate the positive and eliminate the negative. So I asked Asian teachers, "Why do you take the negative approach to the same goal?" And they said, "If you focus on the positive virtues, they are way out there and you're striving. But the poisons are right here and we have to deal with them every day. That's what we should work on, with the assurance that incrementally, drop by drop, to every extent the poisons are eliminated, they will create a vacuum into which the virtues will flow automatically." So, I feel sort of the same way about society. Let's target what we want to tone down, get rid of as much as we can, and then the visions of a good society will emerge in greater clarity as we succeed.

At the present time there are large numbers of people who are taking entheogenic substances, and many of them are quite young. What would you want to say to them?

What bubbles up is, "Be cautious, go slow, but do not give up the quest." But I don't know. I don't have much confidence in myself as an advice giver. It depends so much on the individual and what the person is seeking, and I wouldn't want to impose my world-view. And that too sort of hobbles me in terms of giving advice.

In religious circles this is known as a pastoral question. A pastoral question is one where you don't just flip out stock answers. You enter into the actual situation of the person that you are conferring with, and then as that comes to light, some suggestions might be applicable. So, I think I'd rather leave that there.

What does it mean for you to be an elder in today's society?

I heard that somebody asked Robert Maynard Hutchins, president of the University of Chicago while I was getting my degree there, "What is it like to be old?" And with his typical ironic way, he said, "Just like it was to be young—not good." [laughs] Now, granted, that's just a glib response.

If I'm moved to ultimate seriousness, I'll tell a story about someone I've known for a decade. Last week he called up the police and said, "I'm going into my backyard to shoot myself, and it would be good if you came and cleared up the mess before my wife returns home." Now this was a person who was not depressed. He was eighty-two years old, but vigorous in one of the churches around here, and conducted a weekly public affairs session. He had a wonderfully varied career, with achievements in several directions, and was very well liked. He didn't want to be a burden on people, and one could even look at it as an act—in his eyes—of generosity.

However, this is where it bears on your question. Kendra and I both feel that it's part of life to accept one's limitations, which grow in the advancing years steadily every year, every month sometimes. And part of the total life experience is to accept being dependent, and to move out of the mold of giving, giving, giving, that one has poured oneself into for so many years, into one of being helpless and receiving. So even though his act, I feel sure, was prompted by altruism on his part, from our standpoint, why, there's still a limitation in that particular response to life.

But that's no general answer to what it means to be an elder. I've given you a flip answer and I've gone to the other extreme, in the serious vein. I think the best thing that the elderly can give to the world is a model of how it is possible to accept life's inevitable limitations in good cheer. That's what we're working for. [laughs] Wiser than despair—that's another phrase that has come over the horizon just recently. I don't know where it came from, but there it is: "Wiser than despair."

One final question. What role would you like to see psychedelics have in our society?

Minimally, I would like to begin with a touch of rationality in our absurd drug laws, which make no sense from any possible angle and do so much damage. Once a year I visit my one remaining brother in Detroit. He's very conservative, but when I asked, "Well, what do you propose for the ills of the world?" I was surprised to hear him say, "Legalize drugs." And he's very Republican—conservative politically. We disagree on every other issue I can think of, but these laws are so absurd. I'd like to see them changed.

Beyond that, I would like to see entheogens legally available to serious spiritual seekers. Of course, there are other aspects of it, like the recreational use of these substances. I don't take a puritanical view towards that. After all, I enjoy wine, which is a pleasurable aspect of life. So I wouldn't draw any sharp line there, but recreational use is not the area of my first concern.

NOTE

1. On April 20, 1962, twenty theology students participated in Walter Pahnke's Good Friday Marsh Chapel Experiment. In a double-blind study, half of the students took thirty milligrams of psilocybin, the other half got a placebo, and they all attended a Good Friday worship service. Pahnke hypothesized that a psychedelic drug might generate a mystical experience when consumed in a religious setting by a group of spiritually-inclined subjects. And indeed, this seems to have been the case. In "Pahnke's 'Good Friday Experiment': A Long-term Follow-up and Methodological Critique," published in the *Journal of Transpersonal Psychology* 23, no. 1, (1991): 1–28, author Rick Doblin found that even twenty-five years later, all participants that he spoke with who had consumed the psilocybin still felt that they'd had genuine and beneficial mystical experiences.

In Conclusion

What Did These Elders Learn, and What Can We Learn from Them?

Roger Walsh and Charles S. Grob

This book contains the reflections of people who probably saw a wider array of powerful and profound human experiences than any other group in history. In the thousands of psychedelic sessions they supervised, the whole gamut of human experience unfolded before their eyes. Agony and ecstasy, pathology and health, the sensual and sublime, the satanic and the transcendent—all this and more exploded in their subjects with rare intensity and power.

What did these pioneering researchers learn? What did their explorations reveal about human nature and the human condition, about its potentials and pitfalls, depths and heights, good and evil? What did they learn of the mind and its many layers, of defenses and denial, of pleasure and pain, suffering and ecstasy? What did they conclude about the possibilities of therapy and transformation, help and healing, health and pathology, about the merits of Freud and Jung, Skinner and Sartre? And what did they decide about religion and spirituality, soul and spirit, Buddha nature and Christ consciousness?

These are among the most profound and important questions that we can ask. What answers do these researchers offer us? And how were these witnesses and midwives of transformation transformed themselves?

They describe five broad arenas of insight and transformation. The first was their understanding of the nature of psychedelics and how to use them, the second their understanding of the workings of the mind. The third concerned psychological transformation and therapy, and the fourth their relationship to religion and spirituality. A final effect was the impact psychedelics exerted on their professions.

THE NATURE OF PSYCHEDELICS

The exact nature of psychedelics—what they do, and how they do it—has been a topic for debates and battles almost since their discovery. The names given to these drugs reflect both these battles and the evolution of researchers' understanding. Though originally marketed as "psychotomimetics" and labeled "hallucinogens," their remarkably variable effects soon led Stanislav Grof and others to recognize them as "nonspecific amplifiers" of mental processes that brought previously subliminal experiences to conscious awareness. Hence the name "psychedelic," meaning "mind manifesting." This amplification was particularly true of psychodynamically charged issues and conflicts, and this was one observation that led to the recognition of their therapeutic potential. More recently, they have been described by the term "entheogen," in recognition of their capacity to elicit spiritual experiences.

Initially, they were employed for treatment of major psychopathology. However, they soon also proved effective for other uses, such as for catalyzing psychological growth in normal individuals, for confronting existential threats such as terminal illness, and for spiritual opening.

Two distinct approaches emerged: low-dose "psycholytic" and high-dose "psychedelic" therapies. The psycholytic method fostered the emergence and exploration of psychodynamic issues and levels of the unconscious. As such, it served to facilitate work with personal issues. However, over multiple sessions, deeper layers of the unconscious might emerge and unveil transpersonal or even mystical experiences.

The psychedelic approach, on the other hand, tended to quickly catapult subjects through the psychodynamic levels and on to transpersonal, spiritual, and mystical experiences. Psychodynamic issues might emerge and remain at the forefront of awareness, particularly if they were severe, but they might also be bypassed and transcended in a powerful spiritual awakening. Researchers using the high-dose psychedelic approach concluded that therapeutic and growth benefits occurred in large part as a result of these transpersonal experiences. As such, they rediscovered Carl Jung's conclusion that "the approach to the numinous is the real therapy, and inasmuch as you attain the numinous experience you are released from the curse of pathology."[1]

THE NATURE OF MIND

Researchers of psychedelics found that their understanding of the mind deepened and transformed. They felt compelled to recognize the importance of altered states of consciousness, the multilayered aspects of the unconscious, spiritual depths of the psyche, and a positive view of human nature. All of these researchers concluded that we have hugely underestimated the variety, power, and potential of altered states, as well as their profound transformative abilities. So closely did their conclusions mirror those of William James of a century earlier that is worth repeating his famously eloquent statement on this topic, written after he had himself experienced the impact of nitrous oxide:

> One conclusion was forced upon my mind at that time, and my impression of its truth has ever since remained unshaken. It is that our normal consciousness, rational consciousness as we call it, is but one special type of consciousness, whilst all about it, parted from it by the filmiest of screens, there lie potential forms of consciousness entirely different. We may go through life without suspecting their existence; but apply the requisite stimulus, and at a touch they are there in all their completeness, definite types of mentality which probably somewhere have their field of application and adaptation. No account of the universe in its totality can be final which leaves these other forms of consciousness quite disregarded. How to regard them is the question,—for they are so discontinuous with ordinary consciousness. Yet they may determine attitudes though they cannot furnish formulas, and open a region though they fail to give a map. At any rate, they forbid a premature closing of our accounts with reality.[2]

James, widely regarded as America's greatest psychologist, exquisitely captured the conclusions of psychedelic researchers who followed him a century later.

A second compelling recognition was the multilayered nature of the mind and the vastness of the unconscious. Layer after layer was often peeled away, to quote Betty Eisner, "like one can do with an onion. You

can sit there and watch the Freudian or Jungian principles manifest themselves. Then you can go deeper and deeper and deeper, until finally the ego
cracks completely and you transcend it . . ."

No one theory or school proved adequate for all these layers. Rather,
psychedelic sessions unveiled experiences consistent with psychodynamic
theories as diverse as those of Freud, Rank, and Jung, and often in that
order. From this perspective, most schools of psychology and psychotherapy seemed incomplete, and Stanislav Grof summarized this dilemma as
follows:

> the major problem in Western psychotherapy seems to be that,
> for various reasons, individual researchers have focused their
> attention primarily on a certain level of consciousness and gener-
> alized their findings for the human psyche as a whole. For this
> reason, they are essentially incorrect, although they may give a
> useful and reasonably accurate description of the level they are
> describing, or one of its major aspects.[3]

Spirituality

But even the several varieties of psychodynamic experiences did not
exhaust the layers and depths of the psyche. For after these personal layers,
there frequently emerged transpersonal ones. Here experiences were consistent, not with the theories of Western clinicians, but rather with those
of contemplative traditions. The personal layers of the psyche rested, it
seemed, on still deeper transpersonal layers.

These transpersonal depths opened realms of mind comparable to
those discovered by the world's great spiritual teachers and mystics.
Descriptions of ecstasy, mystical union, pure consciousness, the void, or
satori were suddenly transformed from esoteric mumbo jumbo into
potent, life-changing experiences. The result was a new and deeper appreciation of the world's religious traditions. Some researchers and their subjects alike had such experiences, and many reoriented their lives
accordingly.

For example, James Fadiman "discovered that [his] disinterest in spiritual things was as valid as a ten-year-old's disinterest in sex: it came out of
a complete lack of awareness . . ." Likewise, when asked about long-term
changes in his subjects, Myron Stolaroff concluded:

I think that the most distinguishing mark is accepting spirituality in their lives, a conviction that life has a spiritual basis. They fashioned their lives to live in harmony with that idea as much as they could, and because of this, they really stand apart from most folks.

This interest in spirituality could emerge even in people who had previously been intensely hostile to it, as Stanislav Grof observed:

It would appear that everybody who experiences these levels develops convincing insights into the utmost relevance of the spiritual dimension in the universal scheme of things. Even positivistically oriented scientists, hard-core materialists, sceptics and cynics, uncompromising atheists and antireligious crusaders such as Marxist philosophers and politicians, suddenly become interested in the spiritual quest after they confront these levels in themselves.[4]

All the researchers therefore ended up at least sympathetic to, and in several cases deeply committed to, a spiritual world-view. A striking feature of this world-view was its nondenominational, or perhaps transdenominational, perspective. Even those originally committed to a specific tradition—such as Huston Smith to Christianity or Rabbi Zalman Schachter-Shalomi to Judaism—clearly honored the value of all authentic traditions. As such, their views were consistent with the *sophia communalis*, the common ground of understanding and wisdom at the contemplative core of each of the world's great religious traditions.

A POSITIVE VIEW OF HUMAN NATURE

Not surprisingly, the researchers' views of human potentials and possibilities expanded greatly. All of them concluded that we have seriously underestimated human nature, creativity, and consciousness.

Part of this appreciation of human potentials entailed coming to a more positive view of human nature. Several researchers, such as Stanislav Grof and Gary Fisher, had been trained in psychoanalysis and had adopted its painful view of human nature as largely id driven, conflict ridden, defensive and destructive. However, this view did not long survive the repeated recognition of layers of the psyche far deeper and more benign. It was not that they found Freudian descriptions necessarily incorrect. Rather, the aspect of the psyche that Freud described seemed to be only one level among many, and a relatively superficial level at that. Certainly, researchers saw all too clearly the inner sources of incalculable human savagery and suffering. However, they also concluded that these were produced largely due to alienation from our deeper, more benign nature, and that this deeper nature, when recognized, tended to reframe and heal the sources of pathology.

Limits of Psychedelically Derived Theories

Researchers struggled to create psychological theories capable of encompassing the expanded vision of the mind and human nature suggested by psychedelic experiences. The most comprehensive of the psychedelically derived theories was that of Stanislav Grof. His synthesis encompassed multiple psychological schools, philosophical traditions, and contemplative disciplines of both East and West, and applied them to his extensive clinical observations.[4] The result is a system that is remarkable for its scope and vision.

Of course, all psychologies have their limits, and psychedelically derived ones are no exception. Among other things, the method used for obtaining information sets inherent limits on the types of information acquired, and this is obviously true of information obtained by observations of psychedelic experiences.

The idea that our perspective sets unavoidable limits on knowledge is an ancient one, which was perhaps articulated most precisely by Chinese Hua-yen Buddhism. Every perspective, says Hua-yen, yields both the "revealed" and the "concealed." In contemporary philosophical language, each epistemological method reveals/unveils/enacts corresponding and congruent observations, while leaving others latent and invisible.

The method used by these psychedelic researchers was primarily phenomenological. Phenomenology has obvious merits for this work and yields crucial "revealed" observations. However, it cannot detect those that remain "concealed." This raises an obvious crucial question: What *types* of experiences—of all those that *are* potentially available for phenomenological inspection—do psychedelics reveal, and what do they conceal?

Social and cultural contexts are one type of important "concealeds" that are not available to phenomenology. Cultural contexts—including world-views, ethical systems, language, and socioeconomic factors—all provide background contexts that frame, color, and control the experiences which arise in an individual. Yet these background contexts cannot be detected by phenomenology alone.[5]

Likewise, phenomenology is ill equipped to detect gradual, long-term development. Consequently, it cannot identify adult psychological developmental stages such as those of cognition or morality.

So the phenomenology of psychedelic experiences has inherent limitations, as does any epistemology. Consequently, any psychological or philosophical theory derived primarily from them will also be limited and partial. This is not to belittle such theories, because the same principle applies to other theories. All epistemologies and their resultant knowledge and theories are partial. What is vital is simply to recognize this.

Having noted their limits, we can now honor their contributions. And psychedelically derived theories, especially those of Grof, contribute a great deal. For example, they provide a wealth of clinical information, novel insights into psychological, psychodynamic, and spiritual issues, new understandings of psychopathology and therapy, and an exceptionally encompassing map of the mind.

PSYCHOTHERAPY AND TRANSFORMATION

All those researchers who employed psychedelics clinically had their views of psychotherapy and transformation significantly altered. All of them concluded that in selected clients treated under appropriate conditions, beneficial change could occur more quickly and deeply than with conventional therapies, and in many cases, more quickly and deeply than had previously been assumed possible. Clinical literature on psychedelics contains multiple accounts of dramatic alleviations of major and even seemingly intractable disorders.

The list of disorders that seemed amenable is long. It includes chronic alcoholism and drug addiction, depression and assorted neuroses, personality and psychosomatic disorders, and the emotional and physical suffering in people approaching death. It even included some of the most extreme and intractable forms of pain and disability. For example, those with post-traumatic stress and concentration camp syndrome sometimes benefited, as did some with severe childhood disorders, even apparently including autism and schizophrenia.

Radical changes were not limited to the psychologically disturbed. Many normal subjects also reported positive transformations. Each of the researchers experienced these themselves, and these benefits played a major part in their enthusiastic support and research of psychedelic therapy.

Of course, all these claims need to be accepted cautiously. Many studies were not rigorously designed or controlled and most were only case histories. Nevertheless, the number, variety, and extent of transformations that these researchers describe are dramatic to say the least. Given the all too well known limitations of conventional therapy, and the amount of suffering that might be alleviated, further research seems more than warranted.

The researchers also reached intriguing conclusions about therapeutic approaches and exactly what is beneficial in therapy. As in practically all therapies, a trusting relationship proved crucial—"the basic element of LSD therapy is *trust*," concluded Betty Eisner. However, dialogue between client and therapist, which most therapies view as central and supreme, appeared less important. Indeed, in high-dose sessions it sometimes seemed more distracting than beneficial.

Rather, what seemed most healing and actualizing was a deep embracing of whatever experiences arose. Crucial above all else was the capacity of awareness to metabolize, transform, and heal the experiences brought to it.

Psychedelic researchers therefore independently discovered a crucial principle of healing and growth which lies at the core of diverse therapies. For Jungians, it is the principle that: "Therapeutic progress depends upon awareness; in fact the attempt to become more conscious is the therapy."[6] Fritz Perls, the founder of gestalt therapy summarized it as: "Awareness—by and of itself—can be curative,"[7] while the psychosynthesis writer Piero Ferrucci went further to claim that: "Awareness not only liberates, it also integrates."[8] For humanistic psychologist Carl Rogers, fully experiencing is crucial for transformation and for what he called a "moment of movement."[9]

This recognition is not confined to psychotherapies. It is also central to most major contemplative traditions, which urge students to give careful awareness to each moment and each mental movement. For example, Judaism urges "attend to this moment here and now,"[10] and in Islamic

Sufism, "The best act of worship is watchfulness of the moments."[11] Likewise, Christian contemplatives are urged, "Above all, guard the intellect and be watchful,"[12] while Buddhists are told that, "The best instruction is always to watch the mind."[13] In fact, the central contemplative practice of Buddhism is called "mindfulness meditation."

Clinicians employing psychedelics came to a similar appreciation of the importance and power of awareness. They also came to appreciate the value of several adjunctive therapies. Music, particularly classical music, became an inherent part of most psychedelic therapy, and artistic expression and representation of important experiences proved helpful as well.

Somatic approaches also found a place. The ancient yogic art of modulating breathing was found to soothe or intensify the therapeutic process. Movement could help express emerging energies, while physical therapies such as massage relaxed muscle spasm and chronic holding patterns, thereby releasing the psychodynamic conflicts they expressed.

Psychedelic therapists therefore rediscovered psychoanalyst Wilhelm Reich's concept of "character armor" and the muscular tension which expresses and maintains it. They also rediscovered the therapeutic power of relaxing this muscle armor. Reich wrote that:

> It never ceases to be surprising how the loosening of a muscular spasm not only releases the negative energy, but, over and above this, reproduces a memory of that situation in infancy in which the repression of the instinct occurred.[14]

Combined with prolonged hyperventilation, these adjunctive therapies proved so effective that they would become, in the hands of Stanislav and Christina Grof, a novel and extremely potent therapeutic approach: holotropic breathwork. This in turn led to the founding of a new clinical area: the study and treatment of transpersonal crises or spiritual emergencies.

In the course of their work, the Grofs were approached by people experiencing significant psychological or spiritual difficulties related to practices such as meditation, yoga, or shamanism. In many cases, these crises seemed similar to classic difficulties described in spiritual traditions for centuries, and also to some of the experiences that emerged in psychedelic or holotropic therapy.

Drawing from both the classic resources and their own experiences in working with such experiences the Grofs were able to create a systematic description of, and approach for working with, these transpersonal crises. When treated skillfully, many of these apparent pathologies turned out to be valuable developmental crises that opened new areas and stages of growth. This has been recognized in contemplative traditions by terms such as "purification" or "unstressing," and in psychology by terms such as "crises of renewal," "positive disintegration," "creative illness," and "spiritual emergence."[15]

A further common conclusion concerned a fundamental capacity and drive of mind. The mind increasingly came to be seen as a self-organizing, self-optimizing system. The researchers concluded that, given supportive conditions, the mind tends to be self-healing, self-integrating, self-individuating, self-actualizing, self-transcending, and self-awakening.

These innate tendencies for the mind to flower, unfold, and develop its potentials had been recognized before in both East and West, psychology and philosophy. Long ago, Plato spoke of Eros and Tibetan Buddhism of the self-liberating nature of mind. More recent recognitions include neuroanatomist Kurt Goldstein's "actualization," Carl Rogers' "formative tendency," Carl Jung's "individuation urge," Abraham Maslow's "selftranscendence," Erik Erikson's "self-perfectibility," philosopher Ken Wilber's "eros," and Aldous Huxley's "*moksha* drive." These tendencies of mind had been repeatedly recognized throughout history, but they became unavoidably evident with the catalytic power of psychedelics. Stanislav Grof later coined the related term "holotropism" to describe the mind's tendency to move towards holotropic or transcendent experiences and thereby heal and integrate. One practical result of this recognition of holotropism was that these researchers came to emphasize a relatively non-interfering approach in therapeutic sessions, based on a deep trust in the psyche's self-healing capacities.

Professional Impact

In some areas the impact of psychedelics, both positive and negative, on Western society are well known. Art and music, culture and counter-culture, meditation and yoga, Eastern religions and spirituality, and movements for peace and civil rights, are but a few of the arenas they influenced.

Not so well-known is the extent to which some other disciplines were also affected. Indeed, many of the researchers in this book had a significant impact on their own professions. Psychology, psychotherapy, anthropology, religious studies, shamanism, Judaism, and pharmacology were all affected.

For example, James Fadiman and Stanislav Grof played a major role in founding transpersonal psychology. Concerned that the psychology of the time was dominated and limited by psychoanalytic and behavioral approaches, which focused almost exclusively on pathology, they shared the philosopher Jacob Needleman's concern that "Freudianism institutionalized the underestimation of human possibility."[11] Having seen possibilities and potentials of mind beyond those acknowledged by prior approaches, they urged psychology to expand to recognize and research these potentials.

Transpersonal psychology was not designed to dismiss or replace earlier schools. Rather, it aimed to complement them and set them in a larger context. This context was open to topics such as states of consciousness, exceptional health, well-being, and maturity, as well as to the practices that cultivate them, and to the contributions of Eastern psychologies and disciplines such as meditation and yoga. These topics were famously summarized by another cofounder, Abraham Maslow, as "the farther reaches of human nature."[17] Maslow described the aims of this new psychology with the words:

> This point of view in no way denies the usual Freudian picture, but it does add to it and supplement it. To oversimplify the matter somewhat, it is as if Freud supplied to us the sick half of the psychology, and we must now fill it out with the healthy half. Perhaps this health psychology will give us more possibility of controlling and improving our lives and for making ourselves better people.[19]

Maslow's shift to a transpersonal orientation was itself in part the result of his own psychedelic experience.

The term "transpersonal psychology" was chosen to reflect the therapeutic and actualizing power of transpersonal experiences—experiences in which the sense of self expands beyond (trans) the individual or personal to encompass wider aspects of psyche, humankind, life, and cosmos.[19] Such experiences have been recognized and valued in most cultures throughout history—for example, as unitive experience, mystical experience, yogic *samadhi*, or union with the Tao. Western psychologists periodically rediscover unitive experiences and their benefits, as exemplified by William James' and William Bucke's "cosmic consciousness," psychotherapist Erich Fromm's "at-onement," and Abraham Maslow's "peak experience."[20] "It is chiefly our ignorance of the psyche if these experiences appear mystic," claimed Jung.[21]

Transpersonal psychology exerted an ongoing but modest influence on mainstream psychology. Its modest impact was probably because some of its topics, such as spirituality, ran counter to dominant mainstream assumptions, such as materialism and reductionism, which attempt to explain all experiences as neuronal fireworks, and in the case of spirituality, probably disordered fireworks at that. In addition, it did not develop a large base of supportive experimental data. However, it played other roles, such as validating meditation, feeding the popular human potential movement and the emerging cultural interest in spirituality, and lending impetus to the birth of the recent schools of positive psychology and integral psychology.

Psychotherapy was also impacted. Psychedelic researchers experimented to find the optimal conditions for fostering healing, actualization, and transcendence. They also explored nondrug alternatives for altering consciousness and fostering growth, from which new therapies emerged, the best known probably being Stanislav and Christina Grof's holotropic breathwork.

Anthropologists such as Michael Harner and Peter Furst added new dimensions to their disciplines. Their studies of psychedelic use among tribal cultures, plus their own personal experiences, helped to widen anthropology's understanding of consciousness and culture. The fields of transpersonal anthropology and the anthropology of consciousness emerged from questions and concerns such as these.

Altered states of consciousness were now recognized as central to many cultures and practices. Anthropologists began to study the methods (including psychedelics) for inducing them, healings and rituals for applying them, religions and myths derived from them, and beliefs and worldviews for explaining them.

It became increasingly apparent that societies approve and institutionalize some states of consciousness, while disparaging and prohibiting others, and that societies differ in the number and variety of states they value. Western culture is relatively *monophasic*, meaning that we privilege the usual waking state, derive our world-view almost entirely from it, and marginalize other states, a bias that Michael Harner calls "cognicentricism."[22] By contrast, most societies are more *polyphasic*, drawing their knowledge and world-view from additional modalities of consciousness, such as trance, shamanic, meditative, or yogic states.[23] Likewise, their psychologies and philosophies tend to be multistate and multistage, drawing on and analyzing multiple states of consciousness and stages of development. Western disciplines, however, tend to almost exclusively draw from, and focus on, the normal waking state and conventional, personal stage of development, largely overlooking transpersonal states and stages.[24]

These recognitions raised serious concerns about the extent to which Western researchers could adequately comprehend multistate cultures and disciplines. Limiting factors such as state-specific learning and state-specific communication suggested that researchers who had not themselves experienced these other states might be seriously handicapped in *cross-phasing*. The result? Much of the richness and meaning of these states might be missed. The psychologist Charles Tart therefore argued in the journal *Science* that we may need "state-specific scientists," "yogi-scientists," or "meditative philosophers," who are experts in both multiple states and conventional Western disciplines.[25]

An amusing example and partial validation of Tart's viewpoint came from the psychiatrist Gordon Globus. On reading Tart's article, Globus found the argument unconvincing and wrote a critique. Shortly thereafter, when in an altered state himself, Globus reread Tart's article and this time found it compelling. He immediately wrote another response, this one favorable, while still in the altered state. But when the altered state ended, he yet again found Tart's argument lacking and wrote a response to his response.[26] The staid journal *Science* declined to publish any of them.

In subsequent years, shamanism became a vital spiritual practice for a surprising number of people throughout the Western world, and the spread of this ancient tribal discipline can largely be attributed to Michael Harner. After his initiation with ayahuasca in the Amazonian jungle, Harner's appreciation of shamanic cultures was so profoundly deepened that he undertook shamanic training himself, and subsequently taught thousands of others. In a curious cultural reversal, he and his students have even reintroduced shamanism to some societies where it had been lost or suppressed.

Other researchers impacted other spiritual traditions. Inspired by his psychedelic experiences, Rabbi Zalman Schachter-Shalomi deepened his study of Jewish mysticism and then played a major role in inspiring the Jewish Renewal movement.

Searching for people and traditions to help make sense of his psyche-delic experiences, Ram Dass traveled to India. There he found a guru, and he later returned to the West to become a major popularizer of Hinduism and Buddhism, meditation and yoga, and inspired a whole generation of spiritual seekers.

Psychedelics also led to new interest into the role of drug experiences in religions. It became clear that drugs have played a major part through-out history in multiple traditions, and continue to do so today in ones such as shamanism and the Native American Church. Some people even suggested that psychedelics may have been instrumental in the creation of certain religions.

Huston Smith's influence was key in this regard. His writings were among the first and most persuasive to question the initial tendency of religious scholars to dismiss psychedelic experiences as pseudo-spiritual and insignificant.[27] After Smith's writings, it was hard for any serious scholar to hold these positions.

Stanislav Grof's research also illuminated religious practices and stud-ies. His multitude of contributions defy brief description. However, they include the rediscovery of Jung's principle that "the deeper 'layers' of the psyche . . . become increasingly collective until they are universalized,"[28] and that these deeper layers are associated with religious experiences that have been goals of spiritual practices the world over.

Drawing on the deepest experiences of his several thousand subjects, Grof synthesized their insights into a comprehensive ontocosmology.[29] This is a novel scheme of the cosmos and realms of beings, a map of what the ancient Greeks called the *Kosmos*—the totality of existence, both mate-rial and immaterial. This psychedelically derived map shows clear similar-ities to aspects of the Perennial Philosophy, especially to the variant found in Kashmir Shaivism (the mystical form of Hinduism). The scope of Grof's map and the "cosmic game" it describes is awesome, encompassing (among other things), consciousness, cosmogony, evolution, teleology, enlightenment, evil, and more. It offers numerous unique observations, especially into the dynamics of evil and *maya, maya* being the Hindu term for the encompassing illusion that clouds our awareness.

Of course, there are major epistemological challenges for such a map. Several of these have already been discussed in the analysis of the limits of psychedelically derived theories. An additional challenge for any meta-physical system is the leap from phenomenology to ontology (from expe-rience to claims about the nature of reality). But whatever verdict history may pass on its validity, this map certainly places Grof among the grand theorists attempting to present a "big picture."

The impact of these researchers on their professions was clearly impressive, but it was not limited to these professions alone. Their findings and ideas spread out across the culture, producing new disciplines, practices, and areas of interest.

Many of the researchers in this book took up practices such as meditation, contemplation, and yoga in their search for nondrug methods of transformation, and in order to stabilize and deepen the spiritual insights they had glimpsed. They then played a significant role in popularizing these practices. Professionals and the public eventually took up meditation practices to an extent that would have been unimaginable only a few decades earlier and initiated a quiet but potentially profound revolution in Western culture. These practices in turn led to still further and continuing cultural changes in areas as diverse as therapy, medicine, and technology. The ripple effects from the work of these early psychedelic pioneers continue to touch and transform us in ways we are still struggling to fully appreciate.

NOTES

1. C. G. Jung, *Letters*, ed. G. Adler (Princeton, NJ: Princeton University Press, 1973), 377.

2. W. James, *The Varieties of Religious Experience: A Study in Human Nature* (New York: New American Library, 1958), 298.

3. S. Grof, *Beyond the Brain: Birth, Death and Transcendence in Psychotherapy* (Albany: State University of New York Press, 1985), 142.

4. S. Grof, *LSD Psychotherapy* (Sarasota, FL: Multidisciplinary Association for Psychedelic Studies, 2001), 70. S. Grof, *The Adventure of Self-discovery* (Albany: State University of New York Press, 1988). S. Grof, *Realms of the Human Unconscious* (New York: Viking Press, 1975).

5. K. Wilber, *The Eye of Spirit* (Boston, MA: Shambhala, 1997).

6. E. Whitmont, *The Symbolic Quest* (Princeton, NJ: Princeton University Press, 1969).

7. F. Perls, *Gestalt Therapy Verbatim* (Lafayette, CA: Real People Press, 1969).

8. P. Ferrucci, *What We May Be* (Los Angeles, CA: J. Tarcher, 1982), 54.

9. N. J. Raskin, and C. R. Rogers, "Person-centered therapy," in *Current Psychotherapies*, 6th ed., ed., R. Corsini and D. Wedding (Itasca, IL: F. E. Peacock Publishers, 2000): 155.

10. Rabbi Jacobs in R. Shapiro, ed., *Wisdom of the Jewish sages: A modern reading of Pirke Avot* (New York: Bell Tower, 1993), 88.

11. Abu Bakr Muhammad Al-Wasiti, in *Travelling the Path of Love: Sayings of Sufi Masters*, ed. L. Vaughan-Lee (Inverness, CA: Golden Sufi, 1995): 84.

12. Abba Philemon, *Prayer of the Heart: Writings from the Philokalia*, trans. G. Palmer, P. Sherrard, and K. Ware (Boston, MA: Shambhala, 1993), 97.

13. Patrul Rinpoche, *The words of my perfect teacher* (Boston, MA: Shambhala, 1998).

14. W. Reich, *The Function of the Orgasm* (New York: Touchstone, 1973), 300.

15. S. Grof, *The Cosmic Game* (Albany: State University of New York Press, 1998). S. Grof and C. Grof, eds., *Spiritual Emergency: When Personal Transformation Becomes a Crisis* (Los Angeles, CA: J. Tarcher, 1989).

16. J. Needleman, *Lost Christianity* (Garden City, NY: Doubleday, 1980), 60.

17. A. Maslow, *The Farther Reaches of Human Nature* (New York: Viking, 1971).

18. A. Maslow, *Towards a Psychology of Being* 2nd ed. (Princeton, NJ: Van Nostrand, 1969), 5.

19. R. Walsh and F. Vaughan, eds., *Paths beyond Ego: The Transpersonal Vision* (Los Angeles, CA: J. Tarcher, 1993).

20. W. James, *William James on Psychical Research* (New York: Viking, 1960). R. Bucke, *Cosmic Consciousness* (New York: Dutton, 1969). (Original work published in 1901.) See also note 17.

21. C. G. Jung, "Mysterium conjunctionis," in *Collected Works of Carl Jung*, vol. 14 (Princeton, NJ: Princeton University Press, 1955), 535.

22. M. Harner, *The Way of the Shaman* (New York: Bantam, 1982).

23. C. Laughlin, J. McManus and J. Shearer, "Transpersonal anthropology," in *Paths Beyond Ego: The Transpersonal Vision*, ed. R. Walsh and F. Vaughan (Los Angeles, CA: J. Tarcher, 1993): 190–95.

24. R. Walsh, "Can Western Philosophers Understand Asian Philosophies? The challenge and opportunity of states of consciousness research," *Crosscurrents* 39 (1989): 281–99. K. Wilber, *Integral Psychology: Consciousness, Spirit, Psychology, Therapy* (Boston, MA: Shambhala, 2000). See also note 19.

25. C. Tart, "States of Consciousness and State Specific Sciences," *Science* 176 (1972): 1203–10.

26. G. Globus, "Different views from different states," in *Paths beyond Ego: The Transpersonal Vision*, ed. R. Walsh and F. Vaughan (Los Angeles, CA: J. Tarcher, 1993): 182–83.

27. H. Smith, "Do drugs have religious import?" *Journal of Philosophy* 61 (1964): 517–30. H. Smith, *Cleansing the Doors of Perception: The Religious Significance of Entheogenic Plants and Chemicals* (New York: Tarcher/Penguin, 2000).

28.C. G. Jung, "The Psychology of the Child Archetype," in *Collected Works of C. G. Jung* vol. 9, Pt. 1, Bollingen Series XX, 2nd ed. (Princeton, NJ: Princeton University Press, 1968).

29. See note 15 (Grof 1998).

Contributors

ALISE AGAR-WITTINE (June 8, 1950–June 6, 2001) was the coordinator for the "Psychedelic Elders" project and the midwife for this book. During the last three years of her life she worked tirelessly on this project, handling production duties for the 1998 Gathering of the Elders conference, facilitating interviews with the researchers, and arranging for the publication of some of these interviews.

Her contributions to this project were consistent with her life. A woman of enormous intelligence, heart, wit, and charm, Alise placed the well being of others before her own, even when she was ill. She found enormous pleasure in facilitating meetings between the individuals like those whose interviews are featured in this book. The conferences she worked on always combined diverse areas of consciousness studies: science, philosophy, spirituality, and the arts. She loved this work, and was not only an extraordinary networker, but also a researcher herself in nonordinary states of consciousness. Alise coordinated conferences for the Fetzer, Esalen, and Omega institutes, among others. She was director of operations for the Institute of Noetic Sciences, director of public relations for two health care organizations, and executive director for the Study of Human Consciousness, in Berkeley.

Alise died in 2001 after a long illness. This book, *Higher Wisdom*, is a tribute to her.

GARY BRAVO, MD graduated from Harvard University with a degree in biology and did his medical and psychiatric training at the University of

California at Irvine, College of Medicine. While serving there on the clinical faculty he did research with Drs. Walsh and Grob on the subjective effects of MDMA (Ecstasy), and helped develop the first government approved research protocol on the clinical effects of MDMA. He has published papers and lectured internationally on psychedelics. He currently works as a public psychiatrist, practicing in Santa Rosa, California.

CHARLES S. GROB, MD is director of the Division of Child and Adolescent Psychiatry at Harbor-UCLA Medical Center, and professor of psychiatry and pediatrics at the UCLA School of Medicine. He did his undergraduate work at Oberlin College and Columbia University, and obtained a BS from Columbia in 1975. He received his MD from the State University of New York, Downstate Medical Center in 1979. Prior to his appointment at UCLA, Grob held teaching and clinical positions at the University of California at Irvine, College of Medicine, and The Johns Hopkins University School of Medicine, departments of psychiatry and pediatrics. He conducted the first government approved psychobiological research study of MDMA, and was the principal investigator of an international research project in the Brazilian Amazon studying the visionary plant brew, ayahuasca. He is currently conducting an approved research investigation on the safety and efficacy of psilocybin treatment in terminally ill patients with anxiety. He is the editor of *Hallucinogens: A Reader* and he has published numerous articles on psychedelics in medical and psychiatric journals and collected volumes. Grob is a founding board member of the Heffter Research Institute, which is devoted to fostering and funding research on psychedelics.

ROGER WALSH, MD, PhD is professor of psychiatry, philosophy and anthropology, and adjunct professor of religious studies at the University of California at Irvine. He graduated from the University of Queensland, in Australia, with degrees in psychology, physiology, psychology, neuroscience, and medicine before coming to the United States as a Fulbright scholar. His writings and research have received over two dozen national and international awards and honors, while his teaching has received one national and six university awards. His publications include *Paths beyond Ego: The Transpersonal Vision, The Spirit of Shamanism,* and *Essential Spirituality: The Seven Central Practices.*

On-line Resources

Albert Hofmann Foundation • www.hofmann.org
Association for Transpersonal Psychology • www.atpweb.org
California Institute of Integral Studies • www.ciis.edu
Children: Our Ultimate Investment • www.children-ourinvestment.org
Council on Spiritual Practices • www.csp.org
Drug Policy Alliance • www.dpf.org
Drug Reform Coordination Network • www.stopthedrugwar.org
EastWest Retreats • inservice@earthlink.com
The Entheogen Review • www.entheogenreview.com
Erowid • www.erowid.org
Esalen Institute • www.esalen.com
Foundation for Shamanic Studies • www.shamanism.org
Grof Transpersonal Training, Inc. • www.holotropic.com
Heffter Research Institute • www.heffter.org
Institute of Noetic Sciences • www.noetic.org
Marijuana Policy Project • www.mpp.org
Media Awareness Project • www.mapinc.org
Mind States Conferences • www.mindstates.org
Multidisciplinary Association for Psychedelic Studies • www.maps.org
Norml • www.norml.org
Toward a Science of Consciousness • www.consciousness.arizona.edu

Name Index

Alpert, Richard, 14, 15, 25, 26, 34, 98, 197

Buber, Martin, 208

Cameron, Ewen, 8
Castaneda, Carlos, 37, 112, 153, 154, 175
Cohen, Sidney, 9, 91, 93

Ditman, Keith, 94, 95
Doblin, Rick, 47

Eisner, Betty, 9, 13, 91–101

Fadiman, James, 14, 23, 25–44, 96, 244, 251
Fisher, Gary, 103–117, 138
Freud, 87, 120, 121, 130, 137
Furst, Peter T., 16, 151–157, 252

Ginsberg, Allen, 209
Grof, Stan, 2, 13, 119–144, 229, 242, 244–246, 251

Hari Das, 15
Harman, Willis, 14, 25, 27, 28, 29, 30, 32, 96

Harner, Michael, 16, 147, 159–177, 252, 253
Hoffer, Abram, 94,95, 103, 197
Hoffman, Albert, 12, 21, 47–52, 121
Hubbard, Al, 14, 28, 30, 55, 92, 95, 96, 103
Huxley, Aldous, 7, 21, 51, 70, 91, 97, 99, 196, 210, 211, 226
Huxley, Laura, 13, 179–188

James, William, 243
Janiger, Oscar, 32
Jung, Carl, 2, 60, 87, 133

Kesey, Ken, 31

Leary, Timothy, 8, 10, 15, 26, 28, 34, 49, 93, 97, 103, 108, 109, 184, 197, 198, 202, 207, 209–213, 217, 226
Leo Zeff, 69
Ling, Tom, 96

Maharajji, 15, 17, 18, 19, 213
Maslow, Abraham, 119, 137, 138, 201, 251
Metzner, Ralph, 210
Mogar, Bob, 56

263

Subject Index